*Landscapes of the Islamic World*

# Landscapes of the Islamic World

*Archaeology, History, and Ethnography*

EDITED BY

Stephen McPhillips
and Paul D. Wordsworth

PENN

*University of Pennsylvania Press*

*Philadelphia*

Published by
University of Pennsylvania Press
Philadelphia, Pennsylvania 19104-4112
www.upenn.edu/pennpress

Printed in the United States of America on acid-free paper
10 9 8 7 6 5 4 3 2 1

Library of Congress Cataloging-in-Publication Data
Names: McPhillips, Stephen, editor. | Wordsworth, Paul D., editor.
Title: Landscapes of the Islamic world : archaeology, history, and
   ethnography / edited by Stephen McPhillips and Paul D. Wordsworth.
Description: Philadelphia : University of Pennsylvania Press, [2016] | 2016
   | Includes bibliographical references and index.
Identifiers: LCCN 2015039596 | ISBN 9780812247640 (alk. paper)
Subjects: LCSH: Land use, Rural—Middle East—History. | Middle East—Rural
   conditions—History. | Water-supply, Rural—Middle East—History. | Rural
   development—Middle East—History. | Islamic countries—Commerce—History.
   | Islamic civilization.
Classification: LCC HD846.Z7 L36 2016 | DDC 330.917/67—dc23
LC record available at http://lccn.loc.gov/2015039596

# Contents

Preface    ix
*Stephen McPhillips and Paul D. Wordsworth*

Introduction    1
*Tony J. Wilkinson*


PART I. HYDROECONOMIES: MANAGING
AND LIVING WITH WATER

Chapter 1. The Materiality of Ottoman Water Administration
in Eighteenth-Century Rural Damascus: A Historian's Perspective    19
*Astrid Meier*

Chapter 2. The Islamic Occupation of Qatar in the Context
of an Environmental Framework    34
*Phillip G. Macumber*

Chapter 3. Water Management in Desert Regions: Early Islamic
Qasr Mushash    50
*Karin Bartl*


PART II. AGRICULTURE, PASTORALISM, AND SUBSISTENCE

Chapter 4. Faunal Distributions from the Southern Highlands of Transjordan:
Regional and Historical Perspectives on the Representations and Roles of Animals
in the Middle Islamic Period    71
*Robin M. Brown*

Chapter 5. Zooarchaeological Perspectives on Rural Economy
and Landscape Use in Eighteenth-Century Qatar    94
  *Pernille Bangsgaard and Lisa Yeomans*


PART III. LANDSCAPES OF COMMERCE AND PRODUCTION

Chapter 6. Beyond Iron Age Landscapes: Copper Mining and Smelting
in Faynan in the Twelfth to Fourteenth Centuries CE    111
  *Ian W. N. Jones*

Chapter 7. Ceramic Production in the Central Highlands
of Yemen During the Islamic Period    129
  *Daniel Mahoney*

Chapter 8. Harnessing Hydraulic Power in Ottoman Syria:
Water Mills and the Rural Economy of the Upper Orontes Valley    143
  *Stephen McPhillips*


PART IV. TRANSIENCE AND PERMANENCE:
MOVEMENT AND MEMORY IN THE LANDSCAPE

Chapter 9. The Architectural Legacy of the Seasonally Nomadic Ghurids    169
  *David C. Thomas and Alison L. Gascoigne*

Chapter 10. The Northern Jordan Project and the "Liquid Landscapes"
of Late Islamic Bilad al-Sham    184
  *Bethany J. Walker*

Chapter 11. "Presencing the Past": A Case Study of Islamic Rural Burial
Practices from the Homs Region, Syria    200
  *Jennie N. Bradbury*

Chapter 12. Sustaining Travel: The Economy of Medieval Stopping Places
Across the Karakum Desert, Turkmenistan    219
  *Paul D. Wordsworth*

Conclusion. Some Reflections on Rural Islamic Landscapes    237
  *Alan Walmsley*

Glossary    243

List of Contributors    245

Index    249

Acknowledgments    255

# Preface

## An Interdisciplinary Approach to Landscapes

Landscapes have occupied an increasingly prominent place in the study of the premodern Islamic world over the last three decades. An exponential increase in the study of primary materials, both historical and archaeological, directly relating to rural societies means that many key assumptions based primarily on the studies of cities must be fundamentally reassessed. The shift in focus toward small settlements and agricultural and transhumant communities has necessitated the development of new theoretical and methodological approaches, which are still undergoing critical review and development. One of the most important outcomes of this process is the increasing tendency toward multidisciplinary initiatives that facilitate the combination of evidence derived from several alternative and complementary sources.

Bringing together a variety of data not only provides a more nuanced assessment of the nature and role of extraurban societies but addresses previously encountered problems of a fragmentary record or one that is underrepresented by historical media or material culture. For example, a traditional critique of historical narratives has been their strongly urban perspective, contrasted against archaeological data, which might in many cases "fill the gaps." This volume includes examples of predominantly historical studies of the rural world, but there is indeed a strong reliance on archaeological data in the reconstruction of nonurban societies. All the studies presented here are, however, necessarily reliant on historical and ethnographic data. Only by considering these three disciplines in parallel is it possible to attempt to understand the complexity of rural socioeconomic processes and their chronological context.

This volume aims to invoke a broad interdisciplinary and comparative discussion on studies of Islamic landscapes, with an explicit agenda that seeks to bridge the disciplines of archaeology, history, and ethnography. The intention is not to produce a collection of contributions on one particular field, region, or chronological period, but rather to reflect the scope and diversity of academic studies in this subject, with an emphasis on new and original contributions arranged thematically. The resulting chapters cover a wide geographical area and a long chronological span, bringing together data on rural populations whose fundamental and complex roles in societies are perhaps only beginning to be understood.

## Landscapes in the Islamic World

For the purposes of this volume, *Islamic* refers to those lands where Islam was the predominant but by no means the exclusive religion. More specifically, the categories of Islamic history and archaeology are defined chronologically as post-seventh century CE and focus chiefly on the lands that came to be permanently occupied by empires and states that professed the Muslim faith. Although some religious factors had a demonstrable impact on rural settlements, including the endowment and location of religious structures and the establishment of burial grounds, it is important not to lay too much stress on the discontinuity caused by religion, as the persistence of traditional practices is well attested, possibly even more so in nonurban zones than in cities. It is also important to reinforce the point that Islamicate societies (rural or otherwise) cannot be viewed in isolation, illustrated in the following chapters through the connections with pre-Islamic and contemporary non-Islamic communities. Although the regions analyzed by these articles are geographically diverse, they fall within a zone that can be seen as climatically comparative, allowing us to profile some of the critical issues that arise in these regions, including dryland irrigation and desert water provision. In the same way, rural technologies employed across the Islamic lands were certainly adapted to specific regional needs, but premodern societies also had access to extensive knowledge bases that cut across regularly redefined political boundaries, reinforced, for example, by use of the Arabic script for much of this area.

In many instances, rural landscapes are seen as synonymous with agricultural hinterlands, often centered on cities. While much rural land can be defined as food producing, in this volume we aim to document the variety inherent within extraurban economies, incorporating other crucial elements, such as extraction and production activities. The chapters presented here are not restricted to sedentary fertile zones. Seasonal and transhumant use of rural landscapes is discussed, without constructing a rigid dichotomy between these forms of land use and those perceived to be more permanent or based on agriculture. Such a broad approach can inevitably only hint at the great complexity of rural socioeconomic systems, but it is hoped that these case studies will lead to further debates and studies that cut across traditionally defined social boundaries.

## Reorientation of Studies in Islamic Material Culture

New directions in archaeological fieldwork after the 1960s have widened perspectives on the Islamic world, with large regional surveys demonstrating the crucial role of landscapes in constructing multiperiod models of past economies and society. Just as the appearance of Islam in cities is increasingly viewed in the context of long, complex processes of socioeconomic change, new archaeological evidence encourages an equally nuanced reading of life in the countryside from the middle of the seventh century CE. Likewise, the relationship between rural and urban components of Islamic societies has been shown by studies from the 1990s onwards to be highly complex, challenging preconceived ideas about the passive role of the countryside in relation to the "center" or the state in center-periphery paradigms. At an interregional scale, world systems models of understanding global economic trends have been challenged in the explanations they provide in the historical Islamic world just as they have for pre-Islamic periods. Consideration of the active role of the extraurban has highlighted the agency of these communities in defining the dynamics of societies in the Islamic world. Other hypotheses, such as the observation that rural material culture undergoes a more conservative diachronic change than that of towns and cities, can now be tested by new methodological approaches.

## The Significance of Islamic Landscapes in New Research

Twenty-first-century developments in archaeological and historical theory have been instrumental in raising awareness of the potential for landscape studies in many areas of the Islamic world. In addition to survey work, many rural sites have themselves been the subject of excavation, frequently offering alternative interpretations for places that may in the past only have been considered in terms of their monumental architecture. Interest has also shifted with regard to the study of object classes that have previously been neglected, such as ceramic coarsewares, which have now begun to be incorporated into chronological sequences spanning the periods after the coming of Islam. A significant trend toward multidisciplinary research projects is also producing important new results across the field of Islamic landscape studies, spurred on in part through a more discursive relationship with other archaeological specializations, particularly prehistory. This has involved the use of a wide range of scientific analyses, remote sensing, and computer-generated modeling integrating archaeological and textual data sets. The increased emphasis given to early modern periods in Islamic archaeology, especially in the burgeoning field of Ottoman studies, has also opened up new possibilities for collaboration between archival research, field-based investigation, and ethnography.

The countryside represents the primary production sector of most premodern Islamic entities, and its investigation is highly relevant to pursuing broader themes of socioeconomic enquiry from a time-deep perspective. The chapters in this volume consider a range of production activities in a rural setting, demonstrating that the countryside could in fact act as an engine of artisanal and technical innovation of broad societal significance. This may concern the way in which natural resources are used, but also the complex layers of meaning landscapes may hold for different groups or individual actors.

This volume was in part inspired by an awareness of the widespread and rapid destruction of ancient, medieval, and early modern landscapes across much of the Islamic world. The effects of modern agrarian practices, rapid urbanization, and perhaps most significant, the lack of resources available to those responsible for safeguarding archaeological remains on the ground, mean that Islamic rural sites are often threatened. In some senses, we hope to draw attention to the scientific importance of this heritage and to provide an indication of the current state of research into the field.

In the introduction, Tony Wilkinson discusses the themes covered by the papers in this volume with regard to the discipline of historical archaeology in the Near East, in what we hope is a first step in a new direction, breaking down the barriers of traditional disciplinary research and constructing holistic studies of the rural world.

## Note on Transliteration and Dates

The geographic coverage and cross-disciplinary range of the contributions in this book requires the transliteration of personal and place names and specialized vocabulary in a number of languages. We have adopted a pragmatic approach using the *International Journal of Middle Eastern Studies* (*IJMES*) guidelines when dealing with Arabic and Persian, but omitting the macron over the long vowels and the dots employed under consonants. We have also avoided the use of Arabic language plurals, preferring the addition of an unitalicized "s." Similarly, the spelling of place-names conforms to commonly accepted English forms. Russian transliteration follows the Library of Congress guidelines.

All dates are given as BCE/CE unless stated. Corresponding dates in AH are given where specifically relevant.

# Introduction

*Tony J. Wilkinson*

This volume presents new research in Islamic archaeology and history, discussing the nature of the Islamic rural economy. Topics range from fishing to desert water management and from burial practice to milling, and any distillation of such a diversity of perspectives is bound to be partial. Therefore, here I simply attempt to sketch some common themes from the chapters and place them in a broader context. In places, I extend the temporal range somewhat in order to tease out a comparative perspective because, as Jeremy Johns has reminded us, "The geographical and temporal range of the world of Islam is far greater than that of the Roman Empire" (2010: 1188). Consequently, the big questions are compelling, challenging, and highly relevant to broader historical themes.

Although early Islamic rural settlements have long been investigated, an explicitly rural perspective on the economy was lacking until the 1990s. Rural sites are often covered, perhaps incidentally, by archaeological surveys, but such surveys frequently focused simply upon rural settlement rather than the entire range of rural landscape features. But what constitutes the countryside? In Chapter 12, Wordsworth sidesteps the restrictions imposed by the countryside of sedentary communities alone by referring to a "continuous region, not restricted to just the fertile zone." This frees up the discussion for the consideration of the realm of the nomads, which makes it possible to explore regional interactions more systematically. Nevertheless, there remains the difficulty of reconciling information retrieved by different methods: excavation, survey, and historical texts. Because each class of data has a different modality and temporal range, the concept of materiality might therefore form a unifying thread connecting what would otherwise be rather disparate classes of information. Thus, Meier suggests that until recently, many historians tended to take for granted the material world and how it came about. Historians, unlike archaeologists, do not often venture out to see the material objects they write about (Chapter 1). In order to bring these different academic strands together, integrative paradigms are required, and Bangsgaard and Yeomans suggest that ethnographic and historical sources can be used as analogies for archaeological evidence, although there should be a high degree of similarity in living conditions, subsistence, and geographical setting (Chapter 5).

To some degree, this volume complements an earlier volume devoted to the Late Antique and Abbasid periods of the Near East (Borrut et al. 2011) by providing a finer-grained perspective on rural economies as well as a temporal coverage of the entire Islamic period. The 2011 volume also included several broad syntheses (Kennedy 2011a; Decker 2011; Heidemann 2011) that provide conclusions that can be tested by the present volume.

## Investigations of the Islamic Countryside

Although often regarded as a neglected field, there is nevertheless a substantial literature on the Islamic countryside extending back to the original surveys of Sarre and Herzfeld (1911–1920), as well as the influential surveys of Adams in the Diyala (1965). The latter, as Whitcomb rightly acknowledges, contributed significantly to the growth of Islamic archaeology (2007: 259). In addition to the surveys of Adams (1981) within the Abbasid heartland, al-Rashid's investigations of the Darb Zubayda and Rabadaha (1980 and 1986) in Saudi Arabia and those of Andrew Williamson in Fars and Oman (1987) provided valuable insights into the economies of the deserts and maritime fringes. Milwright's summary of key developments in the countryside (2010: chap. 4) could hardly develop all subtopics, but gratifyingly, a range of historically informed regional investigations are now appearing: for example, Heidemann (2011) and De Jong (2012) in the Balikh, Geyer and Rousset (2011) in central Syria, Eger (2011) in the Hatay, Power and Sheehan (2012) in southeastern Arabia, and Johns (1995), Kaptijn (2010), Walker (2005), and Amr and al-Momani (2011) in Jordan. Broader perspectives are now provided by Kennedy (2011a and b) and Decker (2009; 2011), among others.

## The Role of Archaeological Surveys

Although archaeological and landscape surveys play an important role in the investigation of the Islamic countryside, it is evident from the essays in this volume that they are not the only, or even the primary, sources of information. Of the twelve chapters, five are survey based (Chapters 7, 8, 10, 11, and 12) and three (Chapters 1, 2, and 6) include a survey or landscape component. In other words, about two-thirds have benefited from the growth in archaeological survey since the early 1980s. Because of their broad-brush nature, archaeological surveys ideally need to be "run" several times because initial investigations that establish the structure of settlement over a long temporal range frequently require a second or third fine-tuning to establish period-specific details. Hence Whitcomb's analysis of the ceramics of two sites in the Sweyhat survey (2004), Bartl's study of settlement in the Balikh (1996), McPhillips's analyses of the Homs survey (2012), and Eger's of the Amuq Valley in the Turkish Hatay (2011) all brought greater precision to the earlier surveys, as well as a considerable degree of historical insight.

The alternative to such a two-stage approach is for the Islamic specialist to embark immediately on the investigation of the Islamic remains in a region at the expense of other periods. Although seemingly the most efficient approach, this loses the long perspective that is one of the strengths of archaeological survey (see Mahoney, Chapter 7, and Bradbury, Chapter 11). Pre-Islamic settlement is important, not simply because it provides a yardstick against which the Islamic phases can be measured but also because of the role of some sites and landscape features to act as "stores" of social memory for the inhabitants (Bradbury, Chapter 11).

Satellite imagery is an important tool in landscape survey because it provides an invaluable information source for mapping landscape features and burials, but an understanding of any area through fieldwork is equally essential. Not only do satellite images provide information on archaeological features, such as canals, roads, and fields; they also supply insights into thornier problems not always dealt with by conventional studies. For example, in the Jabbul region of Syria, high-resolution KH7 satellite photographs from the 1960s suggest why there a decline in population is frequently seen in the Middle to Late Islamic period. They demonstrate that "modern" villages often overlie Late Antique or Islamic settlements, which then become obscured by the expanded modern villages, so that the original sites are lost from view and are undercounted (Fig. I.1; also Whitcomb 2006).

Surveys also demonstrate the dynamic nature of settlement. For example, whereas the region southwest of Samsat in Turkey experienced a precipitous decline from the Late Roman–Byzantine to the Early Islamic period (Wilkinson 1990), the Balikh Valley south of Edessa (Urfa) experienced massive growth (Bartl 1996). However, even where decline was apparent, as around Tell Sweyhat or in the Amuq, some lands were evidently newly settled (Wilkinson et al. 2004; Eger 2011). The dynamic nature of Islamic settlement is further discussed below.

I now examine some themes common to the chapters in this volume.

Figure I.1 Satellite image of the area north of the Jabbul in Syria, showing the houses of a village and an extensive spread of an earlier Islamic or Late Antique village to the east (KH7 image, courtesy of USGS).

## Connectivity

Connectivity, namely, the way in which change in any one area may have a significant impact upon developments in physically discrete and often distant regions through specific social, political, or economic connections (Horden and Purcell 2000: 123), is a significant theme in at least four chapters. The Islamic period witnessed the growth and integration of extensive global maritime and terrestrial networks of trade and information flow over vast areas (Burke 2009: 185). In some locations, this led to the development of "cities without hinterlands" or settlements in marginal areas that in most periods would have been regarded as uninhabitable.[1] Cities lacking a robust means of local agricultural support occur throughout the Islamic world but are particularly evident in the Persian Gulf: for example, early Islamic Siraf and fourteenth- to fifteenth-century Hormuz, both with meager and arid agricultural hinterlands, were partly dependent upon imported goods from the maritime routes or the more verdant interior of Fars. In the case of the latter emporium, Kennet suggests that the parallel growth of Julfar in the United Arab

Emirates was intended to supply Hormuz with food (2003: 121–22), a point that suggests a degree of codependency among maritime settlements.

Similarly, regarding the Ghurids (Chapter 9), Thomas and Gascoigne point out that the estimated population of Jam (Afghanistan) would have exceeded the carrying capacity of the surrounding landscape, which lacked agricultural potential. The Ghurids did not seem to regard this as a problem, however, because their mobile strategies formed part of a highly connected world that enabled their settlements to develop and survive, at least as long as such connectivity remained in place.

The site of Qasr Mushash (Jordan), discussed by Bartl (Chapter 3) illustrates the combined role of water management and connectivity. Not only was this desert site dependent upon water management for its survival; it was also a product of its position as a caravanserai. Without the development of long-distance pilgrimage and other communication routes, there would have been no reason for sites such as Qasr Mushash to develop, but importantly, they were dependent upon the technologies of water extraction to be sustainable.

Similarly, Wordsworth's investigations of "stopping places" in the Karakum (Chapter 12) highlights the importance of connectivity: "The trilateral interdependence between urban centers, travelers and the stopping places, is thus a defining characteristic of movement in the desert, and the data presented here suggests that it was not restricted to single highways, but can be seen across a complex network of tracks and pathways." Again, water supply and its management play a major role, not only in the sustenance of such settlements but also by making such connectivity work. Similarly, in Arabia, where religion provided the focal point for the radial pattern of *hajj* routes, the gathering of water from the arid terrain enabled people to use the routes as a means of access to the holy places of Mecca and Medina (al-Rashid 1980). In addition to allowing religious rites to be observed, by connecting Iraq with the Hijaz, the Darb Zubayda also formed a route for information flow and trade.

Conversely, the apparent lack of communications can also be considered under the banner of connectivity. Thus, Mahoney's case study from Yemen (Chapter 7) shows profoundly how a densely populated rural Islamic landscape can manifest its materiality despite meager connections with the outside world. Not only did the paucity of imported ceramics demonstrate a degree of isolation for the local rural population, the traditions of local ceramic wares, which extended back for millennia, point to both conservatism and independence.

The apparent lack of connectivity of the Yemeni highlands cannot be the whole story though, because, as shown at a recent conference by Damgaard,[2] Late Antique amphorae from Aqaba in Jordan are recognized at the Himyarite capital of Zhafar in highland Yemen.[3] This suggests that the communication systems were at least episodically used. Nevertheless, these highland communities developed their own traditions and identities that manifested fewer links with mainstream currents of trade. Moreover, on the Darb Zubayda, glazed and unglazed wares from Iraq, as well as other high-status items, occur within the southern Nejd part of the route, demonstrating the role of the pilgrim route as a conduit for commerce and prestige goods (al-Rashid 1986). Only a minority of these types of items found their way into the Yemen highlands, however. Mahoney therefore successfully demonstrates how local factors and traditions continued to play a significant role in the development of Islamic communities.

## Land and Settlement

Although connectivity played a significant role in the development of the Islamic economy, local land resources and access to them remained important. The interplay between the nucleation and dispersal of communities as well as the role of land tenure emphasizes how changes in social and political factors as well as land availability can result in marked changes in the archaeological visibility of settlements and land use (Walker, Chapter 10). Walker's concept of "liquid landscapes," adopted from Sutton (2000), also resembles concepts of "fluidity of rural adjustment" as laid out by Adams (1981: 250). In the case of northern Jordan, Walker's use of fine-grained archaeological surveys combined with textual evidence suggests that rather than experiencing wholesale population decline, there may have been shifts from nucleated settlement toward more dispersed, less visible patterns of living. Again, the notion of connectivity comes into play because the local movements toward fields, religious places, festivals, and markets set the stage for population flux, which could then be nested within larger frameworks of connectivity.

## Water Management

Water and its management, as well as supporting the tax base of state structures (Adams 2006: 32–35), is central to an understanding of the organization of the rural economy of the Middle East. Here the fine-grained resolution of textual evidence (Meier, Chapter 1), geological investigations (Macumber, Chapter 2), and case studies of water-management structures (Bartl and McPhillips, Chapters 3 and 8, respectively) provide insights on water use over some thousand years. In her chapter on eighteenth-century Ottoman court registers, Meier explicitly recognizes the relevance of the materiality of the remains discussed in the texts: not only in the paper trail left in the registers that contribute details on water distribution but also, for example, in reference to "stones" at off-takes for water division. These references resonate with field evidence from the River Balikh where anomalously large stones occur at intervals along the otherwise subtle traces of canals (Wilkinson 1996). These too were inferred as indicating the location of water off-takes, but the evidence from the Ottoman texts not only supports interpretations about their use but goes further by providing a wealth of information about their position in the organizational framework of irrigation.

Ottoman records also supply crucial information on the role of the state in water management, a question long debated by anthropologists, archaeologists, and historians. Meier points out that the Judge of Damascus played a key role in the water administration of the city and its rural surroundings, whereas the authorities in Istanbul were only rarely involved. This indicates that state authorities, at least at the local level, played a significant role in water management.

The material evidence for water management is also well in evidence in McPhillips' investigation of Ottoman water mills in western Syria. Water mills exhibit their own materiality, well illustrated by their durability in the landscape where they can form conspicuous features of water management that can persist even when their supply channels become obscured (Fig. I.2). The sheer quantity of mills in northwestern Syria is indicative of the investment in milling, as well as the cereal production of the region. Whether early Islamic mills were as frequent in the same landscape appears unlikely. Further afield, however, water mills were common in the hinterlands of both Siraf and Sohar (sixteen for Siraf and five for Sohar), as well as in the Deh Luran plain of Iran (Neely 2011). It can therefore be inferred that mills were significant installations in much of the early Islamic countryside, at least in those areas favored by high investment.

Whereas major canals and water works have received considerable attention (e.g., in Berthier 2001), the rather less glamorous role of groundwater is less evident in the literature on Islamic water management. Macumber's perspective on the role of groundwater in the distribution of Islamic rural settlement is therefore not only valuable in itself; it also supplies context for the chapter on animal husbandry in Qatar (Bangsgaard and Yeomans, Chapter 5). Access to groundwater was a crucial factor in settlement location, and "the history of Qatar is strongly reflected in the history of its wells" (Macumber, this volume). Macumber also extends the argument by suggesting those areas where wells were probably involved in garden irrigation, which elsewhere in Arabia have proved an important part of oasis development (Costa and Wilkinson 1987).

Perhaps surprisingly, despite their lack of rainfall, many desert landscapes often supply a wealth of opportunities for gathering water. As described by Wordsworth (Chapter 12) for the Karakum desert of Central Asia, water-gathering opportunities can take the form of extensive clay flats, or *takyr*, which by providing water sources in the desert, can supply livestock and travelers with essential

Figure I.2 The prominent penstock of an Islamic water mill at Jam, in the hinterland of Siraf, Iran (photograph by Donald Whitcomb).

sustenance. Similarly, in Arabia, numerous minor wadis, or enclosed basins, can collect and conduct water to cisterns (*birka*), which exhibit a remarkable locational flexibility. On the other hand, pasture resources to sustain the camels and other transport animals can be less common; therefore, it was the availability of pasture that often dictated the positioning of cisterns and stopping places on pilgrim routes (Wilkinson 2003: 166–68). Overall, the water systems in the Karakum and around Qasr Mushash discussed by Bartl in Chapter 3, made connectivity possible, and the increased connectivity provided an essential link between otherwise isolated communities.

## Agriculture, Pastoralism, and Rural Subsistence

Whereas in recent years there have been significant advances in our understanding of settlement and agricultural production (Borrut et al. 2011), there remains a need for detailed research on rural provisioning. The two chapters in this volume on the archaeological remains of animal use and fishing therefore provide considerable insights into aspects of food procurement.

Using data from six sites in Jordan occupied in the Middle Islamic period (1100–1516), Brown discusses the type of information on animal use that is rarely addressed in historical sources (Chapter 4). According to Brown, whereas medieval memoirs frequently present lush landscapes populated with wild animals and traversed by high-value horses and other pack animals, such observations reflect the perceptions of an elite social class that tended to disregard mundane livestock that supported the rural economy. Evidence from animal bones supplies an important source of information on, for example, increased use of sheep and goats, but also on the very rich range of fauna that still remained during this period. Such regional-scale investigations therefore provide a valuable complement to regional land use and archaeological surveys.

In Chapter 5, Bangsgaard and Yeomans, although focusing on only part of a site (110 ha. al-Zubara), demonstrate the importance of the sea to this eighteenth-century community in Qatar. Essential context is added by their presentation of data on the plethora of fish traps along the coast. The authors also raise the point that the lack of agriculturally productive land in Qatar made the population dependent on food imported from elsewhere. Therefore, not only did the sea provide one of the main resources, namely, fish, but it also supplied the medium of transport for importing food products that could not be grown locally. Does this mean that al-Zubara, like Siraf and Hormuz, was highly dependent upon food imported from elsewhere, or might the wells (discussed by Macumber in Chapter 2) have serviced such settlements by providing small irrigated gardens for the supply of supplementary food? Whether this was the case or not, such communities could potentially buy their way out of a crisis using networks of maritime communication.

## Technology

In his review of "technological complexes" in the Islamic world, Burke (2009) identifies a pyrotechnological complex, which must have played a significant role in the development of Islamic industry. Whereas archaeologists have lavished considerable attention on early Islamic pyrotechnology (e.g., Henderson et al. 2005; Weisgerber 1987), the Middle Islamic period has remained rather underexplored. What had been a major industry in the ninth to tenth centuries CE, had frequently withered by the fourteenth or fifteenth century to a small-scale operation. Nevertheless, the industry did continue and Jones (Chapter 6), by focusing upon metal production in the Middle Islamic period at Khirbat Nuqayb al-Asaymir in Wadi Faynan (Jordan), demonstrates a degree of conservatism in the use of such technologies as furnaces. In fact, these installations resemble those in use in Oman during the early Islamic boom (Chapter 6), and it seems that the use of this technology was widespread, presumably because of the extensive networks of technological exchange current throughout the Islamic world.

## Burial and the Rural Landscape

Landscapes of the dead are often conspicuous in the Middle East, with countries such as Oman that adjoin the Arabian deserts sometimes appearing to have more ancient tombs than settlements. In the Homs area, as demonstrated by Bradbury, not only do burial monuments cover huge areas of "sub-optimal land," they also form a component part of the large-scale agrarian landscape (Chapter 11). Not only did Islamic burial monuments and cairns represent continuity with the past; they also provided a memory bank that could be harnessed to address land claims and tenure. Burial areas could therefore continue in use long after neighboring settlements had been abandoned. This is of considerable significance for the understanding of Islamic settlements because it means that elements of the landscape can continue to be held by a community after its demise. Burial and land use should not therefore be seen as separate but rather as sometimes belonging to intertwined worlds.

## Broader Questions

Many studies in this volume might be described as fine-grained case studies or regional summaries, which in addition to their intrinsic value, must be seen as forming essential building blocks for broader synthetic studies. Moreover, regions exhibit historical depth and are important parts of cultural and political developments, as argued for Iraq by Visser and Stansfield (2008). Because of the sheer scale of the Islamic imperial domains, it is appropriate, however, to consider how such extensive polities and their cities contributed to the development of the countryside.

In a compelling synthesis, Hugh Kennedy argues that insufficient attention has been paid to the economics of demand, specifically as generated by major Islamic cities, and that the expansion of settlement into climatically environmental lands has resulted from the expansion of the market to much larger regions (2011a: xii). As Kennedy points out, in the eighth to tenth centuries CE, such expansion was not evenly spread but included pockets of decline. Evidence for growth of canals and agriculture is manifest in many areas, including Raqqa and the Balikh Valley (Heidemann 2011; Bartl 1996, parts of the Middle Euphrates (Berthier 2001), and of course the Baghdad area, the latter being for Kennedy "the real engine of economic growth" (Hugh Kennedy pers. comm.). In addition to these loci of expansion, Samarra (and adjacent parts of the Adhaim), Wasit, Basra, Siraf, and Sohar (and its copper-rich hinterland) all witnessed growth during this period, often in the form of a rapid boom followed by decline. In addition, considerable growth occurred along arteries of communication, such as the *hajj* roads, as well as other cross-desert routes as demonstrated here by Bartl and Wordsworth. What emerges from this volume is that to some degree the remarkable connectivity and capacity for information flow in the early caliphates enabled such linked areas of growth to develop further. The integration of maritime networks with systems of riverine and overland transport enabled products to move more freely and growing cities to be sustained more readily by imported supplies within this monetized economy. Hence, cities such as Hormuz and Siraf, and indeed al-Zubara and al-Rabadaha, could all be sustained (at least for a while) by such flows of goods.

Arguably, the expansion of Islamic cities relied on an even greater connectivity than the preceding empires, in part because of the increased capacity of maritime traffic. More generally, the increased utility of transport systems discussed by Kennedy (2011b) forms an extension of the "Mesopotamian advantage" concept applied by Algaze to the growth of fourth- and third-millennium BCE Mesopotamian cities (2008); moreover, the Islamic empires form excellent examples of "network" empires as discussed by Liverani (1988) for the Neo-Assyrian and Smith (2005) for the Maurian empires.

The increased number of regional surveys allows us to compare trends in the Islamic countryside against earlier periods in order to assess the degree of growth or decline of certain regions. Investigations in the Balikh and those areas subjected to Indian Ocean trade discussed above demonstrate that cities not only structured developments in the surrounding countryside; they also presumably sucked in populations from elsewhere. Their rulers and elites often invested in new infrastructure rather than simply building upon the backs of earlier Sasanian or Roman Byzantine antecedents.[4] The population dynamics of such cycles of growth and decline are therefore well captured by the term *fluid* or *liquid landscapes* (Walker, Chapter 10).

To what degree the "Islamic green revolution" contributed to or was part of this growth continues to be debated (Watson 1983; Decker 2009), but the discussion would be strengthened by more studies of carbonized plant remains. Because agricultural growth was to some degree driven by the increase in the scale and distribution of irrigation systems, I suggest that this apparent "revolution" was part of a longer period of growth under the later territorial empires, starting with the Assyrian empire in the early first millennium BCE. This is shown by the spread of canals and water-management systems into moister parts of the Fertile Crescent over some three millennia, namely, from the period of Assyrian empire and later (Fig. I.3). Over this period, the extension of an "umbrella of imperial power" enabled water-management structures to extend into both wetter and drier landscapes, in part because it was possible to administer water and exercise power over multiple drainage catchments and ever larger areas, which was never possible under less extensive or unstable polities (Wilkinson and Rayne 2010).

Although evidence from the late 1980s onward suggests that in many regions, canal construction actually expanded in the early Islamic period, because the investigation of ancient canals is in its early stages, the history of water supply during the Islamic period requires more research. It is also crucial to appreciate just how important wells (Chapter 2) or the local harnessing of water and power was at different times (Chapters 3 and 8), and that more fine-grained studies of historical texts really do inform us about the local or regional management of such systems (Chapter 1). This is not simply because they contribute more data but rather because of the intertwined and mutually reinforcing nature of these different factors. In other words, developments and investments in water supply enable route networks to expand through deserts. This increased connectivity allowed technologies and information to be diffused more widely, and trade to increase; moreover, the extraordinarily dynamic growth of cities such as Baghdad and Sammara was made possible by the increased connectivity within the settlement landscape, and it is hardly surprising that many of the

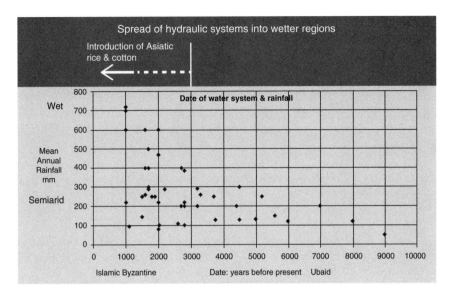

Figure I.3 The increase through time of irrigation systems into progressively moist regions in northern Mesopotamia. The approximate date of introduction of cotton and rice are indicated by the broken line, and the crops of the "Islamic Green Revolution" by the solid line (after Wilkinson and Rayne 2010).

poles of growth described above were linked together by riverine, terrestrial, and maritime links that were both more integrated and more effective than during preceding empires.

Rather than end with the impression that the Islamic world was one of uninhibited growth, which was not the case,[5] the studies in this volume remind us that local people also had to wrestle in their own way with the changes wrought by a dynamic economy: by adapting their animal procurement strategies, by retaining rights to the land (even if they had to move), and in some cases, such as highland Yemen, just continuing on with life, as had been the case in previous eras.

## Notes

1. In fact, there are three particularly noteworthy episodes of settlement of the arid steppe in the Fertile Crescent: the mid to late Early Bronze Age, the Late Roman–Byzantine and the early Islamic periods. To this may be added localized settlement of the marginal "zone of uncertainty" in the Neo-Assyrian period.

2. "Rural Periphery or Economic Dynamo? Production Mercantilism and Connectivity in Early Islamic South Palestine," presented at the Materiality of the Islamic Rural Economy Workshop, Copenhagen, August 2012.

3. This was also the case in some of the larger surrounding settlements.

4. Witness the investments in conduits, qanats, and water mills around both Siraf and Sohar. The canals of Maslama recorded in the Balikh Valley and by Dibsi Faraj were also apparently new undertakings (Wilkinson and Rayne 2010: 125–28; Heidemann 2011: 45).

5. "Boom and bust" may more accurately characterize elements of the Early Islamic economic landscape.

## Bibliography

Adams, Robert McC. 1965. *Land Behind Baghdad*. Chicago: University of Chicago Press.

———. 1981. *Heartland of Cities*. Chicago: University of Chicago Press.

———. 2006. "Intensified large-scale irrigation as an aspect of imperial policy: strategies of statecraft on the Late Sasanian Mesopotamian plain." In *Agricultural Strategies*, edited by Joyce Marcus and Charles Stanish, 17–37. Los Angeles: Cotsen Institute of Archaeology.

Algaze, Guillermo. 2008. *Ancient Mesopotamia at the Dawn of Civilization: The Evolution of an Urban Landscape*. Chicago: University of Chicago Press.

Amr, Khairieh, and Ahmad al-Momani. 2011. "Villages of the early Islamic period in the Petra region." In *Le Proche-Orient de Justinien aux Abbassides: Peuplement et dynamiques spatiales*, edited by Antoine Borrut, Muriel Debié, Arietta Papaconstantinou, Dominique Pieri, and Jean-Pierre Sodini, 305–13. Turnhout, Belgium: Brepols.

Bartl, Karin. 1996. "Baliḫ Valley Survey: settlements of the late Roman/early Byzantine and Islamic period." In *Continuity and Change in Northern Mesopotamia from the Hellenistic to the Early Islamic Period,* edited by Karin Bartl and Stefan R. Hauser, 333–48. Berlin: Dietrich Reimer.

Berthier, Sophie. 2001. *Peuplement rural et aménagements hydroagricoles dans la moyenne vallée de l'Euphrate, fin VIIe–XIXe siècle: région de Deir ez Zor-Abu Kemal, Syrie. Mission Mésopotamie syrienne, archéologie islamique, 1986–1989*. Damascus: Institut Français d'Études Arabes de Damas.

Borrut, Antoine, Muriel Debié, Arietta Papaconstantinou, Dominique Pieri, and Jean-Pierre Sodini, eds. 2011. *Le Proche-Orient de Justinien aux Abbassides: Peuplement et dynamiques spatiales*. Turnhout, Belgium: Brepols.

Burke, Edmund III. 2009. "Islam at the center: technological complexes and the roots of modernity." *Journal of World History* 20(2): 165–86.

Costa Paolo, M., and Tony J. Wilkinson. 1987. "The hinterland of Sohar: archaeological surveys and excavations within the region of an Omani seafaring city." *Journal of Oman Studies* 9: 1–238.

Decker, Michael. 2009. "Plants and progress: rethinking the Islamic agricultural revolution." *Journal of World History* 20(2): 187–206.

———. 2011. "Settlement and agriculture in the Levant, 6th–8th centuries." In *Le Proche-Orient de Justinien aux Abbassides: Peuplement et dynamiques spatiales,* edited by Antoine Borrut, Muriel Debié, Arietta Papaconstantinou, Dominique Pieri, and Jean-Pierre Sodini, 1–6. Turnhout, Belgium: Brepols.

De Jong, Lidewijde. 2012. "Resettling the steppe: the archaeology of the Balikh valley in the early Islamic period." In *Proceedings of the 7th International Congress on the Archaeology of the Ancient Near East, 12 April–16 April 2010, the British Museum and UCL, London*, edited by Roger Roger and John Curtis, vol. 2: 517–31. Wiesbaden, Germany: Harrassowitz.

Eger, A. Asa. 2011. "The swamps of home: marsh formation and settlement in the early medieval Near East." *Journal of Near Eastern Studies* 70(1): 55–79.

Geyer, Bernard, and Marie-Odile Rousset. 2011. "Déterminants géoarchéologiques du peuplement rural dans les Marges arides de Syrie du Nord aux viiᵉ–ixᵉ siècles." In *Le Proche-Orient de Justinien aux Abbassides: Peuplement et dynamiques spatiales,* edited by Antoine Borrut, Muriel Debié, Arietta Papaconstantinou, Dominique Pieri, and Jean-Pierre Sodini, 77–92. Turnhout, Belgium: Brepols.

Heidemann, Stefan. 2011. "The agricultural hinterland of Baghdād, al-Raqqa and Sāmarrāʾ: settlement patterns in the Diyār Muḍar." In *Le Proche-Orient de Justinien aux Abbassides: Peuplement et dynamiques spatiales*, edited by Antoine Borrut, Muriel Debié, Arietta Papaconstantinou, Dominique Pieri, and Jean-Pierre Sodini, 43–57. Turnhout, Belgium: Brepols.

Henderson, Julian, K. Challis, S. O'Hara, S. McLoughin, A. Gardner, and G. Priestnall. 2005. "Experiment and innovation: early Islamic industry at al-Raqqa, Syria." *Antiquity* 79: 130–45.

Horden, Peregrine, and Nicholas Purcell. 2000. *The Corrupting Sea: A Study of Mediterranean History.* Oxford: Blackwell.

Johns, Jeremy. 1995. "The longue durée: state and settlement strategies in southern Transjordan across the Islamic centuries." In *Village, Steppe and State: The Social Origins of Modern Jordan,* edited by Eugene Rogan and Tariq Tell, 1–31. London: I. B. Tauris.

———. 2010. "Islamic archaeology at a difficult age." *Antiquity* 84: 1187–91.

Kaptijn, Eva. 2010. "Communality and power: irrigation in the Zerqa Triangle, Jordan." *Water History* 2: 145–63.

Kennedy, Hugh. 2011a. Introduction. In *Le Proche-Orient de Justinien aux Abbassides: Peuplement et dynamiques spatiales*, edited by Antoine Borrut, Muriel Debié, Arietta Papaconstantinou, Dominique Pieri, and Jean-Pierre Sodini, 43: xi–xv. Turnhout, Belgium: Brepols.

———. 2011b. "The feeding of the five hundred thousand: cities and agriculture in early Islamic Mesopotamia." *Iraq* 73: 177–99.

Kennet, Derek. 2003. "Julfar and the urbanization of Southeast Arabia." *Arabian Archaeology and Epigraphy* 14(1): 103–25.

Liverani, Mario. 1988. "The growth of the Assyrian empire in the Habur/Middle Euphrates area: a new paradigm." *State Archives of Assyria, Bulletin* (Padua) 2: 81–98.

McPhillips, Stephen. 2012. "Islamic settlement in the Upper Orontes Valley, Syria: recent fieldwork (2009)." In *Proceedings of the 7th International Congress on the Archaeology of the Ancient Near East, 12 April–16 April 2010, the British Museum and UCL, London*, edited by Roger Roger and John Curtis, vol. 2: 691–710 Wiesbaden: Harrassowitz.

Milwright, Marcus. 2010. *An Introduction to Islamic Archaeology.* Edinburgh: Edinburgh University Press.

Neely, James. 2011. "Sasanian period drop-tower gristmills on the Deh Luran Plain, southwestern Iran." *Journal of Field Archaeology* 36(3): 232–54.

Power, Timothy, and Peter Sheehan. 2012. "The origin and development of the oasis landscape of al-ʾAin (UAE)." *Proceedings of the Seminar for Arabian Studies* 42: 291–308.

al-Rashid, Saʾad. 1980. *Darb Zubayda: The Pilgrim Route from Kufa to Mecca.* Riyadh: University Libraries.

———. 1986. *Al-Rabadahah: A Portrait of Early Islamic Civilization in Saudi Arabia.* Riyadh: King Saud University.

Sarre, Friedrich P. T., and Ernst E. Herzfeld. 1911–1920. *Archäologische Reise im Euphrat-und Tigris-Gebeit.* 4 vols. Berlin: Dietrich Reimer.

Smith, Monica L. 2005. "Networks, territories, and the cartography of ancient states." *Annals of the Association of American Geographers* 95(4): 832–49.

Sutton, Susan Buck. 2000. "Liquid landscapes: demographic transitions in the Ermionidha." In *Contingent Countryside: Settlement, Economy, and Land Use in the Southern Argolid Since 1700*, edited by Susan Sutton, 84–106. Stanford: Stanford University Press.

Visser, Reidar, and Gareth Stansfield, eds. 2008. *An Iraq and Its Regions: Cornerstones of a Federal Democracy?* New York: Columbia University Press.

Walker, Bethany J. 2005. "The Northern Jordan Survey 2003—agriculture in Late Islamic Malka and Hubras villages: a preliminary report on the first season." *Bulletin of the American Schools of Oriental Research* 339: 67–111.

Watson, Andrew. 1983. *Agricultural Innovation in the Early Islamic World: The Diffusion of Crops and Farming Techniques.* Cambridge: Cambridge Studies in Islamic Civilization.

Weisgerber, Gerd. 1987. "Archaeological evidence of copper exploitation at 'Arja." *Journal of Oman Studies* 9: 145–238.

Whitcomb, Donald. 2004. "Khirbet Dhiman (SS 11), Khirbet al-Hamrah (SS 7) (Sweyhat Survey Period XIV." In *On the Margin of the Euphrates: Settlement and Land Use at Tell es-Sweyhat and in the Upper Lake Tabqa Area, Syria,* edited by T. J. Wilkinson, N. F. Miller, C. D. Reichel, and D. Whitcomb, 98–99, 124–30. Oriental Institute Publications 124. Chicago: University of Chicago Press.

———. 2006. "Archaeological evidence of sedentarization: Bilad al-Sham in the early Islamic period." In *Die Sichtbarkeit von Nomaden und saisonaler Besiedlung in der Archäologie: Multidisziplinäre Annäherungen an ein methodisches Problem,* edited by Stefan R. Hauser, 27–43. Halle: Orientwissenschaftliche Hefte 21, Mitteilungen des SFB.

———. 2007. "Islamic archaeology and the 'Land Behind Baghdad.'" In *Settlement and Society: Essays Dedicated to Robert McCormick Adams,* edited by Elizabeth C. Stone, 255–59. Los Angeles: Cotsen Institute of Archaeology and the Oriental Institute.

Wilkinson, Tony J. 1990. *Town and Country in SE Anatolia, vol. 1: Settlement and Land Use at Kurban Hoyuk and Other Sites in the Lower Karababa Basin.* Chicago: Oriental Institute Publications 109.

———. 1996. "Sabi Abyad: the geoarchaeology of a complex landscape." In *Tell Sabi Abyad the Late Neolithic Settlement,* edited by P. M. M. G. Akkermans. Istanbul: Netherlands Historical and Archaeological Institute.

———. 2003. *Archaeological Landscapes of the Near East.* Tucson: University of Arizona Press.

Wilkinson, Tony J., Naomi F. Miller, Clemens D. Reichel, and Donald Whitcomb. 2004. *On the Margin of the Euphrates: Settlement and Land Use at Tell es-Sweyhat and in the Upper Lake Tabqa Area, Syria.* Oriental Institute Publications 124. Chicago: University of Chicago Press.

Wilkinson, Tony J., and Louise Rayne. 2010. "Hydraulic landscapes and imperial power in the Near East." *Water History* 2: 115–44.

Williamson, Andrew. 1987. "Regional distribution of mediaeval Persian pottery in the light of recent investigations." In *Syria and Iran: Three Studies in Medieval Ceramics,* edited by James Allan and C. Roberts, 11–22. Oxford: Oxford Studies in Islamic Art 4.

# PART I

# Hydroeconomies

Managing and Living with Water

# CHAPTER 1

# The Materiality of Ottoman Water Administration in Eighteenth-Century Rural Damascus

## A Historian's Perspective

*Astrid Meier*

At the beginning of April 1708, a group of about fifty men from the village of al-Kanakir, situated to the southwest of Damascus (Fig. 1.1), arrived, fully armed (*bil-'udda al-kāmila*), at the point where the water channel of the village of al-Rujm (also Rujm al-Khayyat) departed from the main canal. They came to confront an official delegation sent by the Judge of Damascus who, as the head of the judiciary of the province, also fulfilled eminent administrative functions. Threatening violence, the group of armed men made it impossible for the "engineer" (*ḥaysūb*) present on the spot to proceed with the repairs of the diversion mechanism the delegation had been sent to inspect.[1]

Nearly five years later, another court document sheds more light on the water-related conflict that seems to be behind the incident. It involved not only the two villages of al-Kanakir and al-Rujm but also the villages of al-Husayniyya, Mu'azzamiyyat Darayya, Sahnaya, al-Judayda, Shaqhab, and al-Nufur, all situated along the A'waj River between Sa'sa' and Darayya, two of the water nodes of the region that were also implicated in the case. In December 1712, the Judge of Damascus sent another delegation to Sa'sa' to inspect the canal system and repair the equipment that regulated the flow of water toward these villages (MSD 32/207/561 [27 Dhu l-Qa'da 1124]). On both occasions, tangible things, objects or assemblies of objects—in particular, the stone blocks that diverted the water into the secondary canals[2]—were the focus of the interest. In 1712, repairs were successfully completed, yet not by simply restoring them to their previous condition, as became

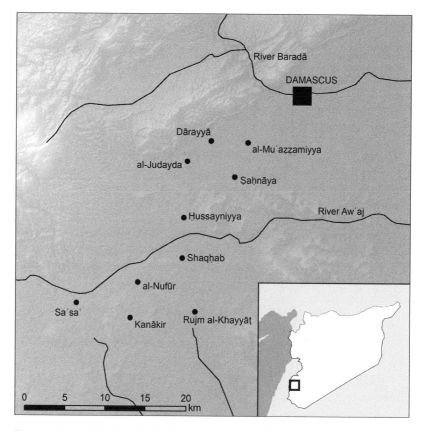

Figure 1.1 Map showing the locations mentioned in the text (base map courtesy of USGS).

clear during the proceedings. At the end of that day, the water was redistributed in a new manner, and al-Kanakir seemingly came out of the conflict as the winner, as it successfully claimed shares of water from its immediate neighbors, including al-Rujm, al-Nufur, and Shaqhab.

With respect to the material, this rearrangement was orchestrated easily enough. However, it had proven more difficult when it came to gaining the consent of all the interested parties to the changes effected by the new arrangements. The use, or at least the threat, of violence in 1708 is proof enough of the difficult back-history of the operation. That incident, read as a moment of systemic crisis or disruption, brings to the forefront the complex social, political, and material mechanisms of control that made up the Ottoman system of water administration. It also sheds light on the reasons for the elaborate administrative proceedings that accompanied the repairs mentioned in 1712 (MSD 32/207/561 [27 Dhu l-Qaʿda 1124]) that are one point of interest of this chapter. What was going on evidently was not about the technology in use but a question of legitimation and an expression of shifting power relations in this rural environment.[3]

Both moments, captured in the formal and rather sterile language of the Ottoman court registers, highlight the importance of materiality in water administration but not in terms of a simple presence of things or objects or of objects possessing agency of their own. Behind the material lay the manifold processes connected to the "socialization of water," a term that points to the societal dimensions of resource management and its complexities.[4] The stone blocks mentioned in the eighteenth-century court documents therefore seem an appropriate starting point for a historian's contribution to this volume combining archaeological, anthropological, and historical approaches to the rural Islamic world. As, for the most part, the Ottoman period has remained outside the concerns of archaeologists, projects that combine the expertise of both textual and material sources are only just beginning and concern mainly urban contexts.[5]

I would like to draw attention to the rich and variegated aspects of materiality that can be found in the Ottoman archival sources (Hopwood 2000). I shall start with some remarks as to the "state of the art" of water-related research in Ottoman studies. Following this is a close reading of the documents in order to highlight what can be learned from them for the study of materiality but also to name some of the difficulties one encounters in this undertaking. I shall conclude with some thoughts about the methodological issues this type of study opens for interdisciplinary cooperation.

## Water

Water and accessibility to it are decisive factors in shaping human, animal, and plant life. This simple truth is even more evident in a setting where water is scarce and where access to it is difficult and contested. Though the city of Damascus and its surrounding oasis have been renowned for their generous supply of water through the historical record,[6] competition about water triggered numerous conflicts. In the eighteenth century, there is ample documentation in court and administrative archives and contemporary historiography for a high frequency of wide-ranging, water-related confrontations.[7] When and how such conflicts developed, in what manner they were resolved, and how materiality figures in such settlements are all questions that go beyond the material: the rules and norms of water distribution, the handling of this sensitive resource by both the people concerned and the Ottoman authorities on various levels. The hydroeconomies of early modern Damascus need to be understood in a framework that also encompasses what today is called law and politics.

The case of the two villages of al-Kanakir and Rujm al-Khayyat in the A'waj valley thus raises questions of how materiality is integrated into the realms of politics, law, and administration. All have been important fields of inquiry in Ottoman studies, but water administration has only recently become an object of extensive study (Mikhail 2010, 2011; Lemire 2010; for a more comprehensive bibliography, see Marino and Meier 2012). This "hydrographic" turn is also an expression of a higher sensitivity to environmental factors in historical analysis (e.g., White 2011; İnal 2011; Tabak 2008). Addressing various issues in different times and places and working with different source material, these studies are too diverse to allow drawing a conclusive picture of the workings of Ottoman water administration. One aspect has become evident, though: if one follows not only the physical flow of water but also the paper trail it left in the various archives and repositories, one is brought from a specific locality to the provincial and regional levels of administration, sometimes even to the imperial capital, and back again.

In eighteenth-century Damascus, the various spheres meet in the main court of the city, the Mahkamat al-Bab, the seat of the judge of the province of Damascus. He was appointed by the central administration and came from Istanbul for a term usually not longer than one year. Next to the governor, the judge occupied one of the key positions in the administration of the province, fulfilling many functions that today would be those of a municipality. This becomes evident if one looks through the documentation entered into the judicial registers that were kept in the judge's court for further use. These records (which Ottomanists call *sijill* after the usage of the time) are one of the most important sources available for the writing of history (for an introduction, see Faroqhi 1999).

Only a few important cases related to water issues were heard in the Governor's Council (*diwan*), of which the *qadi* was a member ex officio. A greater number of cases, all inspection missions, also implicated some of the governor's staff in the proceedings. Only rarely did a case from the Damascus hinterland seem to have reached Istanbul and the central authorities, although this topic awaits further investigation in the central archives (Marino and Meier 2012: 381–88; for the differing case of Egypt, see Mikhail 2010, 2011).

The Judge of Damascus played a key role not only in the water administration of the city but also in its rural surroundings. When problems related to the water supply came to his attention, he sometimes went in person to see what was happening, or he sent his substitutes as in the two cases mentioned above. Inspection missions (*kashf wa-wuquf*) were usually solicited by one of the interested parties, but they seem to have become one of the most important measures related to water administration in eighteenth-century Damascus. The key function of this simple procedure and its potential for accommodating adaptation and change have been underrated so far in the scholarly literature on rural societies, politics, and economies.

This oversight stems to a high degree from the views that have dominated water-related research since the early twentieth century. Many studies, inspired by anthropological approaches that stressed the importance of local custom, claim that the prevalence of such practices and the weight that they simply called "tradition" was the main reason why the systems seemed to be unchangeable and were so difficult to "modernize."[8]

Such arguments were reinforced by references to Islamic law, for instance to a well-known maxim that says that the old order of things should be maintained (*yutrak al-qadim 'ala qidamihi*), as long as there is no legal proof that contradicts the status quo.[9] In conflicts about taxes, another contested field in which the usually invisible rural communities frequently make an appearance, this maxim is often invoked by the village representatives, and judges invariably hold up its validity (Meier 2005). Water rights, however, are a more complicated issue that can only be sketched out here briefly.[10]

According to all schools of Islamic law, water itself is considered *res nullius* (*mubah*) and cannot be owned, apart from small quantities that can be kept in receptacles. However, the land water is found upon or flows through can be owned, as well as all types of canals, wells, pipes, and drains. The A'waj River counts in Hanafi legal thought—which is the most relevant for the understanding of the documents in question—as a great river (*nahr kabir*). This means it is considered common property (*'amm*: general, common), and its water can be used by anybody. The secondary and tertiary canals that are fed by the A'waj belong, however, to a different category and are considered the property of particular village communities or groups of communities (*khass*: specific, particular).

In terms of access to water, this legal categorization has the following consequences. Everybody has the right to use the water of the A'waj in its natural bed as long as this does not harm anybody else's interests. The water of the smaller canals can be used to quench one's thirst or to a certain extent to water one's flocks (right of *shafa*, pertains to persons and animals) but not for irrigation (right of *shirb*, pertains to land) except by those entitled to such use. Canals thus are considered as a type of co-owned property (*milk mushtarak*). Rights and obligations are shared by all those who are entitled to a share, however loosely defined this incorporated group is. In the cases in question, these corporate bodies mainly appear in the form of village communities (*qarya*), represented by a number of men who are listed by name in the documents. In legal theory, such corporate groups can freely decide on the distribution and redistribution of water rights, as long as this occurs unanimously.

This conception of rights and obligations led the Hanafi jurists to the perhaps surprising tenet that in the case of such communitarian canals, there is no such thing as precedence or custom that fixes water shares and access to it. At any time, a group of users has the right to make new arrangements under the one condition that they all agree. This important aspect is not made explicit in the court acts, which is intriguing considering that it is a central point of the cases under investigation. It probably does not need to be spelled out here that the condition of general agreement is nearly impossible to meet and does not resemble the "democratic" principle of majority rule.[11]

## To Make Stones Speak: The *Qadi*'s Experts and a Moving Public

To return now to the stone blocks themselves: what exactly was done with them on the two occasions? To find out, it is necessary to take a closer look at the documents and how they describe the assessment of damage and the repair operations, as well as the legitimating procedures in which the repairs were embedded.

The mechanism that regulated the diversion of the water between the main canal and its derivation is described in the court documents by several elements: a "window" (*ṭaqa*), an "off-take" (*basṭ*), and an "opening" set inside the canal (*al-farḍ al-mawḍuʿ min baṭin al-nahr*). All of them are described in both acts as damaged and in need of repairs. This is already evident in the stated aim of the first, aborted mission, which was to "inspect the 'off-take' (*basṭ*) for the water of the village of al-Rujm from the canal of al-Kanakir (which derives from the river Aʿwaj) and to repair the 'opening' (*farḍ*) in the middle of the canal." On the ground, the delegation found that a number of stones were missing in this "opening" and had to be reset. Furthermore, the "gate of the off-take" (*fam al-basṭ*) as well as the "banks of the canal" (*ḥaffat al-nahr*) had to be repaired (MSD 29/178/386 [11 Muharram 1120]).

The second document gives a more elaborate description of the water diversion and followed an inspection tour involving at least ten village communities that all shared the water of the Aʿwaj. The tour begins outside the village of Saʿsaʿ, at locations where some of its inhabitants seem to have diverted the water to their fields without legal claim; then the tour comes to the main diversion inside the village, called a *qubba*, and proceeds first with the resetting of the main division of the canals leading to Darayya and to al-Kanakir. The delegation then turns off to inspect three different village off-takes, one after the other. I shall concentrate here on the diversion of al-Kanakir and al-Rujm.[12] The "window" (*ṭaqa*) and the "off-take" (*basṭ*) are introduced by the measurement of a "circular divider" (*daʾira*) through which the water was supposed to flow (Shaʿbān 1997–98: 87). Standing on the banks of the canal, the delegation then found that the whole off-take was out of working order and its stones broken. The building experts then cleared the spot of all debris and set down the new stones, fixing them with mortar (*mun*). The circular divider was reset in its old place "exactly as it was before."

Yet the repairs did not stop there. After an exchange of contradictory statements, as to whether the mosque of al-Kanakir held water rights in this off-take or not, the proceedings take a surprising about-turn, which is not explained further in the document. The parties agree (*tawafaqu*) upon setting another new stone on the western side of the off-take from which water would flow into the canal toward al-Kanakir and its mosque. The document ends this whole section with the laconic statement, "The engineer cut [the stone to the specified dimensions] and deposited it in the 'off-take' toward the west (*fa-nahatahu al-ḥaysub wa-wadaʿahu fi l-basṭ min jihat al-gharb*)."

This is the end of the story that began nearly five years earlier with the dramatic appearance of about fifty men at arms. The village of al-Rujm seems to have lost some of its former share of water to al-Kanakir. Yet as long as there is no other information available, we are left to speculate about the reasons for their agreement to the change. Environmental stresses might have played a role in this shift in power relations as these were years of rather severe drought (Shaʿban 1997–98: 97, 101, 105–106).

It is, however, possible to explore the strategies that were used by the different parties to legitimize the change. This means turning from the stones to the people involved. The document lists a considerable number of individuals who were implicated in the proceedings. The first inspection mission had been solicited by an Ottoman official in the name of the people of Rujm al-Khayyat, some of whom were certainly present at the diversion when the group of about fifty armed men came from al-Kanakir to stop the proceedings. The second document lists, besides the *qadi*'s delegation and groups of unnamed bystanders, the names of about fifty people, arranged in groups of three to five, said to represent the ten villages (in order of their mention in the document): al-Kanakir, Darayya, al-Husayniyya, Muʿazzamiyyat Darayya, Sahnaya, al-Judayda, Shaqhab, Rujm al-Khayyat, al-Nufur, and Saʿsaʿ. These men take on different roles during the long inspection tour of the day: when standing at their own diversion, they act as the interested party and have the power to make far-reaching decisions, such as the agreement explained above. Agreements (*tawafuq*) are often accompanied by other declarations of consent (*riḍaʾ*, *taṣdiq*) and recognitions of rights (*iqrar*), powerful legal instruments (Linant de Bellefonds 1971). In most cases, an agreement brings the legal process to a close, which leaves the historian to speculate about the motivations of the parties at this juncture and the possible use of economic or political force if not outright military strength or violence as manifest in the case of al-Kanakir and al-Rujm. Ottoman jurists and judges, however, consider agreements as if all parties entered them freely and without any kind of constraint, and usually do not question the contexts of such declarations.

The incorporation of the attendants into groups fluctuated and mirrored the flow of the water in the form of a network of tributary canals: whereas those depending on the same canal were united in their interests against those of another, they could become opponents when it came to the distribution of water among themselves. In the case described here, the village representatives first all stood united against Saʿsaʿ before splitting up into two groups: al-Kanakir and its co-owners on the one side, and Darayya and its co-owners on the other. Then the first group was further divided into its components, when the inspection and the repairs reached the water diversions between single villages. Yet it seems that the whole group of people moved along with the delegation from one place to the other, maybe acting as witnesses. All in all, the whole group of attendants can be seen as a kind of "moving public" that lent authority to the proceedings. I will come back to this aspect in the last section of the chapter.

On the ground, the most active participants were the building experts who were present in all such missions. The same "engineer" (*ḥaysub*) and his two colleagues, all of them Christians according to the names and titles given in the document, were present on both occasions. The second delegation was accompanied even by the head engineer (*miʿmarbashi*) of Damascus, a Muslim, as well as by a delegate of the governor of the province. As already described, the building experts were there for practical reasons: they cut stones to measure and set them in the right positions, and this in front of the "public" that moved along with them from one spot to the next. Yet they also provided expertise in cases when it was needed: at another stop on the tour, they had to render an informed opinion as to whether a water leak had caused damage to a village or not. They were the ones who were supposed to be able to read the situation and make the material speak.

This role of experts in legal and administrative procedures has long been known, but its importance for the working of administrative structures is probably underrated even today (Shaham 2010). Although it takes experts to make them speak, things and objects also have a voice that can be taken into account in the communitarian readjustment of rights that is done in the setting of a court session or an inspection tour (Johansen 1998). The basic skill for making things speak is the expert's ability to see (van Staëvel 2001). The importance of looking and seeing is highlighted time and again in the documentary record because the outward appearance of things cannot be taken for granted. They change over time, sometimes naturally, sometimes by lawful or unlawful manipulation. It was the job of the experts to see through this and to make the judges and their delegates see the difference, as well as to examine whether the arrangements of stone blocks resulted in the desired and agreed-upon distribution or not. Therefore, the experts were responsible for the activities of measuring the water debit, cutting stone blocks to measure, and positioning the stones, all under the eyes of their moving public.

The records of the various courts are another prop that experts and interested parties could rely on to tell the stories of things. These acts were written for those familiar with the situations and the words used to describe them. Therefore, it is not easy for modern historians to grasp the exact meaning of the technical terms, as their use is far from unambiguous and scholarly explanations are rather inconsistent.[13] Moreover, words are a rather inadequate instrument for conveying the exact proportions of a water-diversion mechanism. This can be gleaned from the fact that even in Ottoman times the experts and the legal personnel used drawings to record the exact shape and dimensions of a hole in a water distributor.[14] Unfortunately, such drawings seem not to have been copied into the court registers. This is why it is impossible for me to give exact translations of the technical terms used in the documents, and so I provide only vague and general descriptions: *bast*, translated here as "off-take," is described either as an alignment of huge stone blocks set in the middle of a waterway at a certain distance from each other to divide the water flow and branch it off (see Figs. 1.2 and 1.3),[15] or, in another case, as something resembling a small basin (*ḥawḍ ṣaghīr*) with a floor paved with stones and an opening called *ṭāqa*, "window," in its side (Shaʿbān 1997–98: 87). *Daʾira* is given as a water divider in circular form, usually a stone block with one or more circular holes.[16] *Farḍ* is not explained in the literature; the translation "opening" comes from *furḍa*, "opening" in a river or canal.[17]

Figure 1.2 Photograph of the diversion of the Darani (Planche V, Thoumin 1957: 71).

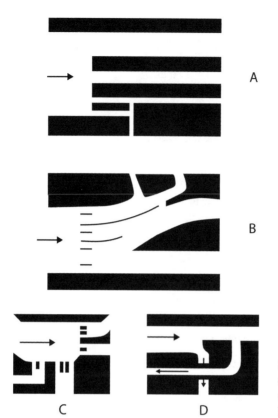

Figure 1.3 Sketch of various water diversions (Thoumin 1957: 69). Dividers on the following rivers: A. Tura; B. Darani; C. and D. in the Zur.

## "Making Things Public"

The exact circumstances of how the stone blocks of the water divider between al-Kanakir and al-Rujm first were set, then ended up broken—maybe by violence—and reset again, might remain obscure, but this history is proof enough that they were "objects of politics." These politics created occasional and momentary types of assemblies of people, maybe even a "public," and, on the second occasion, a kind of a moving "parliament" that went with the inspection mission from one place to the next (Marres 2005). Seen from this perspective, it is fairly easy to connect the two cases with a discussion that in another context and in another time frame, has been labeled "making things public" (Latour and Weibel 2005). Although inspections such as those described in the Ottoman court documents of Damascus were not exactly "public experiments" in the manner of the assays performed by scientists in early modern England and described by Simon Schaffer, they certainly were "vital sites and performed indispensible political roles" (2005: 299). And, *mutatis mutandis*, Schaffer's next words also pertain to the Ottoman case in question:

We still lack an entirely adequate history of the relation between the assays run in early modern states and the diagnostic trust vested in experimental experts. Such a history would take very seriously the consideration
that social institutions are made through communal performances and that
the knowledge made in such performances is itself constitutively communitarian. . . . The right to speak, and to have some activities count as truth,
are the basic political questions here. (ibid.)

In this competition over truth, entitlements, and resources, objects and things
played a vital role. Until recently, many historians have tended to take for granted
the material world and how it came about. If they want to understand how things
became issues of "public" concern—and to address what "public" might mean in
the Ottoman context through such performances as inspections and court
sessions seems a promising starting point—they have to develop the ability to see
things and objects in their contexts (Trentmann 2009). This basic requirement is
stressed in many debates about materiality in history writing, as, for instance, in
Daniel Miller's introduction: "The surprising conclusion is that objects are important not because they are evident and physically constrain or enable, but often
precisely because we do not 'see' them. The less we are aware of them, the more
powerfully they can determine our expectations by setting the scene and ensuring
normative behavior, without being open to challenge. They determine what takes
place to the extent that we are unconscious of their capacity to do so" (2005: 5).
Historians, unlike archaeologists, but also unlike Ottoman judges of the eighteenth
century and their substitutes, do not often venture out to see the material objects
they write about. In many cases, admittedly, such a mission would prove futile,
as there is nothing left to see. Yet in some other instances, historians could learn
from archaeologists or art historians what to look for in order to make the connections with what they read in their texts, and so start to understand them more
thoroughly so that archaeologists in turn could profit more from the results of
that joint undertaking.[18]

   Both the material and the social worlds described in the court records do not
appear as an exterior made of unchanging things through which people move as
if on a stage but as a carefully balanced system that needed constant attention to
be reset and maintained if one wanted it to remain stable and in functioning order.
The complex proceedings described in the court records can be read as an expression of a "regime of proof" that operated within more encompassing "regimes of
trust and doubt" as described by Schaffer (2005: 299). When a stone block is put
into such a framework, historians and archaeologists together can start to understand why it needed fifty men at arms to put a halt to its being positioned, as was
the case in the water conflict between the people of al-Kanakir and those of Rujm

al-Khayyat. So it is not a question of the technology in use, or pointing to the agency of rural communities, or understanding Ottoman law, politics, and administration: it is a question of bringing all these spheres together and highlighting their interconnectedness.

## Notes

1. This is a document from the Syrian National Archive in Damascus, the Center of Historical Documents (Dār al-wathā'iq al-ta'rīkhiyya), from the Series *al-Maḥākim al-Shar'iyya, Dimashq* (MSD). The documents are cited here in the following format: MSD register no./page no. /document no. (hijri date given in the document). The document quoted here is MSD 29/178/386 (11 Muḥarram 1120).

2. For an illustration of such mechanisms, see the sketches and photographs in Khayr (1966: 183–207) and Thoumin (1936: 41–74).

3. For the terminology and concept of "technology-in-use" that critiques the "innovation-centredness" that dominates the history of technology by stressing the category of "use," see Edgerton (2007: 5–10) in particular.

4. "Water is so closely related to the development of human groups that it becomes entangled in their social world, for which it constitutes a central link. However the 'socialisation' of water is an extremely complicated process . . . and is, moreover, one that has hardly been explored." The observation of Jean-Pierre Le Bourhis (2005: 482) is related to the study of contemporary societies, but it also pertains to historical research.

5. A notable exception is the ongoing study of the rural societies of what is today northern Jordan in late Mamluk and early Ottoman times, by a team of archaeologists and historians under the direction of Bethany Walker: see Chapter 10 in this volume. Cf. Baram and Caroll (2000) and the contributions in *ARAM Periodical* (1997–98).

6. In the first century of Islamic history, the Umayyad Caliph al-Walid b. 'Abd al-Malik (d. 96/715) is said to have listed his famous mosque in Damascus (completed in 87/706) only as the fifth element of pride and splendour of a city that claimed four others: "I see how you, the people of Damascus, pride yourselves on four elements: you are proud of your water, your air, your fruit and your bathhouses, and I would like that your mosque shall be the fifth" (MS. Ta'rikh Masjid Dimashq, quoted in al-Munajjid [1947: 402]).

7. For a discussion of water-related conflicts in early modern Damascus, see, among others, Marino and Meier (2012); Sha'bān (1997–98: 88–101); cf. also Shoshan (2011).

8. This point is very evident in the pioneering studies of water management in the Ghūṭa: see Tresse (1929), Thoumin (1934, 1936), Khayr (1966: 163–66), and cf. Alleaume (1992: 301–303).

9. For details, see Marino and Meier (2012: 379–80).

10. For this and the following paragraph, see Marino and Meier (2012: 372–76), Powers (2002: 103–105), and Young (1986: 860).

11. See also a case of 1806 described by Thoumin (1936: 108–11).

12. MSD 32/207/561 (27 Dhū l-Qa'da 1124): "*fa-wajadū l-basṭ mukassar al-aḥjār, yaḥtāj ilā ta'mīr wa-i'āda fa-qal 'uhu wa-'ammarūhu jadīdan bi-l-aḥjār al-jadīda wa-l-mūn . . . wa-a 'ādū al-dā'ira makānahā kamā kānat awwalan.*"

13. For an explanation of the terminology used in this article, see below. For general introductions to the hydrologic vocabulary in use at the time, see Sha'bān (1997–98: 87–96); Khayr (1966: 160–61), Thoumin (1936: 76, 83–86), and Tresse (1929: 474–525).

14. Drawings of openings, MSD 144/161/286 (18 Dhū l-Qaʿda 1167); ʿAṭṭār (1984: 35–36); Thoumin (1936: 76).

15. *Basṭ:* "répartiteur aux mesures de pierre alignées," in Thoumin (1936: 7); the same as *mazāz,* "alignment of huge stones in set distances in order to divide the water flow," in Khayr (1966: 160); "off-take of a canal at its source," made of stone blocks that are put down at wider distances than in an ordinary diversion called *mazāz* or *maṣāṣ* (*kalimat basṭ wa-huwa fatḥat al-nahr min aṣlihi . . . wa-aḥjār al-basā takūnu mutabāʿida akthar mimmā fī l-mazāzāt al-ʿādiyya*), in Zakariyyā (1957: vol. 2, 32).

16. *Dāʾira:* "répartiteur circulaire," in El Faïz (2005: 297).

17. For *farḍ,* see Shaʿbān (1997–98:87); for *furḍa* and *farḍ,* see Lane (1863: 2374–75).

18. In my own experience, such interdisciplinary teamwork can prove very fruitful, see Meier and Weber (2005: 379–431); and the ongoing project on rural bathhouses with a number of Syrian and French architects and building specialists, that will be on hold for the foreseeable future owing to the war in Syria, cf. Meier (2011 and 2014).

# Bibliography

Alleaume, Ghislaine. 1992. "Les systèmes hydrauliques de l'Égypte pré-moderne: essai d'une histoire du paysage." In *Itinéraires d'Égypte: Mélanges offerts au Père Maurice Martin S.J.,* edited by Christian Décobert, 301–22. Cairo: Institut français d'Archéologie orientale.

*ARAM.* 1997–98: Special issue: "The Mamluks and the early Ottoman period in Bilad al-Sham: history and archaeology." *ARAM Periodical* 9/10, 1997–98.

ʿAṭṭār, Muḥammad Ḥusayn al-. 1984. *ʿIlm al-miyāh al-jāriya fī madīnat Dimashq aw Risāla fī ʿilm al-miyāh,* edited by A. Sabānū. Damascus: Dār Qutayba.

Baram, Uzi, and Lynda Caroll, eds. 2000. *A Historical Archaeology of the Ottoman Empire: Breaking New Ground.* New York: Kluwer Academic/Plenum.

Edgerton, David. 2007 "Creole technologies and global histories: rethinking how things travel in space and time." *HOST, Journal of History of Science and Technology* 1(1): 3–31.

El Faïz, Mohammed. 2005. *Les maîtres de l'eau: histoire de l'hydraulique arabe.* Arles: Actes Sud.

Faroqhi, Suraiya. 1999. *Approaching Ottoman History: An Introduction to the Sources.* Cambridge: Cambridge University Press.

Hopwood, K. R. 2000. "The use of material culture in writing Ottoman history." *Archivum Ottomanicum* 18: 195–208.

İnal, Onur. 2011. "Environmental history as an emerging field in Ottoman studies: an historiographical overview." *Osmanlı Araştırmaları Dergisi* 38: 1–26.

Johansen, Baber. 1998. "La découverte des choses qui parlent: la légalisation de la torture judiciaire en droit musulman (xiiie–xive siècles)." *Enquête* 7: 175–202.

Khayr, Ṣaffūḥ. 1966. *Ghūṭat Dimashq: Dirāsa fī jughrāfiyya al-zirāʿiyya.* Damascus: Wizārat al-Thaqāfa wa-l-Irshād al-Qawmī.

Lane, Edward William. 1863. *An Arabic-English Lexicon.* London: Willams & Norgate.

Latour, Bruno, and Peter Weibel, eds. 2005. *Making Things Public: Atmospheres of Democracy.* Cambridge, MA: MIT Press.

Le Bourhis, Jean-Pierre. 2005. "Water parliaments: some examples." In *Making Things Public: Atmospheres of Democracy,* edited by Bruno Latour and Peter Weibel, 482–85. Cambridge, MA: MIT Press.

Lemire, Vincent. 2010. *La soif de Jérusalem: essai d'hydrohistoire (1840–1948).* Paris: Publications de la Sorbonne.

Linant de Bellefonds, Y. 1971. "Iḳrār." *Encyclopaedia of Islam 2*, vol. 3, 1078–81. Leiden: Brill.

Marino, Brigitte, and Astrid Meier. 2012. "L'eau à Damas et dans son environnement rural au XVIIIe siècle." *Bulletin d'études orientales* 61: 363–428.

Marres, Noortje. 2005. "Issues spark a public into being: a key but often forgotten point of the Lippmann-Dewey debate." In *Making Things Public: Atmospheres of Democracy*, edited by Bruno Latour and Peter Weibel, 208–17. Cambridge, MA: MIT Press.

Meier, Astrid. 2005. "'Le plus avantageux pour le waqf': villages, fondations et agents fiscaux aux environs de Damas dans la première moitié du 18ᵉ siècle." In *Sociétés rurales ottomanes/ Ottoman Rural Societies*, edited by Mohammad Afifi, Rachida Chih, Brigitte Marino, Nicolas Michel, and Işık Tamdoğan, 47–64. Cairo: Institut français d'Archéologie orientale.

———. 2011. "Bathing as a translocal phenomenon? Bathhouses in the Arab-speaking provinces." In *Bathing Culture of Anatolian Civilizations: Architecture, History and Imagination*, edited by Nina Ergin, 169–97. Leuven, Belgium: Peeters.

———. 2014. "Bathhouses in the countryside of Ottoman Damascus: a preliminary enquiry." In *25 Siècles de Bain Collectif en Orient: Proche-Orient, Égypte et Péninsule Arabique. Balaneia=Thermae=Hammāmāt. Actes du 3ᵉ Colloque International Balnéorient (Damascus 2009)*, edited by Marie-Françoise Boussac, Sylvie Denoix, Thibaut Fournet and Bérangère Redon, 745–61. Cairo: Institut français d'Archéologie orientale.

Meier, Astrid, and Stefan Weber. 2005. "Suq al-Qutn and Suq al-Suf: development, organization and patterns of the everyday life of a Damascene neighbourhood." *Bayt al-'Aqqad: The History and Restoration of a House in Old Damascus*, edited by Peder Mortensen, 379–43. Aarhus, Denmark: Proceedings of the Danish Institute in Damascus IV.

Mikhail, Alan. 2010. "An irrigated empire, the view from Ottoman Fayyum." *International Journal of Middle East Studies* 42: 569–90.

———. 2011. *Nature and Empire in Ottoman Egypt: An Environmental History*. New York: Cambridge University Press.

Miller, Daniel. 2005. "Materiality: an introduction." In *Materiality*, edited by Daniel Miller, 1–50. Durham, NC: Duke University Press.

al-Munajjid, Ṣalāḥ al-Dīn. 1947. "Ḥammamāt Dimashq." *al-Mashriq* 41: 401–25.

Powers, David S. 2002. *Law, Society and Culture in the Maghrib, 1300–1500*. Cambridge: Cambridge University Press.

Schaffer, Simon. 2005. "Public experiments." In *Making Things Public: Atmospheres of Democracy*, edited by Bruno Latour and Peter Weibel, 298–307. Cambridge, MA: MIT Press.

Sha'bān, 'Abd al-Majīd. 1997–98. *Rīf Dimashq min khilāl sijillāt al-maḥākim al-shar'iyya, 1700– 1725*. Unpublished doctoral dissertation, University of Tunis I, Department of History.

Shaham, Ron. 2010. *The Expert Witness in Islamic Courts: Medicine and Crafts in the Service of Law*. Chicago: University of Chicago Press.

Shoshan, Boaz. 2011. "Mini-dramas by the water: on irrigation rights and disputes in fifteenth-century Damascus." In *Histories of the Middle East: Studies in Middle Eastern Society, Economy and Law in Honor of A. L. Udovitch*, edited by Roxani Margariti, Adam Sabra, and Petra Sijpesteijn, 233–44. Leiden: Brill.

Tabak, Faruk. 2008. *The Waning of the Mediterranean, 1550–1870: A Geohistorical Approach*. Baltimore: Johns Hopkins University Press.

Thoumin, Richard. 1934. "Notes sur l'aménagement et la distribution des eaux à Damas et dans sa Ghouta." *Bulletin d'études orientales* 4: 1–26.

———. 1936. *Géographie humaine de la Syrie centrale*. Paris: Ernest Leroux.

Trentmann, Frank. 2009. "Materiality in the future of history: things, practices, and politics." *Journal of British Studies* 48: 283–307.

Tresse, René. 1929. "L'irrigation dans la Ghouta de Damas." *Revue des études islamiques* 3: 461– 574.

van Staëvel, Jean-Pierre. 2001. "Savoir voir et le faire savoir: l'expertise judiciaire en matière de construction, d'après un auteur tunisois du 8e/XIVe siècle." *Annales Islamologiques* 35: 627–62.

White, Sam. 2011. *The Climate of Rebellion in the Early Modern Ottoman Empire*. New York: Cambridge University Press.

Young, M. J. L. 1986. "Art. Mā': 2. In classical Islamic law." In *Encyclopaedia of Islam 2*, vol. 5, 860. Leiden: Brill.

Zakariyyā, Aḥmad Waṣfī. 1957. *al-Rīf al-sūrī. Muḥāfazat Dimashq*. 2 vols. Damascus: al-Maṭbaʿa al-ʿumumiyya bi-Dimashq.

# CHAPTER 2

# The Islamic Occupation of Qatar in the Context of an Environmental Framework

*Phillip G. Macumber*

With its arid to hyperarid climate, high temperatures, and absence of surface water, environmental conditions for occupation in Qatar are exceedingly harsh. Potable water has to be obtained from the groundwater system. While regional groundwater in Qatar is brackish to saline, in the north, there is an overlying freshwater lens. The disparity in water quality between north and south is reflected in the occupation patterns across Qatar; it is especially notable in the distribution of settlements and the nature of the mosques. Settlements mostly occurred in the north, especially closer to the coast where the water table was within ready reach by hand-dug wells. Perhaps the earliest of the Islamic settlements are the Abbasid linear villages, most occurring in a discrete zone of shallow groundwater in the northwest.

By contrast, in the south, occupation appears to have consisted largely of nomadic visitations, probably during periods when ephemeral surface or groundwater became temporarily available in response to storms or favorable seasons. However, even when there was no potable surface or groundwater, wells with brackish groundwater enabled year-round nomadic visitations since the water was suitable for camels. This is reflected in one of the more significant architectural features of the south, the predominance of small open mosques consisting only of a *qibla* wall and *mihrab* niche.

## Physical and Hydrological Constraints
## on the Occupation of Qatar

Central to any holistic archaeological study is the relationship between occupation and the natural environment—why people live where they do. This is especially the case in early Qatar, where low rainfall and high temperatures coupled with low topographical relief results in the absence of fresh surface water and a relatively hostile natural environment. The only water source is from groundwater occurring in the Tertiary marine limestone aquifers. Rainfall is mostly in winter, from winter westerlies, allowing recharge into the Tertiary aquifer system, especially following storm events. The arid to hyperarid climatic setting across Qatar has been in place since the end of the hydrological optimum (Macumber 2011b) in early mid-Holocene times, from about 7,500 to 6,000 years BP, during which time rainfall was greater and sea levels were up to one to three meters above those at present. The distribution of the many Neolithic coastal sites containing Ubaid pottery and an Arabian Bifacial Tradition (Kapel 1967) are a feature of a more favorable climate in early to mid-Holocene times. The 7,000-year-old Shagra site, excavated on the shores of the mid-Holocene high sea level in the 1980s (Inizan 1988), fits into this pattern (locality: Fig. 2.1). The subsequent decline in rainfall and later fall in sea levels after 4,000 years BP ushered in the present, significantly more inhospitable climatic regime, which persisted throughout Islamic times up to and including the present.

Qatar lies on a limestone peninsula extending northward from the mainland of the Arabian peninsula into the Arabian-Persian Gulf along a north–south anticlinal structure and referred to as the Qatar Arch. Almost all of Qatar has a relief of less than 100 meters, with a dissected plateau in the south at elevations of about 40 to 60 meters. It has an arid to hyperarid climate with a highly variable annual rainfall, averaging 80 millimeters in the north and less in the south. Rainfall is unpredictable and highly erratic across the country, often falling during storms. Temperatures during summer are high (greater than 40°C), with annual average evaporation rates of 2,200 millimeters, very strong northwest winds, and high relative humidity (Abu Sukar et al. 2007).

The absence of permanent surface water dictates that occupation in the past was dependent on groundwater, accessible only by hand-dug wells. Even where groundwater was shallow and readily accessible, water quality was the crucial factor in determining the potential for settlement. In more recent times, the use of modern drilling techniques has enabled water to be exploited from deep within the aquifer; however, this was not the case in earlier times. An indication of the general distribution of usable groundwater may be had by examining the location of the main farming areas across Qatar (most established during the modern era),

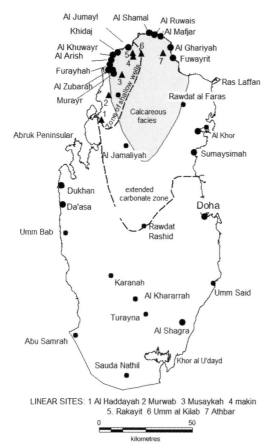

LINEAR SITES: 1 Al Haddayah 2 Murwab  3 Musaykah  4 makin
5. Rakayit  6 Umm al Kilab  7 Athbar

0                    50

kilometres

Figure 2.1 The locations of selected towns and early Islamic linear sites (numbered) (prepared by author).

with the bulk of the farms in the north. Since water availability is central to permanent settlement, the farm distribution reflects the relative habitability over the past four thousand years. One important rider is that the farm well distribution is a reflection of the presence of better-quality groundwater but not necessarily of the availability of potable (drinking) water, with the farm bores commonly used for agricultural produce or stock and domestic purposes.

In practice, a combination of groundwater depth and fresh groundwater presence determined the location and extent of Islamic settlement in Qatar up to the modern era of drilled wells and desalination plants. This relationship is clearly seen in the groundwater salinity map of Qatar (Fig. 2.2) and the depth of the water table across the country (Fig. 2.3), taken together. The earliest determined water table configuration across Qatar was in 1958; this predates the modern era of groundwater development, which saw significant falls in groundwater levels and the resulting seawater encroachment into the coastal aquifer system. The 1958 setting is deemed to represent a steady-state condition that was present throughout the late Holocene period continuing up to the modern era. On the 1980 salinity

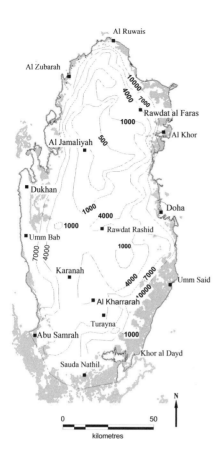

Figure 2.2 Salinity map of Qatar in 1980 in milligrams per liter total dissolved solids (TDS) (modified from Dastane and Al-Faihani 1980). The position of coastal *sabkha* are shown in gray.

map, data from deeper bores drilled after 1958, which penetrate more saline groundwater, have partially masked the presence of an overlying shallower coastal freshwater lens in salinity maps. This problem is greatly exacerbated by heavy groundwater pumping, with the consequent seawater intrusion replacing the freshwater lens in coastal aquifers, leading to the abandonment of most existing coastal settlements.

Eccleston and colleagues (1981) produced an early depth-to-the-water-table map for only northern Qatar, and another map of all Qatar was produced by Macumber (2012). Both constructions show that beneath Qatar, the water table was relatively flat, being "tied" to sea level at the coast in a manner similar to that of an oceanic island (Fig. 2.3). This stems from Qatar being a peninsula surrounded on three sides by the sea and only connected by land to Saudi Arabia in the south.

An oceanic island analogy is further strengthened by the presence of the freshwater lens in the north, produced and maintained by rainfall-derived groundwater recharge. Stable isotope data show that the lens is not fossil groundwater, as is the case elsewhere in the Gulf where fresh water is at times attributed to the recharge

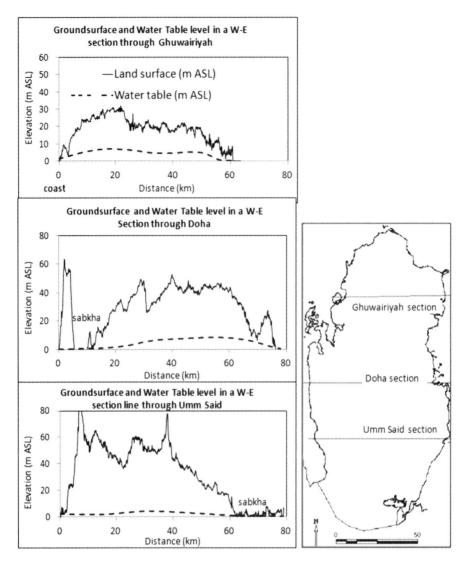

Figure 2.3 West to east sections showing measured surface levels and water-table levels across Qatar in the north, center, and south. The water table is at the top of the zone of saturation (Macumber 2011a).

during the wet period between 9,000 and 6,000 years BP. The flatness of the lens relative to sea level is a product of the low rainfall and recharge or the high permeability of the varyingly karstic aquifer system, or both. The fresh water in northern Qatar is associated with the presence of a calcium carbonate limestone facies representing shallow water marine deposition astride the north–south Qatar Arch (Fig. 2.1). Lateral to this zone, the aquifer is highly gypseous and the groundwater brackish to saline. A southern extension of the fresher zone to Rawdat Rashid occurs in response to gypsum solution within the Rus Formation. The several hundred *rawda* depressions dotting the Qatari landscape represent the surface expression of collapse in the underlying gypseous aquifer.

In northern Qatar, the *rawda* vary from small basins to large, elongated composite depressions in the Dammam Limestone, ranging in area from 0.25 to 45 square kilometers. Thin colluvial sequences with loam to sandy clay-loam soils have accumulated in the *rawda* to depths ranging from 30 to 150 centimeters. The *rawda* collect surface water from direct rainfall, from runoff from surrounding bedrock areas, and from flow from small drainage lines; they are the main source of groundwater recharge. This process maintained the lens throughout premodern Islamic times. During recharge, the underlying water table varyingly mounds up beneath the depressions. Groundwater mounding beneath *rawda*, both seasonally and intermittently after discrete storm events, was described by Eccleston and colleagues (1981), from Musayka and Rawdat al-Faras, where water tables were initially between 8 and 8.5 meters below the surface. Over the winter and spring periods in 1976 and 1977, seasonal recharge caused 3- to 4-meter mounds in the water table, and similar rises were measured at Rawdat al-Faras after storm events. Superimposition of discrete rainfall events during wetter seasons or simply prolonged seasonal rainfall may cause groundwater levels to rise to the surface wherever water tables are shallow. The presence of standing water at the surface in such instances is therefore not simply a surface ponding effect of rainfall and runoff but also a reflection of the response of the water table to wet events. The rate of decline of the underlying groundwater mound determines the period for which water remains visible at the surface.

The *rawda* provide the basis for much of the occupation of the north, being sites for shallow wells; the grassy *rawda* plains are used extensively for grazing and at times agriculture. This was also the case in the past as shown by the location of the early Abbasid linear villages adjacent to *rawda* (Macumber 2011b).

The extent and distribution of the coastward-flowing fresh groundwater in the north is reflected in the many small towns that occurred between al-Zubara and Fuwayrit (Fig. 2.1); this closely matches the distribution of the calcareous limestone zone. The pattern is similar to that shown on Brucks's map of coastal settlements in the 1820s (Brucks 1865: 531, chart no. 6). Groundwater flows from recharge areas in the hinterland toward the coast, where the groundwater discharges into the numerous fringing *sabkha*, where it is lost to the surface by capillarity and evaporation leaving behind the salt. As a consequence, the *sabkha* are underlain by hypersaline groundwater where salt is continuously accumulating. This process is readily seen in the case of the *sabkha* at al-Zubara, where small excavated pits fill with hypersaline water in which halite (salt) precipitates under the extreme evaporative regime; it is then harvested as small discrete blocks. The *sabkha* initially developed along the coast after the fall in sea levels from their mid-Holocene highs during the Flandrian transgression and have therefore formed relatively recently, from circa 4,000 years BP to the present. They are most commonly developed as deflation surfaces on mid-Holocene shallow marine and beach sediments but may also be cut across Dammam Formation bedrock, initially formed as wave-cut rock platforms across which the sea transgressed.

An understanding of the nature of groundwater occurrence nearer the coast is important to an understanding of the distribution and roles of coastal settlements. De Cardi (1978: 188) noted the presence of water closer to the coast and its significance for settlement, observing that "the overriding need to produce results in terms of sites and finds also meant that our survey had to be concentrated upon those localities most likely to have attracted settlers, namely, the coastal regions where water and sustenance would have been available." (ibid.: 181). For Qatar, groundwater salinity ultimately determines the occupational potential, both now and in the past. In the southwest, there is brackish to saline fossil groundwater, which flows upward from deeper aquifers; it is sourced in Saudi Arabia and exists under flowing artesian conditions in the Salwa area. Stable isotopic data show that across the south, the brackish groundwater is a mixture of Saudi Arabian sourced regional groundwater and limited modern-day recharge. However, in the south, there is no comparable freshwater lens as in the north, and hence a dearth of drinking water, making settlement unfeasible, especially in earlier times.

Thus, the south with its brackish to saline groundwater was always an area where occupation was extremely limited and best represented by a nomadic existence. The relief is much greater, and in such areas, the water table lies beyond reach of hand-dug wells; conversely, where the relief is low, as in the southeast, *sabkha* predominate, and the groundwater is mostly saline. This is especially clear in the area south beyond Umm Said, where there are broad *sabkha* and paleo-*sabkha* landscapes, representing former embayments present during mid-Holocene times (Fig. 2.2). Ironically, it is in on the edge of this landscape, at Shagra on a mid-Holocene shoreline now lying well inland of the present coast, that the oldest house in Qatar exists, a seven-thousand-year-old fisherman's hut (Inizan 1988). This too was a site where visitations rather than occupation occurred.

Three west--east slices through Qatar show the 1958 relationship between water-table level and land surface at Ghuwairiya, Doha, and Umm Said. All three show that the greatest depth of the water table is in southern and central Qatar, where there is the greatest relief. The water table is shallowest in the north, and its depth continues to decrease on approaching the coast. Therefore, apart from groundwater salinity, a second parameter, landscape relief, determines the availability of water. Given the flatness of the water table beneath Qatar, the higher the relief, the deeper the water table below the surface (Fig. 2.3). Since, in practice, the depth of hand-dug wells is limited, the absence of early wells over much of the higher interior areas, both in the north and especially in the south, can be accounted for by depth of the water table alone, notwithstanding the groundwater salinity.

Whatever the broad hydrological framework indicated here, there are exceptions. For instance, a further factor is that while the calcareous facies, with which fresh water is associated in the north, is largely absent from southern Qatar, a narrow calcareous band occurs passing southeastward through Umm Bab toward Turayna. This is associated with the northward-trending Dukhan anticline. Here, however, the groundwater would have been too deep for hand-dug wells.

Otherwise, in limited cases, localized fresh groundwater may develop through the infiltrating storm water perched over a rock or soil layer with low permeability, in coastal systems where dune recharge may occasionally occur, or further inland where bare limestone surfaces provide a localized catchment funneling rainfall runoff into an adjacent sandy wadi. The latter appears to be the case near San al-Fuzayra in the southeast, where a small, now abandoned settlement was established along such a wadi. The importance of the site, and probably its unusual freshwater supply, is demonstrated by the presence of a large open mosque on the hill overlooking the settlement (see Fig. 2.5:1). The mosque is an open-air, multiarea feature that otherwise resembles the numerous small mosques found across the south. A smaller, more typical open mosque consisting only of a short *qibla* wall and *mihrab* occurs in the nearby wadi bed, as do a number of small house structures and an enclosed well. Shade is provided by small trees and large bushes, relying on whatever moisture might accumulate or perhaps tapping a shallow water table. The presence of the large mosque suggests that it was a central meeting point in the region, its presence likely due to the nearby freshwater well, an unusual occurrence in the south.

## The Nature of Premodern Occupation in Northern Qatar

While a hydrological and physical framework may be established to examine the broad-scale occupation potential across Qatar, the supporting evidence lies in the actual distribution of the small towns and villages, which are most common in the coastal areas of northern Qatar, and in the small wells scattered across the northern countryside. A dearth of older villages is characteristic of southern Qatar, while hand-dug wells are uncommon.

There is a preponderance of abandoned coastal and near hinterland towns lying between Fuwayrit in the northeast to beyond al-Zubara in the northwest, not seen elsewhere in Qatar (Fig. 2.1). Those in the northwest are contained within a discrete broad zone of shallow wells identified by Lloyd and colleagues (1981) following several detailed hydrogeological studies. The shallow well zone passes from al-Jumayl in the north to al-Haddaya in the south, and extends twelve to eighteen kilometers inland from the coast (Fig. 2.1). It contains a number of seventeenth- to mid-twentieth-century coastal towns, including al-Zubara, Furayha, al-Arish, al-Khuwair and al-Jumayl, and the Ruwayda Fort (Petersen et al. 2010). These were in turn supported by small but intensive irrigation areas, such as that of the Muhayriqat irrigation settlement near Helwan and that to the south of al-Jumayl, near Umm Jassim (Macumber 2011b). In addition, there were probably minor irrigation areas around smaller well fields, as was the case at Murayr. Like the coastal towns, they too are now abandoned.

A significant number of coastal sites have been constructed on raised paleo-beach ridges formed during earlier marine transgressions, which, as at al-Zubara, are located on the coast and bounded on their landward side by *sabkha*. As a consequence of the underlying saline groundwater, they do not have a source of fresh water and instead obtain their drinking water from settlements with freshwater wells located further inland. In this respect, they may be deemed to be "twinned" towns, with the coastal towns providing commerce and fishing, while the inland towns produced farm produce and potable water. In the case of al-Zubara, the water source is Umm al-Shuwayl (De Cardi 1978, although a further freshwater source existed at Musayka, located a little further inland. A number of wells established at Murayr close to the earlier fort were sunk in an area of marine terrace close to the *sabkha* edge. The groundwater was varyingly brackish but would have been suitable for stock and domestic supplies. However, the more southerly Murayr wells also span the marine-bedrock boundary, and it is likely that potable water was obtained from these bedrock wells by skimming the fresh water from the top of the freshwater lens above the brackish water (Fig. 2.4). This approach requires careful management and imposes strict limits on the amount of water extracted. The southern Murayr wells could also have been used for small-scale irrigation, as suggested by the adjacent large enclosures.

Similar inland sources of potable water were at Ain Muhammad, a probable principal water supply for Furayha (although there is also a well in the aeolianite closer to the town). On the northeastern coast, al-'Athba was a likely inland source for the coastal villages at al-Ghariya and perhaps also Fuwayrit. In both cases, additional water sources were located in small settlements closer to the coastal towns. The inland water sources were known and used over extended periods since both al-'Athba and Musayka were sites of earlier Abbasid linear villages; this supports the view that the wells were important permanent fixtures whatever and whenever the occupation. In this respect, the history of Qatar is strongly reflected in the history of its wells.

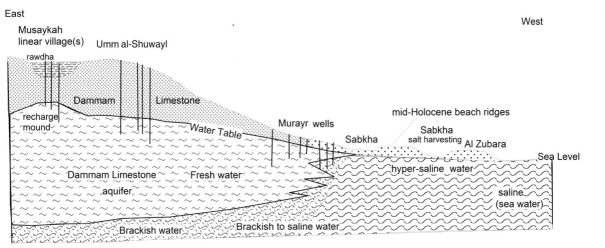

Figure 2.4 Groundwater salinity facies between Musaykah and al-Zubara showing well field locations (diagrammatic).

The coastal sites are now largely ruins, many having been abandoned in the mid-twentieth century in response to the impact of the intense groundwater development, which saw a large number of farms established across Qatar. Using modern drilling techniques to enable large-scale groundwater extraction for irrigation, the freshwater lens was depleted. Intense localized pumping led to upconing into the bores of the deeper, more saline groundwater found beneath the freshwater lens, causing salinization of many of the farms. On a regional scale, groundwater levels fell markedly, and the freshwater lens was partially destroyed. A further response was the retreat of the lens inland from the coastal areas and its replacement by seawater. The wells serving the coastal towns rapidly became saline forcing their eventual abandonment.

The zone of shallow groundwater also contains a large number of older archaeological sites, including six of the seven known sites where Abbasid linear villages occur—al-Haddaya, Murwab, Musayka, Rikayat, Makin, and Umm al-Kilab (locality: Fig. 2.1). Murwab was a ninth-century CE Abbasid settlement (Guérin and al-Naʿimi 2009). Of the known linear settlements, only al-ʿAthba lies outside the zone (Fig. 2.1). Most linear villages lie well inland from the coast at elevations close to the ten meters above sea level contour, guaranteeing fresh water. Other sites within the shallow well zone include Umm al-Maʿ, Yoghbi, and the Neolithic site(s) near the mouth of Wadi al-Dubayan to the west of al-Zubara on the mid-Holocene shoreline. It has artifacts of the Arabian Bifacial Tradition and Ubaid pottery (al-Naimi et al. 2011). The time range for the sites supports the view that favorable conditions for settlement were present along the northwestern coastline for perhaps as long as there has been occupation of Qatar; these conditions persisted throughout Islamic times up to the modern era. The Abbasid linear sites consist of a number of aligned stone houses mostly occurring along parallel northeast–southwest orientations, ranging from about 235° to 245° (Fig. 2.5). This alignment approximates the direction of the *qibla* (Table 2.1). However, the sites also lie at right angles to the predominant northwest–southeast wind direction, which is the preferred orientation adopted for tent lines to minimize the impact of the northwesterly winds in the hotter months. At all linear sites, turquoise-glazed pottery was present.

At al-Haddaya (Fig. 2.5:3), located about seventeen kilometers to the north of Jamaliya (locality: Fig. 2.1), a small outdoor mosque consisting of a *qibla* wall and *mihrab* niche lies at the southwestern end of the settlement (Fig. 2.5:4). This is the most southerly of the Early Islamic linear villages so far identified in northern Qatar, and the mosque firmly establishes an Islamic age for the village. The village lies on a ridge overlooking two treed depressions on the northern and southern sides, the likely sites for wells at the time. The *qibla* wall lies roughly at right angles to the line of the village. There were several graves adjacent to the houses, and coarse-grained and turquoise-glazed pottery were present.

Figure 2.5 1. The four-hundred-meter-long linear village of Umm al-Kilab. 2. Umm al-Kilab looking southwest. 3. Linear village at al-Haddaya looking southwest. 4. Open mosque at southwestern end of al-Haddaya (author image).

Table 2.1. Alignment of selected linear villages (approximate)

| Locality | Alignment of Structures | Direction of Ka'ba (Mecca) |
| --- | --- | --- |
| Umm al-Kilab (Figure 2.5, Photos 1 and 2) | 237° | 248° (−111.81°) |
| Murwab | 241° | 249° (−111.17°) |
| al-Haddaya (Figure 2.5, Photos 3 and 4) | 244° | 249° (−110.66°) |

## Premodern Settlement in Southern Qatar

In southern Qatar, the landscape is dominated by low Neogene hills and limestone plains. A deeply eroded central plateau reaches a height of 103 meters, but the bulk of the plateau lies between 40 and 60 meters. The land connection with Saudi Arabia occurs only in the far south.

Unlike in the north, sand, as both individual dunes and sand sheets, is prevalent. It is assumed to have come from the exposed northern shorelines following the fall in sea levels after 4,000 years BP, driven southward by the dominant northwesterly winds. Across the region, the landscape is subject to intense sandblasting during the frequent sandstorms, which has resulted in scalloped and fluted limestone bedrock and the later Pleistocene limestone strand lines. While *rawda*-like depressions occur in the south, they are fewer and are small and isolated, with sandy floors and scattered vegetation.

A number of very large, deep structural depressions occur in the south, with their rims at elevations of forty to fifty meters above sea level and the floors ten to fifteen meters lower. These include the Turayna Depression and the Karana Depression. Despite the lower rainfall, significant modern-day groundwater recharge occurs in areas of broken limestone. This is shown by Tritium values in the groundwater reaching levels as high as twenty-one to fifty-nine TU[1] recorded in the northern parts of the Karana Depression (Lloyd et al. 1981). Unlike in the north, a discrete freshwater lens does not exist, and instead stable isotope analyses show that whatever recharge occurs mixes with the underlying, more saline regional groundwater, perhaps as a consequence of the deeper groundwater upflow. The large structural depressions in the south might have provided the most favorable areas for occupation given the right hydrological conditions. However, the water table lies only about four meters above sea level, indicating that it was beyond the practical reach of hand-dug wells during late Holocene times.

Whatever the broad hydrological framework indicated here, there are a limited number of isolated areas in the south where fresher-quality groundwater is recorded in an otherwise saline setting—such as to the south of Turayna. This may in part be associated with a narrow band of calcareous facies associated with the Dukhan anticline, which passes southeastward through Umm Bab toward Turayna. Here, however, the groundwater is too deep for hand-dug wells. Otherwise, in other instances, it is likely that the limited freshwater occurrences represent perched groundwater lying above the regional system and maintained by localized storm recharge. The latter situation was earlier suggested by Dastane and al-Faihani (1980), who noted that in southern Qatar, fresh groundwater was confined to perched systems. This is probably the case at the abandoned village of San al-Fuzayra, discussed below.

While there are exceptions, potable groundwater in the south is generally absent, as are settlements. Even so, people regularly traveled through the south, either internally within Qatar or on journeys to and from Saudi Arabia. While this was more likely to occur during favorable seasons when storm water temporarily ponded in depressions or accumulated in shallow basins in the limestone, it was mostly made possible through the utilization of camel wells since camels are able to drink brackish to moderately saline water (Farid 1989) and produce (fresh) milk. In this respect, the camels may be considered as portable desalination plants. While shallow, brackish camel wells enhanced movement throughout Qatar, they were a necessity for traversing much of the south. Sites associated with camel wells are described in De Cardi (1978), and one such well occurs adjacent to a high aeolianite outcrop to the north of Shagra where a number of stone artifacts and pottery were found (Macumber 2012). While there is a limited scattering of cairns and small circular structures of indeterminate age (without excavation) in the south, the next most prominent architectural features are the small open mosques consisting only of a *qibla* wall and a *mihrab* (Fig. 2.6). These are found across the region, commonly occurring in lightly treed areas.

Open mosques are not solely a feature of the south but are also sparsely present across northern Qatar. However, unlike the southern mosques, the northern open mosques are associated with small settlements. These include the Abbasid al-Haddaya mosque and small mosques associated with substantial subrecent ruins near al-Thaqab about four-and-a-half kilometers east of Furayha, and at Fayshakh amid a small group of scattered ruins located about four kilometers west of al-Jamailiya. The al-Thaqab and al-Haddaya mosques are small with a simple *qibla* wall and *mihrab* niche, but the Fayshakh mosque, although small, is rectangular and enclosed all sides; it is a little larger than the others.

A similar variation was observed in the Negev Highlands (Avni 1994, 2014), where twelve sixth- to eighth- or ninth-century CE open mosques were recorded.[2] These include mosques built either within urban settlements or adjacent to rural settlements, and mosques connected with nomadic populations in the southern Negev. An open mosque at Bor Bator not associated with a settlement was deemed to have been used by travelers. This is clearly the case for the majority of mosques

Figure 2.6 Mosques in the south. 1. Large mosque at San al-Fuzayra. 2. Mosque on
the edge of the Turayna Depression. 3. Mosque in the southeastern Karana Depression.
4. Mosque southeast of Turayna (author image).

noted across southern Qatar, with the exception being the two mosques, noted
above, at the village near San al-Fuzayra.

## Conclusion

In Qatar, premodern Islamic settlement depended on the availability of fresh
groundwater accessible by shallow hand-dug wells. However, fresh groundwater
occurs as a freshwater lens found only in the north, where the presence of *rawda*,
*sabkha*, and the depth to the water table, determines the distribution of specific
archaeological sites. Because of its topography, shallow wells in the north are mostly
located closer to the coast, as are the settlements, exemplified by the distribution
and location of most settlements including Early Islamic (Abbasid) linear settlements, found only across northern Qatar.

The groundwater is generally not potable in the south, and settlements were uncommon. However, the presence of permanent fresh water is not necessary for travel or temporary occupation in southern Qatar, which may occur during wetter seasons or after heavy storms. Such visits are facilitated by the presence of brackish to saline camel wells. The nomadic nature of the south is reflected in the basic form of the mosques, which are mostly isolated structures consisting only of a *qibla* wall and *mihrab* niche.

The hydrological regime of the last four thousand years was seriously changed by modern (post-1958) groundwater exploitation, significantly depleting the freshwater lens, causing partial salinization of the aquifer and the consequent demise of coastal settlements and inland farms.

## Notes

1. TU=Tritium units, equivalent to one Tritium ($^3$H isotope) per $10^{18}$ atoms of Hydrogen. Modern groundwater can typically be distinguished from pre-modern groundwater on the basis of >5 TU, owing to the significant increase in this radioactive isotope after the start of atmospheric nuclear testing (Vogel et al. 1974: 131–133).

2. There is now a broad consensus about the relative dating of these structures in the Negev from the seventh century to as late as the eighth or ninth century CE. For recent discussion, see especially Avni (2014: 267–73; 1996: 57) and Magness (2003: 135–38). For further bibliography on the phenomenon of open air, see Insoll (1999: 46–48), and on the recent use of open air mosques in eastern Arabia, see Cole (1975: 127).

## Bibliography

Abu Sukar, H. K., F. H. Almerri and A. A. Almurekki. 2007. *Agro-Hydro-Meteorological Data Book for the State of Qatar.* Doha: Department of Agricultural and Water Research.

Avni, Gideon. 1994. "Early mosques in the Negev Highlands." *Bulletin of the American Schools of Oriental Research* 294 (May 1994): 83–100.

———. 1996. *Nomads, Farmers, and Town-Dwellers: Pastoralist-Sedentist Interaction in the Negev Highlands, Sixth–Eighth Centuries CE.* Jerusalem: Israel Antiquities Authority.

———. 2014. "The Byzantine-Islamic transition in Palestine: an archaeological approach." *Oxford Studies in Byzantium*, 1st ed. Oxford: Oxford University Press.

Brucks, G. B. 1865. "Navigation of the Gulf of Persia." In *Arabian Gulf Intelligence: Selections from the Records of the Bombay Government. Concerning Arabia, Kuwait, Muscat and Oman, Qatar, United Arab Emirates and the Islands of the Gulf,* edited by R. H. Thomas, 531–80. London: Oleander.

Cole, Donald Powell. 1975. *Nomads of the Nomads: The Āl Murrah Bedouin of the Empty Quarter.* Arlington Heights, IL: AHM.

Dastane, N. G., and M. al-Faihani. 1980. *Irrigation Practices: Technical Report No 4.* Doha: State of Qatar, Ministry of Industry and Agriculture, Water Resources Project.

De Cardi, Beatrice, ed. 1978. *Qatar Archaeological Report: Excavation 1973.* Oxford: Oxford University Press.

Eccleston, B. L., J. G. Pike, and I. Harhash. 1981. *The Water Resources of Qatar and Their Development, Doha, 1981. Technical Report No. 5*. Doha, Qatar: Ministry of Industry and Agriculture Water Resources and Agricultural Development Project (Food and Agriculture Organization).

Farid, Mohammed F. A. 1989. *Water and Mineral Problems of the Dromedary Camel (an Overview)*. Cairo: Desert Research Institute, al-Matareya.

Guérin, Alexandrine, and Faysal al-Naʿimi. 2009. "Territory and settlement patterns during the Abbasid period (ninth century AD): the village of Murwab (Qatar)." *Proceedings of the Seminar for Arabian Studies* 39: 181–96.

Inizan, Marie-Louise. 1988. *Préhistoire à Qatar*. Mission archéologique française à Qatar, vol. 2. Paris: Éditions Recherche sur les Civilisations.

Insoll, Timothy. 1999. *The Archaeology of Islam*. Oxford: Blackwell.

Kapel, Holger. 1967. *Atlas of the Stone-Age Cultures of Qatar*. Reports of the Danish Archeological Expedition to the Arabian Gulf, vol. 1. Aarhus, Denmark: Aarhus University Press.

Lloyd, J. W., B. L. Eccleston and J. G. Pike. 1981. *The Hydrochemistry of the Groundwaters of Qatar*. Ministry of Industry and Agriculture, Water Resources and Agricultural Development Project (Technical Note, 14.). Consultant Report to the Government of Qatar. Unpublished report. Rome: Food and Agriculture Organization.

Macumber, Phillip G. 2011a. "Geomorphology, hydrology and occupation across north-eastern Qatar: geomorphological and geoarchaeological results from the Third Season of the Copenhagen University Study in Northern Qatar." In *Qatar Islamic Archaeology and Heritage Project: Archaeology Section, End of Season Report. Stage 2, Season 1. 2009–2010*, edited by Tobias Richter. Copenhagen: University of Copenhagen and Qatar Museums Authority.

———. 2011b. "A geomorphological and hydrological underpinning for archaeological research in northern Qatar." *Proceedings of the Seminar for Arabian Studies* 41: 187–200.

———. 2012. "An examination of the impact of environmental disparity on the occupation of Qatar: season 4, Copenhagen University Study of the Archaeology of Qatar." In *Qatar Islamic Archaeology and Heritage Project, End of Season Report 2011–2012*, edited by Stephen McPhillips. Copenhagen: University of Copenhagen and Qatar Museums Authority.

Magness, Jodi. 2003. *The Archaeology of the Early Islamic Settlement in Palestine*. Winona Lake, IN: Eisenbrauns.

al-Naimi, Faisal, Kathryn M. Price, Richard Cutler and Hatem Arrock. 2011. Reassessing Wādī Debayan (Wādī al-Ḍabayʿān): an important early Holocene Neolithic multi-occupational site in western Qatar. *Proceedings of the Seminar for Arabian Studies* 41: 239–244.

Petersen, Andrew, Tony Grey and Catherine Rees. 2010. Excavations and survey at al-Ruwayḍah, a late Islamic site in northern Qatar. *Proceedings of the Seminar for Arabian Studies* 40: 41–54.

Vogel, J. C., C. Thilo and M. van Dijken. 1974. Determination of groundwater recharge with Tritium. *Journal of Hydrology* 23: 131–140.

# CHAPTER 3

# Water Management in Desert Regions

## Early Islamic Qasr Mushash

*Karin Bartl*

Water utilization, water management, and the technology of hydrological structures in antiquity have been subjects of intensive research for several years now
(Bienert and Häser 2004; Ohlig 2007, 2008; Mouton and Dbiyat 2009; Klimscha et al. 2012). The reasons for this interest are the significance of water as
a basic necessity for human life, and the evident problem in many regions of the
disappearance of water resources and the resulting challenges for the future.
Knowledge about ancient water systems reveals that the use of basic resources
was already the focus of planning initiatives in antiquity and frequently led
to simple yet effective solutions, which possessed a sustainability that is much
evoked today.

A number of contrasting examples of water management in early Islamic times
are known in northern Bilad al-Sham, for instance, at Qasr al-Hayr al-Gharbi, Qasr
al-Hayr al-Sharqi (Genequand 2009, 2012) and Resafa–Sergiupolis-Rusafat al-
Hisham (Brinker and Garbrecht 2007). Of the early Islamic sites in the Jordanian
*badia*, Qasr Mushash is an outstanding representative of water management during
the seventh and eighth centuries CE (Fig. 3.1).[1]

## Site and Setting

Qasr Mushash is located about 40 kilometers east of Amman in the middle of the
desert steppe. The site was first visited and described by Alois Musil in 1901 (Musil
1907), yet owing to its remote location, it is still little known today. Conversely,
the nearby sites of Qasr Kharana (Urice 1987; Bisheh 1986) and Qusayr 'Amra (Musil

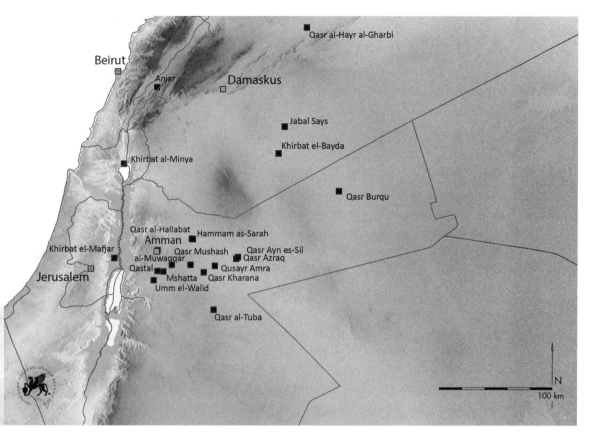

Figure 3.1 Desert castles in Bilad al-Sham, location of Qasr Mushash (map: DAI, Orient-Department, T. Urban, using USGS/NASA 3-arc second SRTM data).

1907; Almagro 1975; Vibert-Guigne and Bisheh 2007) are better known and were in use more or less at the same time as Mushash. Unlike the two "desert castles," Qasr Kharana and Qusayr 'Amra, which are attested through inscriptions, no historical sources or epigraphic evidence has been found at the site itself that would provide information about the date of its appearance or function. Qasr Mushash is an extensive complex with a great variety of structures whose most outstanding feature is the comparatively large number of hydraulic installations. These include reservoirs, cisterns, and dams, which are found both in the central area of the complex and further afield. This site has been assigned to the group of so-called desert castles, characteristic monuments of the Umayyad period (661–750 CE) in Bilad al-Sham (Genequand 2012), although structures and building complexes of this type have received many and varied interpretations. On the one hand, they are considered temporary residences of the Early Islamic ruling elite; on the other, they are seen as caravan stations located along pilgrimage and trade routes (Bacharach 1996: 31).[2]

Recent research has stressed both the economic and political functions of the desert castles. The former are defined by agricultural revenues and traded products, and the latter, by the interaction between the caliphal rulers and the local elites. The nature and frequency of these contacts may have influenced the character and size of the various structures (Genequand 2012). As some of the desert castles are surrounded by dispersed housing units, forming unplanned villages, it was recently suggested that these sites could have served as settlements for people who were still partly nomadic. These "nomadic villages" appeared in the transitional Late Roman through Umayyad periods as a result of changing political structures (Kennedy 2004: 217).

Qasr Mushash is situated within the Saharo-Arabian climate zone, where the annual precipitation is less than 100 millimeters (Bender 1974: fig.19). Characteristic topographical features include separate chains of hills extending east to west. They, like the plain adjoining to the south, are traversed by numerous wadis, some of which are deeper than others. Stable perennial watercourses, springs, and wells are completely absent in this region. Nonetheless, older reports offer information about the procurement of water from holes dug into wadi beds (Moritz 1908: 426; Musil 1907: Abb. 104).[3] These holes are designated as *mshash*, thus suggesting, as Ghazi Bisheh surmises, an association between local names and Qasr Mushash (Bisheh 1989: 82 n. 7). A temporary water supply for the site is provided by so-called flash floods, which emerge after sudden torrential winter rains and turn dry wadi beds into surging rivers. A long-term water supply, however, is only possible by means of a differentiated water management.

Present-day vegetation around Qasr Mushash is exceedingly sparse, consisting of a meager growth of drought-resistant bushes along wadi banks (Amr et al. 2011: 34ff.). Although nomadic Bedouins, often accompanied by large herds of sheep, still live in the region today, stock raising is only possible by feeding animals dried pellets. The few natural resources that are at hand in the springtime do not suffice for animal fodder. Aside from herds of sheep, a few camels are raised here, able as they are to subsist on the dried brush vegetation. Nevertheless, the current dearth of natural vegetation does not in fact mean that restrained crop cultivation is impossible. So-called wadi farming, that is, planting hardy kinds of cereals such as *durra* in wadi beds and banks, where the earth is still moist from winter precipitation, is still a common use of resources. The barren landscape between al-Muwaqqar and Qasr Azraq is indicative, on one hand, of the region's extremely small agricultural capacity as far as the supply of water and food for larger groups of people is concerned. On the other hand, localities like Qasr Mushash demonstrate that the region was indeed capable of long-term occupation.

## Archaeological Investigations

After visits by Aurel Stein in 1938, who gave a particularly detailed description of the site (Gregory and Kennedy 1985: 287), more comprehensive inspections of the *qasr* and its surroundings were undertaken by Geoffrey King in 1980 and 1981 (King 1982: 86–88; King et al. 1983: 386–92). In 1982 and 1983, some of the most important structures, the *qasr* and the bath, were investigated by Bisheh (1989: 81–90, 1992: 37–38; King 1989: 391–95). Research on the prehistory of the surrounding area, particularly of the Paleolithic periods, was undertaken by Copeland and Hours in the 1980s (1989: 21–25, 84–87). The significant potential of the site for answering questions about water management and subsistence economy was recognized by King and Bisheh, leading to the resumption of fieldwork there in 2011 by the Department of Antiquities of Jordan and the German Archaeological Institute.

Work at present entails the systematic documentation of all archaeological remains within a radius of ten kilometers of Qasr Mushash (Fig. 3.2). During two previous seasons of fieldwork, a great number of archaeological sites were recorded. These can be assigned to two temporal horizons: sites dating to prehistoric times, that is, between the Lower Paleolithic and the Neolithic periods, and sites of later historical periods, that is, between the Late Roman and the Early Islamic eras. Sites dating to the sixth to first millennia BCE are almost completely absent. A total of 131 sites date to prehistoric periods. In almost all cases, they are characterized by agglomerations of artifacts, that is, lithics. Sites of actual occupation were attested in very few places (see Bartl et al. forthcoming). Some forty-one findspots date to the late Roman and Early Islamic times. Most findspots, consisting of individual installations or walls, are in the vicinity of Qasr Mushash, that is, they are a component part of this site.

## The Site of Qasr Mushash

The settlement area of Qasr Mushash is structured by three tributary wadis running north to south. The entire expanse covers an area of approximately two square kilometers. It can be divided into two areas: Qasr Mushash West and Qasr Mushash East, about one and a half kilometers to the northeast (Fig. 3.2). Qasr Mushash West and its central area lie directly next to Wadi Mushash and to the south of Tall Hamrat al-Qurayma, a chain of hills that rise up to a hundred meters above the plain. Buildings and installations can be found as far as one kilometer to the north along wadi B. These structures prove that the wadis were an integral part of the entire settlement area.

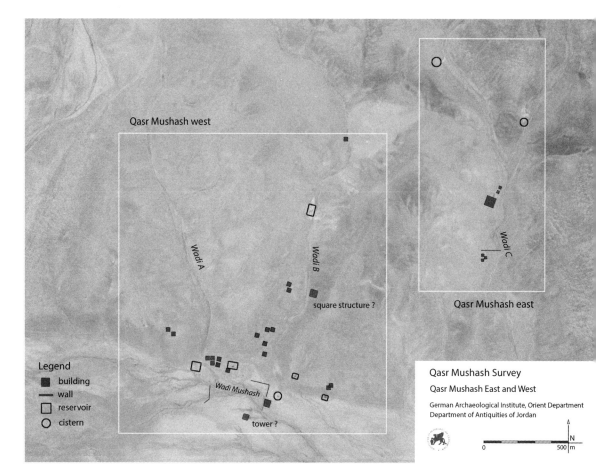

Figure 3.2 Location of Qasr Mushash West and East (map: DAI, Orient-Department, Th. Urban [satellite image: Quickbird/WorldView-1]).

Qasr Mushash East is located at wadi C and consists of a group of buildings, several installations on Wadi Mushash, and two large rock cisterns. The functional connection between the two settlement areas is still unclear. However, pottery finds indicate that these sites were contemporaneous. To date, investigations have been concentrated on Qasr Mushash West. This complex is made up of several areas, each with different building complexes (Fig. 3.3).

*Area A: The Qasr*

The *qasr* itself is a building with a surface area of 26 by 26 meters (Fig. 3.4). Its entrance lies in the southeast and opens onto a central courtyard, which in

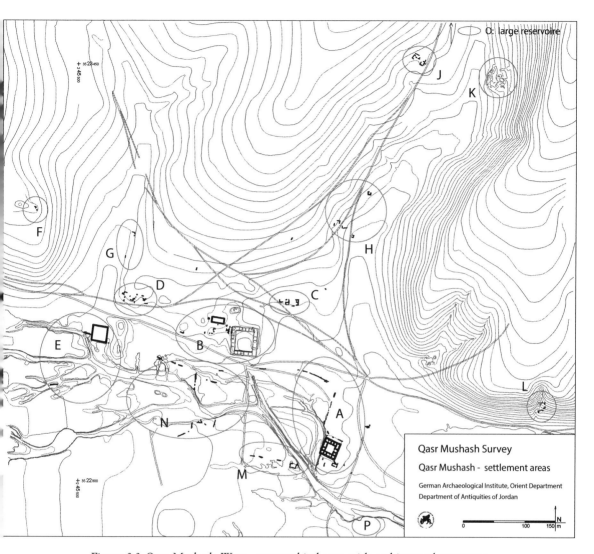

Figure 3.3 Qasr Mushash West—topographical map with architectural structures
(map: DAI, Orient-Department, T. Urban).

turn is surrounded by fourteen rooms. This complex could either have been a
residence or a small fortress. Based on surface pottery found in the immediate
surroundings, the visible part of the building can be dated to the Umayyad period. Yet again, a few red-slipped sherds present the possibility of a predecessor
building from Roman or late Roman times.[4] The *qasr* was surrounded by more
houses in the north, east, and south, of which few remains are preserved. The
original size and structure of these buildings are difficult to deduce, as the terrain bordering immediately to the east of the *qasr* has been severely damaged by
illicit excavations.[5]

Figure 3.4 Qasr Mushash West—Qasr (area A) (photo: APAAME_20080909_0033_ DLK_033. Photograph: David L. Kennedy. Aerial Photographic Archive for Archaeology in the Middle East (APAAME), archive accessible from www.classics.uwa.edu .au/aerial_archaeology).

### Area B: Central Part of the Site

The central part of the settlement lies some 200 meters northwest of the area of the *qasr*; it encompasses a large square building in the east, the bath adjoining in the west, and a rectangular cistern in the northwest. Largely destroyed by looting activities, the square building with its interior division could only be distinguished by means of geomagnetic investigations (Fig. 3.5).[6] South of the cistern are several more buildings, some relatively large in size, revealed by ground penetrating radar investigations.

### Areas C, D, F, G, H, J, L: Remains of Various Buildings

Areas C, D, F, G, J, and L display various remains of building structures of different size and shape. Due to the poor state of preservation, the walls are difficult to recognize.

### Area E: Large Reservoir

Located some 80 meters southwest of area D and directly at Wadi Mushash is a large quadrangular reservoir covering a surface of about 576 square meters.

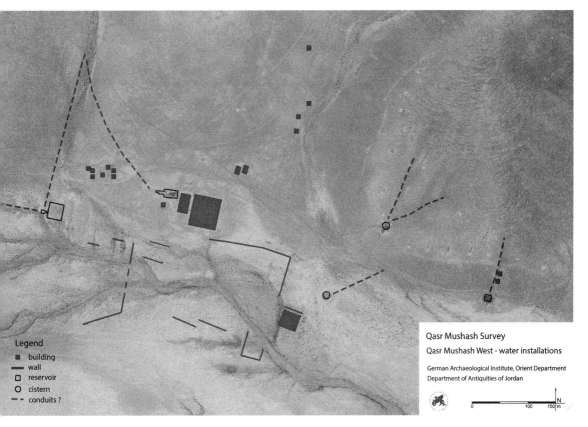

Qasr Mushash Survey

Qasr Mushash West - water installations

German Archaeological Institute, Orient Department
Department of Antiquities of Jordan

0          100    150 m

Figure 3.5 Qasr Mushash West—central area—square structure, results of geomagnetic investigation (area B) (map: DAI, Orient-Department, T. Urban [geomagnetic survey data M. Posselt]).

## Area K: Square Complex

On the east bank of wadi B, across from area J at a distance of 80 meters, stood an extremely desolate larger building. In all likelihood, this was another square complex with a side length of 30 meters. Some larger, coarsely finished ashlars indicate that a large enclosure wall was located here.

## Area M, N: Wall Remains on the South Bank of Wadi Mushash

Opposite the *qasr*, on the south bank of Wadi Mushash, is a severely destroyed building, whose form and size can no longer be determined. Some larger fragments of walls were found west of this building; their function has not yet been clarified.[7]

*Area O: Large Reservoir*

Approximately 900 meters north of Qasr Mushash, another large rectangular reservoir, of 21 by 19 meters, is located on the west bank of wadi B, which today is completely destroyed.

The settlement site of Qasr Mushash therefore constitutes individual groups of buildings that apparently were not associated with one another, and some of which were quite isolated. The two largest units are area A (the *qasr*) and the central area B with the surrounding building structure groups C, D, and G. Separate units include building groups F, H, J, K, L, M, and N, whereas—in view of their proximity—groups J and K probably belonged together. The reservoir in area O represents an isolated structure.

*Water Installations*

Five complexes for storing water are located in the area of Qasr Mushash West. One of these can be labeled a cistern. It lies northeast of the *qasr* and displays a circular shaft with a diameter of 4.8 meters; it is lined with stone and covered by a stone vaulting, of which two arches are preserved. The interior of the cistern is finished with lime plaster. On the eastern side of the cistern above the ground is a rectangular, stone-lined channel, which served as a conduit from the northeast (Bisheh 1989: 84). The depth of the cistern might have been approximately 3 meters. The cistern had a maximum capacity of 54.3 cubic meters.[8] The rectangular structure, 17.8 by 7 meters, in the central area of Qasr Mushash appears today as an open reservoir (Fig. 3.6). A settling basin with lime plaster adjoins it on the western side; a channel within the reservoir was still visible in the 1980s (Bisheh 1989: 85). With an estimated depth of about 2.5 meters, the reservoir had a capacity of 315 cubic meters. Another large reservoir located in the southwest is represented by a basin, whose sides are 25.4 meters long; its inner and outer surfaces are finished with lime plaster. With an estimated depth of 1.5 meters, this basin could have held a maximum of about 940 cubic meters (Bisheh 1989: 84, pl. 3b).

The largest reservoir was found in area O; it measures approximately 21 by 19 meters and is 4.7 meters deep. Although completely destroyed today, King's description states that steps on the northern narrow side provided entry to the reservoir (King et al. 1983: 389). Above the steps, which descended from west to east, was a stone channel that served as a conduit. The reservoir is built of hewn stones, and the surface is completely finished with hydraulic plaster. It had a maximum capacity of 1,890 cubic meters. Two other structures might also be interpreted as hydraulic installations:

Figure 3.6 Qasr Mushash West—central area, reservoir (area B) (photo: DAI, Orient Department, K. Bartl).

- An earthen dam (no longer preserved) at the intersection of two small wadis, northeast of the *qasr*, behind which could have been small collecting basins. However, almost no traces of a basin are now visible.
- A rectangular structure with sides formed by earthen ramps, located at the foot of a very small wadi farther east.

In total, Qasr Mushash West demonstrates a water storage capacity of far more than 3,000 cubic meters. This exceptionally large volume raises the question about possible technical aspects of the hydraulic system as well as the likely function of this location. With regard to so-called water harvesting, there are two possibilities of use, either together or alternating. Imaginable, on the one hand, is that the wadi in the area west of the *qasr* was dammed up. On the other, it is possible that the winter rainfall that accumulated in the north–south flowing tributary wadis A and B was conducted into reservoirs and cisterns. The first possibility is supported by the fact that even today remains of massive stone walls are visible on the banks of Wadi Mushash, which may be interpreted as efforts at damming the watercourse. These walls were still well preserved at the beginning of the twentieth century, as attested in descriptions by Moritz (1908: 426). Accordingly, two long walls running north to south lay to the west of the wadi, at an interval of about 200 meters. The westerly wall was constructed with "wing walls" at both ends in a U-form, which possibly created a kind of basin. However, the way in which the dammed-up water was used and how the constructions were employed to raise the water are still unclear.

All water-storage facilities are clearly located at a higher level than the maximal height of water in the wadi. The conveyance of this wadi water into the basin must have been achieved by such water-lifting devices as a whim or a waterwheel. However, no traces of these have been found. Therefore, it is doubtful whether the water supply came from the main branch of the Wadi Mushash, running west to east. It seems more probable that the wadis running north to south (i.e., wadis A and B) were exploited (Fig. 3.7). It can be presumed that the water inflow into the western reservoir in area E, which lies at the southern end of wadi A, probably came from the north by means of a conduit to a settling basin.[9] The reservoir in the central area was also probably fed by wadi A, supplied by means of a canal

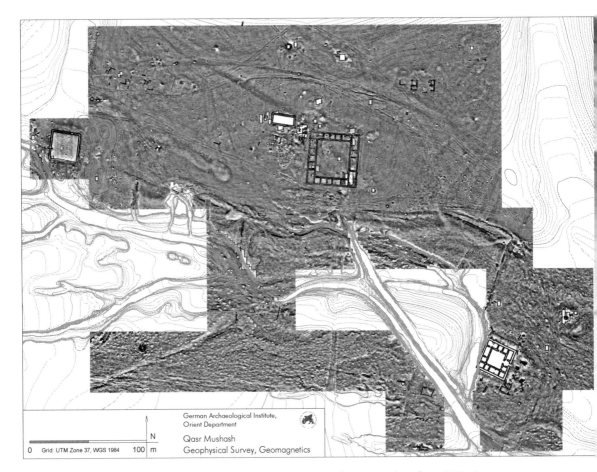

Figure 3.7 Qasr Mushash West—reconstruction of water conduits (map: DAI, Orient-Department, T. Urban [satellite image: Quickbird/WorldView-1]).

from the northwest that is no longer visible. The ground slope would have been sufficient for the flow. Similarly, the cistern near the *qasr* was likely supplied by a canal, which led water from wadi B. Traces of such a structure were still visible during the excavations (Bisheh 1989: 85). The amount of water in smaller wadis was exploited too. This is demonstrated by the dam (no longer existent) near findspot 10 and the depression to the east of it. However, the latter might be of recent date. The fact that the north–south wadis with their incline were intensely exploited is shown by the large cistern in the north. This structure lies on the west bank of wadi B; it was filled from the north with floodwater transported by the wadi.

## The Function and Meaning of Qasr Mushash: Discussion

Considering the entire complex, three different types of buildings can be noted: representative buildings and public buildings—the *qasr*, square complexes 1 and 2, the bath, the large houses in the northeast; simple domestic buildings—structures in the northwest and northeast; and supply installations and hydraulic structures. The core of the site constitutes a central area in which all three building types are present. The square complex is the most outstanding: with dimensions of about 40 by 40 meters, it forms the largest of a total of four square structures in Qasr Mushash West and East. This complex has a large courtyard measuring approximately 20 by 20 meters, which is enclosed on all sides by a row of rooms, apparently all close to the same size. This type of building refers back to a long tradition and served various purposes: a military use as a *castrum* or *castellum* in Roman–Late Roman times, or use as a residence or as a way station or caravan halt.[10] Nonetheless, the definitive assignment of one of these functions to the complex, based on the ground plan alone, is still difficult if not impossible.[11] It can be assumed that the area of the *qasr* and that of the tower on the south bank of the wadi were most likely defensive. However, there is no proof for a military function of these buildings in Early Islamic times. Moreover, the function of the possible Roman–Late Roman predecessor of the *qasr* remains likewise unclear.

The small buildings scattered in the northwest, north, northeast, and east probably formed the actual dwelling areas. It is noteworthy that these habitations apparently had no individual water storage facilities and that the water supply of the "public" as well as "private" structures was achieved by means of large reservoirs or cisterns. The data presented here can be interpreted in two ways: on one hand, the structures could be seen as a palatial complex with an adjoining settlement and accompanying supply facilities. On the other, they could also represent a way station or caravan halt. The latter interpretation is supported above all by the number of water-storage installations, which would seem out of proportion for such a small community. Furthermore, the function of the larger square complex in the center supports this suggestion. The square structure (which may resemble a caravanserai) and the bath together form an interrelated and—according to the pottery typology—probably a coeval complex. The proximity of the bath and the cistern also implies interconnection, but this aspect still needs further investigation. Evidence of a combined caravanserai and bath or reservoir is occasionally found in Ottoman *hajj* forts, for example, in Qutayfa, located forty kilometers from Damascus (Sauvaget 1940: 117–21), and in Qala'at Fassu'a in southern Jordan (Petersen 2012: 112ff.). The interpretation of Qasr Mushash as a halting place for travelers, already proposed by Stein, Bisheh, and Kennedy, seems to be given further confirmation by recent additional data.[12] It is likely that the central area represents the core of a way station. The surrounding smaller buildings, each with one or two rooms, could have constituted a small settlement for the supply of the main building, which might have served as accommodation for travelers. The large water basin in the west can also be correlated with the function of a way station. It is quite plausible that this basin was a watering place for animals, whereas the central cistern was reserved for human necessities. Well-known Ottoman period examples are the very large Birkat al-Hajj and the Birkat an-Nabatiya in Busra, which have Nabataean origins (Dentzer-Feydy et al. 2007: 164–65). The maximum volume of water storage in Qasr Mushash West would have been about 3,200 cubic meters. An estimation of the water supply needed for people and animals demonstrates that the provision of a small settlement and pack animals with water was not problematic—provided that the winter rains were plentiful (Table 3.1).

The question nevertheless arises as to whether the site was used permanently throughout the entire year or temporarily, that is, seasonally. Due to the lack of paleoclimatic data for the seventh and eighth centuries, no definitive statements can be made. However, the Early Byzantine–Early Islamic city of Resafa in the Syrian desert steppe provides an example that a water supply based exclusively on

Table 3.1. Water demands

| Days | Number | Humans | Camels | Sheep/Goats | Total |
|------|--------|--------|--------|-------------|-------|
| 1 | 1 | 10–30 L | 15–20 L | 2–5 L | 27–55 L |
| 1 | 100 | 1,000–3,000 L | 1,500–2,000 L | 200–500 L | 2,700–5,500 L |
| 365 | 100 | 365,000–<br>1,095,000 L | 547,000–<br>730,000 L | 73,000–<br>182,500 L | **985,000–<br>2,007,500 L**<br>(or c. 1000–<br>2000 m³) |

*Note:* Values for human consumption based on sources from Pergamon (Keilholz 2007: 224) estimating a minimum of about 3.5 cubic meters per person per year.

collected and stored winter rainfall is indeed possible, even for a larger number of people (Brinker and Garbrecht 2007: 117ff.).[13] The principle of water storage by means of cisterns and reservoirs has a long tradition in the southern Levant. Especially renowned are the countless examples from the Nabataean era, which are well evidenced in Petra (Bellwald 2008) as well as at other sites. These locations contain simple, yet effective forms of conducting wadi water with the aid of stone channels or pipes to storage installations, which were used in subsequent periods as well (Oleson 1990, 1995, 2007). Consequently, functional and formal parallels in water management in Qasr Mushash can be traced back at least until Hellenistic-Roman or Nabataean-Roman times, signifying that water management was based on older prototypes and adapted to specific local conditions.[14] In addition to the existence of numerous hydraulic installations, the location of Qasr Mushash suggests that it was a caravan station. The site forms one of a total of five places that were founded or used in the Early Islamic period and that extend to the east of the modern town of Sahab near Amman to Azraq on a west–east line: al-Muwaqqar, Qasr Mushash, Qasr Kharana, Qusayr ʿAmra, and Qasr Azraq.[15] The distances between these sites are approximately 15 and 26 kilometers (Table 3.2).

With the exception of Qasr Kharana, where water was supplied exclusively by means of groundwater from the wadi bed (Urice 1979 9 n. 8), all the other sites show different kinds of hydraulic installations, such as reservoirs, wells, cisterns, and dams, which would have facilitated their use as a way station.[16] It therefore seems plausible to reconstruct a historical route to Azraq from al-Muwaqqar to Qasr Mushash via Qusayr ʿAmra and Azraq, while avoiding Qasr Kharana. This track may have in fact formed the main route as no other sites with water sources or installations are known. The watering places al-Muwaqqar, Qasr Mushash, Qusayr Amra, and Azraq permit comfortable day-long marches on a route of about 100 kilometers between ʿAmman and the oasis of Azraq, which forms the access to the Wadi Sirhan, one of the most important corridors through the northern part of the Arabian peninsula.[17]

Apart from Qasr Kharana, which appears today as a solitary building in the steppe, the other four places consist of numerous building structures of different

Table 3.2. Distances separating early Islamic sites between ʿAmman and Azraq

| From | To | Kilometers |
|------|------|------------|
| ʿAmman | al-Muwaqqar | 23.50 |
| al-Muwaqqar | Qasr Mushash | 19.40 |
| Qasr Mushash | Qasr Kharana | 16.40 |
| Qasr Kharana | Qusayr ʿAmra | 14.60 |
| Qusayr ʿAmra | Azraq Süd | 22.00 |

form and size. In each case, one or several constructions suggest official or administrative functions. In al-Muwaqqar, the subconstructions of the *qasr* were still visible at the beginning of the twentieth century (Brünnow and von Domaszewski 1905: 182; Creswell 1969: 493). In Qasr Mushash, the different square structures and enclosures were probably for official use; in Qusayr ʿAmra, official functions are demonstrated in the reception hall with the bath as well as the square *qasr* to the north of it. In the oasis of Azraq, the main building is represented by the large fort existing since the Roman period, while a small square building with connected bath and reservoir named Qasr Ain al-Sil and dated to the Umayyad period might have been used as a farmstead or as a small residence (Bisheh 1989: 90ff.). It is conceivable that the use of these places as way stations was only one function among others. This utilization partially corresponds to the better-known halting places of the *hajj* caravans (Petersen 2012). Here, two types of sites can be distinguished: large forts in the midst of villages and rather isolated places far away from larger settlements[18] that served exclusively for the protection and provisioning (particularly water supply) of the pilgrims and their animals. Concerning Qasr Mushash, further research is needed to clarify the function of the entire site.

## Notes

My sincerest thanks go to Dr. G. Bisheh, former Director General of the Department of Antiquities of Jordan. His constant support is of tremendous importance for our work at Qasr Mushash. I would like to express our thanks to the Acting Director General of the Department of Antiquities of Jordan (DoA), Fares Hmoud, for generous help and support. My sincerest thanks go also to the representatives of the DoA, Ashraf al-Krisha and Mr. Hussein Saleh. I am very grateful to all members of the team for the efforts and the good spirit in the work, and would like to thank Dr. Thomas Urban (surveyor), Abdel-Nasser Hindawi (archaeologist), Dr. Franziska Bloch (archaeologist, pottery specialist), Tobias Richter (archaeologist, lithic specialist), Martin Posselt, and Jona Ostheimer (archaeologists, geophysics). Moreover, I must thank our workmen from Sahab for their contributions to the success of our fieldwork.

1. Hydraulic installations of Early Islamic times are also present in the neighboring communities of al-Muwaqqar (Brünnow and von Domaszewski 1905; Musil 1907: 27ff.; Hamilton 1946; Mayer 1946), Qusayr ʿAmra (Vibert-Guigne and Bisheh 2007), and Qasr Hallabat (Arce 2008; Ghrayib 2003). Whereas the use of the corresponding buildings and installations in the first two sites mentioned can be dated to the Early Islamic period with certainty, the beginnings of Hallabat are presumed to be Roman (Kennedy and Riley 1990: 75).

2. For an overview of the interpretations of the Early Islamic *qusur*, see Bloch (2011: 131ff.).

3. Musil (1907: 115) designated the quadrangular openings in the wadi bed as cisterns.

4. Red-slipped pottery types like Late Roman C/Phocean Ware and African Red Slip, which are common ware types in Late Roman–Early Byzantine times in the Near East, were no longer produced in the Early Islamic period (Hayes 1972). Therefore, the appearance of red-slipped pottery among the surface finds at the *qasr* point to a pre-Islamic foundation of the building.

5. Based on aerial surveys of the ruins since the end of the 1990s within the framework of the Aerial Photographic Archive for Archaeology in the Middle East (APAAME) project, the

looting activities in Qasr Mushash can be traced back to the year 1997 (see APAAME, archive accessible from www.classics.uwa.edu.au/aerial_archaeology.

6. During a visit in 2001, Genequand documented some of the walls of the square structure, which became visible through clandestine excavations (2002: 16, figs. 8–9).

7. Furthermore, during his visit to Qasr Mushash in 1901, Musil reported a tower located west of the *qasr* (1907: 113, fig. 104), but no remains are present today.

8. An exemplary comparison for this type of cistern is located in Humayma in southern Jordan (Oleson 1995: fig.6).

9. King and colleagues (1983: 392) also conjectured that the wadis flowing north to south were mainly used for collecting water.

10. The latter function has been suggested for one of the Umayyad square complexes at Jabal Says (house T), which were connected to the *qasr* (Schmidt 2012: 76). For the typological similarities and functional differences of square buildings in the Roman and Umayyad periods, see Genequand (2006: 3ff).

11. For more on this problem, see Dentzer (1994).

12. Sir Aurel Stein defined the locality as a caravan station on the way from Wadi Sirhan to Amman-Philadelphia and dated it to the Roman period (Gregory and Kennedy 1985: 287). Similarly, Bisheh interprets Qasr Mushash as a halting place for official post caravans but not for *hajj* caravans. In his opinion, this site was in use only during Umayyad times (1989: 88ff., 1992: 40f.). Kennedy sees Qasr Mushash as a small Late Roman site, which was enlarged during Umayyad times; in his view, it also served as a halting place for travelers (Kennedy and Bewley 2004: 221).

13. The four large cisterns at Resafa, which were constructed in the Early Byzantine period have a capacity of more than 20,000 cubic meters. This volume alone would have been more than sufficient for an average population of six thousand, estimated for Resafa, an important pilgrim center (Ulbert 2005: 111). This number increased during the pilgrimage season.

14. Much more complex systems for water management in Early Islamic times, which served for crop cultivation and raising animals, are known in Qasr al-Hayr al-Gharbi and Qasr al-Hayr al-Sharqi (Genequand 2009).

15. It cannot be excluded that Qasr Uweinid, another fort of Roman date, east of Qusayr 'Amra, was used as a halting place in Early Islamic times as well, since the place is mentioned at Muqaddasi in the tenth century (Gregory and Kennedy 1985: 285). Nevertheless, archaeological evidence for this time span is still missing.

16. Several large reservoirs were documented at al-Muwaqqar and its surroundings at the end of the nineteenth century (Musil 1907: fig. 28). One of them can be dated to 720–724 by an inscription of Yazid II on a water gauge (Hamilton 1946; Mayer 1946). Qusayr Amra shows two wells of the *saqiya* type (that is, water lifting with means of waterwheels) as well as a cistern. The nearby Wadi al-Butm is well known for its torrential floods in rainy winters (Vibert-Guigne and Bisheh 2007: pl.2b). In the southern part of the oasis of Azraq, a huge open reservoir made of basalt blocks is located near the spring 'Ayn as-Sawda. The orthostats of the basin seem to be of Umayyad date (Abu Azizeh 2014: 632)..

17. Another route in the south that bypasses the oasis of Azraq might have been from Qusayr Amra via Qasr Uweinid to Qasr Tuba.

18. The medieval settlements of Kiswa, Busra, and Karak were halting places of the former group, while Zarqa, Doshaq, and al-Thaniyya were more isolated places without a settlement nearby (Petersen 2012: 9ff.).

# Bibliography

Abu-Azizeh, Lorriane. 2014. "Azraq: 'Ayn Sawda Reservoir." Contribution in Glenn J. Corbett, Donald R. Keller, Barbara A. Porter, and Christopher A. Tuttle, "Archaeology in Jordan, 2012 and 2013 Seasons." *American Journal of Archaeology* 118: 627–76.

Almagro, Martin, Luis Caballero, Juan Zozaya and Antonio Almagro. 1975. *Qusayr 'Amra: Residencia y Baños Omeyas en el Desierto de Jordania.* Madrid: Instituto Hispano-Árabe de Cultura.

Amr, Zuhair S., David Modry and Mustafa Shudiefat. 2011. *Badia: The Living Desert.* Amman: National Center for Development and Research.

Arce, Ignacio. 2008. "Hallabat: castellum, coenobium, praetorium, qasr: the construction of a palatine architecture under the Umayyads (I)." In *Residences, Castles, Settlements: Transformation Processes from Late Antiquity to Early Islam in Bilad ash-Sham, Proceedings of the International Conference Held at Damascus, 5–9 November 2006,* edited by Karin Bartl and Abdelrazaq Moaz, 153–82. Rahden, Germany: Marie Leidorf.

Bacharach, Jere L. 1996. "Marwanid Umayyad building activities: speculations on patronage." *Muqarnas* 13: 27–44.

Bartl, Karin, Ghazi Bisheh, Franziska Bloch, and Tobias Richter. Forthcoming. "Qasr Mushash survey: first results of archaeological fieldwork in 2011 and 2012." *Annual of the Department of Antiquities of Jordan.*

Bellwald, Ueli. 2008. "The hydraulic Infrastructure of Petra: a model for water strategies in arid land." In *Cura Aquarum in Jordanien, Proceedings of the 13th International Conference on the History of Water Management and Hydraulic Engineering in the Mediterranean Region, Petra/Amman, 31 March–9 April 2007,* edited by Christoph Ohlig, 47–94. Siegburg, Germany: Schriften der Deutschen Wasserhistorischen Gesellschaft, Band 12.

Bender, Friedrich. 1974. *Geology of Jordan.* Berlin: Brüder Bornträger.

Bienert, Hans-Dieter, and Jutta Häser. 2004. *Men of Dikes and Canals: The Archaeology of Water in the Middle East. International Symposium Held at Petra, Wadi Musa (H.K. of Jordan), 15–20 June, 1999.* Rahden, Germany: Marie Leidorf.

Bisheh, Ghazi. 1986. "Some observations on recent Umayyad discoveries" [in Arabic]. *Annual of the Department of Antiquities of Jordan* 30: 10–12.

———. 1989. "Qasr Mshash und Qasr 'Ayn al-Sil: two Umayyad sites in Jordan." In *The History of Bilad al-Sham During the Umayyad Period (Fourth International Conference: 24–29 October 1987, Amman),* edited by Adnan Bakhit and Robert Schick, 81–103. Amman: Bilad al-Sham History Committee.

———. 1992. "The Umayyad monuments between Muwaqqar and Azraq: palatial residences or caravanserais?" In *The Near East in Antiquity,* vol. 3, edited by Susanne Kerner, 35–41. Amman: Kutba.

Bloch, Franziska. 2011. *Das umayyadische "Wüstenschloss" und die Siedlung am Ğabal Says. Band II: Keramik und Kleinfunde.* Darmstadt: Philipp von Zabern.

Brinker, Werner, and Günter Garbrecht. 2007. "Die Zisternen-Wasserversorgung von Resafa-Sergiupolis." In *Antike Zisternen,* edited by Christoph Ohlig, 117–42. Siegburg, Germany: Schriften der Deutschen Wasserhistorischen Gesellschaft, Band 9.

Brünnow, Rudolf E., and Alfred von Domaszewski. 1905. *Die Provincia Arabia, Zweiter Band: Der Äussere Limes und die Römerstrassen von El-Ma'ān bis Bosra.* Strasbourg: Karl J. Trübner.

Copeland, Lorraine, and Francis Hours. 1989. *The Hammer on the Rock: Studies in the Early Palaeolithic of Azraq, Jordan.* Oxford: British Archaeological Reports International Series 540(i).

Creswell, Keppel Archibald Cameron. 1969. *Early Muslim Architecture,* vol. 1, part I: *Umayyads A.D. 622–750.* Oxford: Clarendon.

Dentzer, Jean-Marie. 1994. "Khāns ou casernes à Palmyra? À propos de structures visible sur les photographies aériennes anciennes." *Syria* 71(1–2): 45–112.

Dentzer-Feydy, Jacqueline, Michèle Vallerin, Thibaud Fournet, Ryas Mukdad, and Anas Mukdad. 2007. *Bosra aux portes de l'Arabie.* Beirut: Institut français du Proche-Orient.

Genequand, Denis. 2002. "Projet 'Implantations umayyades de Syrie et de Jordanie: rapport sur une campagne de prospection et reconnaissance.'" *Schweizerisch-Liechtensteinische Stiftung für Archäologie, Jahresbericht* 2001: 3–33.

———. 2006. "Umayyad castles: the shift from late antique military architecture to early Islamic palatial building." In *Muslim Military Architecture in Greater Syria from the Coming of Islam to the Ottoman Period*, edited by Hugh Kennedy, 3–25. Leiden: Brill.

———. 2009. "Économie de production, affirmation du pouvoir et *dolce vita*: aspects de la politique de l'eau sous les Omeyyades au Bilād al-Shām." In *Stratégies d'acquisition de l'eau et société au Moyen-Orient depuis l'Antiquité, Études des cas*, edited by Michel Mouton and Mohamed al-Dbiyat, 157–77. Beirut: Institut français du Proche-Orient.

———. 2012. *Les établissements des élites omeyyades en Palmyrène et au Proche-Orient.* Beirut: Bibliothèque Archéologique et Historique.

Ghrayib, Romel, with a contribution by Maria Elena Ronza. 2003. "The 2002 season at Qasr al-Hallabat: a preliminary report." *Annual of the Department of Antiquities of Jordan* 47: 65–74.

Gregory, Shelagh, and David Kennedy. 1985. *Sir Aurel Stein's Limes Report.* Oxford: British Archaeological Reports International Series 272(i).

Hamilton, Richard W. 1946. "An eighth-century water-gauge at al-Muwaqqar." *Quarterly of the Department of Antiquities in Palestine* 12 (3/4): 70–72.

Hayes, John W. 1972. *Late Roman Pottery.* London: British School at Rome.

Kennedy, David, and Robert Bewley. 2004. *Ancient Jordan from the Air.* London: Council for British Research in the Levant, British Academy.

Kennedy, David, and Derrick Riley. 1990. *Rome's Desert Frontier from the Air.* London: B. T. Batsford.

King, Geoffrey. 1982. "Preliminary Report on a Survey of Byzantine and Islamic Sites in Jordan." *Annual of the Department of Antiquities of Jordan* 26: 85–95, plates 433–44.

———. 1989. "Mushash (Qasr el)." In *Archaeology of Jordan, II.2 Field Reports Sites L–Z*, edited by Denise Homès-Fréderiq and J. Basil Hennessy, 391–96. Leuven, Belgium: Peeters.

King, Geoffrey, Cherie J. Lenzen, and Gary O. Rollefson. 1983. "Survey of Byzantine and Islamic sites in Jordan, second season report, 1981." *Annual of the Department of Antiquities of Jordan* 27: 387–436, plates 85–98.

Klimscha, Florian, Ricardo Eichmann, Christoph Schuler, and Henning Fahlbusch. 2012. *Wasserwirtschaftliche Innovationen im archäologischen Kontext: Von den prähistorischen Anfängen bis zu den Metropolen der Antike. DAI ForschungsCluster 2. Innovationen: technisch, sozial.* Rahden, Germany: Marie Leidorf.

Mayer, Leo Aryeh. 1946. "Note on the inscription from al-Muwaqqar." *Quarterly of the Department of Antiquities in Palestine* 12 (3–4): 73–74.

Moritz, Bertold. 1908. "Ausflüge in der Arabia Petraea." *Université Saint-Joseph, Mélanges de la Faculté Orientale* 3 (fasc. I): 387–436.

Mouton, Michel, and Mohamed al-Dbiyat. 2009. *Stratégies d'acquisition de l'eau et société au Moyen-Orient depuis l'Antiquité, Études des cas.* Beirut: Institut français du Proche-Orient.

Musil, Alois. 1907. *Kusejr 'Amra*, vol. 1: *Text.* Vienna: Kaiserliche Akademie der Wissenschaften.

Ohlig, Christoph. 2007. *Antike Zisternen.* Siegburg, Germany: Schriften der Deutschen Wasserhistorischen Gesellschaft, Band 9.

———. 2008. *Cura Aquarum in Jordanien: Proceedings of the 13th International Conference on the History of Water Management and Hydraulic Engineering in the Mediterranean Region,*

*Petra/Amman, 31 March–09 April 2007*. Siegburg, Germany: Schriften der Deutschen Wasserhistorischen Gesellschaft, Band 12.

Oleson, John Peter 1990. "The Humeima hydraulic survey: preliminary report of the 1989 season." *Annual of the Department of Antiquities of Jordan* 34: 285–312.

———. 1995. "The origins and design of the Nabataean water-supply system." *Studies in the History and Archaeology of Jordan* 5: 707–19.

———. 2007. "The enduring attraction of Hawara/al-Humayma, a multi-cultural site in Arabia Petraea." In *Crossing Jordan: North American Contributions to the Archaeology of Jordan*, edited by Thomas E. Levy, 447–55. London: Equinox.

Petersen, Andrew. 2012. *The Medieval and Ottoman Hajj Route in Jordan: An Archaeological and Historical Study*. Oxford: Oxbow.

Sauvaget, Jean. 1940. "Caravansérails syriens du moyen-âge II: caravanserails mamelouke." *Ars Islamica* 7(1): 1–19.

Schmidt, Kurt. 2012. *Das umayyadische "Wüstenschloss" und die Siedlung am Ğabal Says*, vol. 1: *Architektur*. Darmstadt: Philipp von Zabern.

Ulbert, Thilo. 2005. "Resafa/Sergiupolis." In *Orte und Zeiten: 25 Jahre archäologische Forschung in Syrien, 1980–2005*, edited by Deutsches Archäologisches Institut Damaskus, 110–15. Damascus: Salhani.

Urice, Stephen. 1979. "The Qasr Kharana Project, 1979." *Annual of the Department of Antiquities of Jordan* 25: 5–19.

———. 1987. *Qasr Kharana in the Transjordan*. Durham, NC: American Schools of Oriental Research.

Vibert-Guigne, Claude, and Ghazi Bisheh. 2007. *Les peintures de Qusayr ʿAmra: un bain omeyyade dans le bâdiya jordanienne*. Beirut: Institut français du Proche-Orient, Department of Antiquities of Jordan.

# PART II

# Agriculture, Pastoralism, and Subsistence

# CHAPTER 4

# Faunal Distributions from the Southern Highlands of Transjordan

## Regional and Historical Perspectives on the Representations and Roles of Animals in the Middle Islamic Period

*Robin M. Brown*

It has been well demonstrated that faunal remains from archaeological sites of the Islamic era offer unique information on a variety of cultural practices and social activities. The many studies of animal bone collections from the Islamic Levant have made important contributions to understanding the cultural past at specific sites, while a few of these also address research methods.[1] A recent increase in reporting of faunal data from locations across the Levant provides an exceptional opportunity to explore animal bone distributions at sites that are geographically clustered. This chapter describes a regional approach to faunal distributions that draws on Middle Islamic assemblages from one such cluster of sites in southern Transjordan (Fig. 4.1).[2] While any number of regional studies focus on settlement patterns and ceramic representations in the Islamic Levant, faunal distributions have not been addressed.[3] The specific challenges in synthesizing animal bone data emerge from differences in sampling, choice of analytical procedures, and reporting formats.[4] Nevertheless, the preliminary approaches adopted here demonstrate that collective data, compiled from multiple sources, illustrate regional patterns of animal exploitation that cast new light on animal roles within a broad historical and cultural milieu.

This study of animal use in the Middle Islamic period (1100–1516) has two goals. The first is to examine faunal distributions across the southern highlands of Transjordan with simple techniques that illustrate spatial and temporal patterns. Although this approach lacks statistical authority due in part to variance in

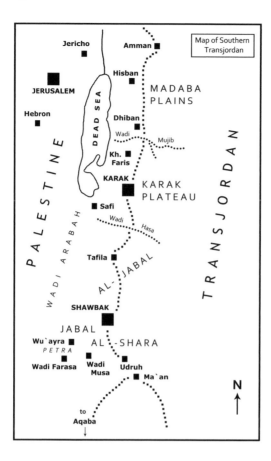

Figure 4.1 Map of southern Transjordan (prepared by author).

sampling and reporting, the results offer important points for discussion and future research. The limitations of the faunal data, which represent only a segment of the extensive realm of human and animal interactions characteristic of Middle Islamic Transjordan, are also a point of consideration. The second goal, therefore, is to extend and recontextualize the value of archaeologically retrieved faunal material by referring to animal representations in historical literature. Even a cursory glance at a few sources provides a fresh view of human and animal dynamics within multiple spheres of cultural practice that reach well beyond food preparation and consumption activities. The narratives consulted here also illustrate the highly distinctive ways that social elites perceived the landscape and its animal life. This and other aspects of human and animal relationships that are potentially relevant to Middle Islamic Transjordan may remain elusive archaeologically, yet they can contribute to the kinds of questions that archaeologists consider. In examining faunal assemblages, the question of why some species are unrepresented is important in constructing a broad vision of the complex social spheres that linked humans and animals within Islamic cultural settings.

## Faunal Data from Settlement Sites
## in the Southern Highlands

The faunal assemblages discussed in this chapter are reported from excavations at Hisban, Dhiban, Karak, Shawbak, Wuʻayra, and Wadi Farasa, as shown in Table 4.1.[5] Each of these sites is situated in the southern highland belt of Transjordan (modern Jordan), where natural districts separated by formidable wadis include the Madaba plains, the rolling hills and plains of the Karak plateau, and the mountainous Jabal al-Shara. The prevailing semiarid Mediterranean bioclimate (al-Eisawi 1985: 48–49; Kürschner 1986: 47, fig. 1; 49, map 1) has hosted a variety of animal and plant life within this area in which dry farming and livestock production have been traditional. Native vegetation is dominated by Mediterranean non-forest scrub (*garrigue*), which followed the degradation of once-wooded lands (al-Eisawi 1985: 52, fig. 9; 54). The area is bounded to the west by the rift valley escarpment and to the east by the arid shrub lands of the desert steppe. Resource exploitation was similar among the settlement communities discussed here as their environmental catchments offered immediate or proximate access to open lands, providing pasture for livestock grazing and fertile soil for the cultivation of grains and other crops. These sites are also situated near springs with riparian growth, where thickets and trees once supported woodland wildlife.[6] This continuity affords fair justification for adopting a regional approach to the faunal collections, although it does not bear any expectation of uniformity among the assemblages, some of which are distinctly unique.

Throughout the Middle and Late Islamic periods, the southern highlands included a continuum of settlement-based communities, semimobile groups, and nomadic tribes, which were linked through cultural traditions, integrating trade and communications routes, and a social order that was maintained by imperial authorities or dominant local coalitions. Overall, a mixed farming economy prevailed, yet shifts in land use had long-term consequences for the social organization of rural production and the distribution of households across the landscape.[7] An expansion of cultivation during the thirteenth to fourteenth century appears to have involved widespread occupation of settlements and some specialized production yielding marketable surpluses (Walker 2011: 150–51, 154–57, 93), yet subsistence farming was certainly an important factor within this economy as well. During the fifteenth century, the region responded to changes in Mamluk administrative and land allocation policies with greater reliance on household-based mixed farming practices, including an apparent emphasis on livestock production (145, 226–32). The use of constructed settlements in open areas diminished sharply in favor of caves, tents, and villages sheltered by rugged terrain, particularly during the Ottoman era. Within this transformative period, local tribes presided from

Table 4.1. Faunal samples from Middle and Late Islamic sites in southern Transjordan

| Site and Year of Excavation | Area, Phase, or Stratum | Description of Faunal Sample |
|---|---|---|
| **Dhiban** [2005] (Kansa 2011) | Phase 2 Mamluk | NISP: 320 identified to species and other taxa. Total reported = 320+. |
| **Hisban** [1968–1976] (Driesch and Boessneck 1995; Boessneck 1995; see also Boessneck and Driesch 1978) | Strata IV, II–III, I Ayyubid and Mamluk Late Ottoman | TF/NISP Strata IV, II–III: 9,911+ identified to species and other taxa. Total reported = 9,911+. TF/NISP Strata I: 1,105 identified to domestic mammals. Total reported = 1,105+. |
| **Hisban-cistern** [1971] (LaBianca 1995) | Cistern (D6) Ayyubid/ Mamluk | TF/NISP: 391 identified sheep/goats (total sample and other taxa are unreported). |
| **Karak** [1987] (Brown and Rielly, forthcoming) | Phases 1b and 2 Mamluk and Ottoman | TF: 404 identified to species and other taxa. 497 listed in categories of bird, fish, sheep-sized, cattle-sized, and cattle/sheep-sized. Total reported = 901. |
| **Shawbak** [1986] (Brown and Rielly 2010a) | Phases 1, 3, and 4 Ayyubid, Mamluk, and Ottoman | TF: 343 identified to species and other taxa. 598 listed in categories of bird, fish, sheep-sized, cattle-sized, and cattle/sheep-sized. Total reported = 941. |
| **Shawbak** [2005] (Mazza and Corbino 2007b; see also Corbino and Mazza 2009) | Area 6000c Crusader | NISP: 722 identified to species and other taxa or categories. 423 unidentified. Total reported = 1145. |
| **Wadi Farasa** [2002] (Schmid and Studer 2003, 2007) | Cistern Crusader/ Ayyubid | NISP: 538 identified to species and other taxa. 398 listed in categories of mammal, fish, and mollusk. Total reported = 936. |
| **Wu'ayra** [1987] (Brown and Rielly 2010b) | Phase Ia and 1b Crusader | TF: 461 identified to species and other taxa. 689 listed in categories of bird, fish, sheep-sized, cattle-sized, and cattle/sheep-sized. Total reported = 1,150. |
| **Wu'ayra** [1993] (Corbino and Mazza 2013) | Area UT 83 Crusader/ Ayyubid | NISP: 444 identified to species and other taxa. 461 unidentified. Total reported = 905. |

*Notes:* NISP = number of identified specimens or number of individual specimens; TF = total fragments. The + symbol follows bone counts where the existence of additional material is indicated. The figure for the Hisban assemblage is calculated from information in Driesch and Boessneck (1995) and Boessneck (1995).

*Chronology:* Crusader era (1115–1188), Ayyubid period (1174–1263), Mamluk period (1263–1516), and Ottoman period (1516–1918).

the seventeenth through the nineteenth century, in the absence of direct state governance (Johns 1994: 25–28). Shifts in food production strategies may have been further encouraged by environmental factors, as suggested by the occurrence of significant wet and dry cycles.[8]

The built environment of the southern highlands accommodated the needs of various sedentary or largely sedentary populations, as reflected in diverse settlement types that fulfilled a range of residential, military, and administrative functions. Among them, the twelfth-century fortress at Wu'ayra was a substantial Crusader military base, and the nearby outpost in Wadi Farasa probably belonged to the Frankish defensive network as well. These garrison communities would have relied on provisions of foodstuffs drawn from local producers. Villages at Hisban and Dhiban thrived as rural agricultural communities through the Ayyubid and Mamluk eras. Households in these communities may have been predominantly subsistence based, although some specialized production of surplus for formal market-based exchange would have supported nonproducers. Karak and Shawbak castles were Ayyubid and Mamluk administrative and military centers standing adjacent to towns. Both sites were embellished with a royal palace complex. Consumption patterns at elite residences were probably distinctive, although this is not apparent at Karak and Shawbak as the deposition postdates the original functions of the dwelling and reception areas. Both castles were reused during the Ottoman period, at which time village households were established within the ruins.

Optimally, Middle Islamic faunal remains from the rural Levant may describe dietary patterns and offer insights on livestock farming and distribution practices in ways that are not addressed in historical sources. However, a few cautions should be acknowledged. Interpretations of livestock-producing strategies generally rely on inferences linking bone refuse from food preparation and dining activities to reconstructions of herd compositions. Animal age and sex profiles may be informative in this regard, yet variability and bias due to taphonomic processes must be anticipated. Furthermore, chronological determinations are extremely important to interpretation as production strategies were by no means static. Cautions are evident here as well, for bone elements from deposits of a given phase are generally treated as coterminous, although such deposits containing faunal debris may represent accumulations over multiple decades. The remains, therefore, may refer to a combination of food production strategies.[9] Sample size is a further consideration, for conclusions based on observations of small collections are most tentative. Of the assemblages discussed here, the only large sample is from the Middle Islamic strata at Hisban (see Table 4.1), yet information on this material is limited as no period-focused study was conducted (see Driesch and Boessneck 1995). While these and other caveats are generic to animal bone studies, the interpretive models offered by faunal specialists are essential in promoting the exploration of Middle Islamic animal representations and roles.

## Species Representations

The discussion of species representations within Middle Islamic faunal assemblages from southern Transjordan is introduced by a complete list of reported taxa and an overview of domestic animal use and documented wild species. Domestic animal use is further described by quantitative distributions of major food-animal remains, according to total fragments or the number of identified specimens and compilations of available data on sheep-to-goat ratios and sheep/goat age distributions.

The species represented in most collections tend to be few in number and fairly redundant across assemblages. Yet the full inventory of species reported from all assemblages shows a more robust picture. The identified taxa listed in Table 4.2 (n=63) include mostly species that are presumed to have been culturally relevant (n=46), while the rest may be considered incidental (amphibians, and some rodents and birds). Each species occurs in one or more of the Middle Islamic assemblages, while fewer (n=12) also occur in Late Islamic assemblages. Some species native to Jordan today or in the past, including several of those eradicated during the early twentieth century, are not represented.[10] Thus the potential for species representation is greater than that expressed archaeologically, yet this is expected as most faunal waste accrued from the preparation and consumption of domestic species, underscoring a persistent and heavy reliance on selected livestock species.

Livestock was critical to the rural economy of southern Transjordan as domesticated breeds provided meat, eggs, dairy products, wool, and hair, in addition to work activity. Ovicaprids were the most common meat source, while pig appears important in Crusader settings, and a few draft animals were consumed at the end of their working lives. The latter included cattle providing traction for plows, threshing sleds, and the like. Equids were also essential for transportation, but as nonfood animals, they are rarely represented in deposits of domestic refuse. Although the significance of horses within the local economy cannot be assessed from bone remains, historical sources show that they were highly valued, playing substantial roles in commerce, communications, religious pilgrimage, and state functions, including the military. Dromedaries performed a similar variety of labors as both horse and cattle and were ultimately consumed.[11] Domestic chicken was common, and some native geese, partridges, and pigeons were probably bred in captivity. Fish and occasional game complemented the livestock-based meat diet.

Table 4.2. Inventory of species represented in Middle Islamic faunal assemblages from Dhiban, Hisban, Karak, Shawbak, Wadi Farasa, and Wu'ayra

**Domestic Animals** (N = 12; 19%)
Sheep (*Ovis orientalis f. aries*)
Goat (*Capra aegagrus f. hircus*)
Cattle (*Bos primigenius f. taurus*)
Pig (*Sus scrofa f. domestica*)
Donkey (*Equus africanus f. asinus*)
Horse (*Equus ferus f. caballus*)
Camel (*Camelus dromedarius f. domestica*)
Dog (*Canis lupus f. familiaris*)
Cat (*Felis silvestris f. catus*)
Chicken (*Gallus gallus f. domestica*)
Graylag goose (*Anser anser f. domestica*)
Domestic pigeon (*Columba livia domestica*)

**Wild Mammals** (N = 16; 25.4%)
Gazelle (*Gazella* sp.)
Persian fallow deer (*Dama dama mesopotamica*)
Red deer (*Cervus elaphus*): non-native
Nubian ibex (*Capra ibex nubiana*)
Wild goat (*Capra aegagrus*): non-native
Wild boar (*Sus scrofa lybicus*)
Syrian onager (*Equus onager hemippus*)
Fox (*Vulpes vulpes*)
Badger (*Mellivora capensis* or *Meles meles*)
Striped hyena (*Hyaena hyaena syriaca*)
Marten or Marbled polecat (Mustelidae)
Wild cat (*Felis silvestris tristrami*)
Leopard (*Panthera pardus*)
Primate (a variety of monkey or ape): non-native
Cape hare (*Lepus capensis*)
Porcupine (*Hystrix indica*)

**Wild Birds** (N = 25; 39.1%)
Chukar partridge (*Alectoris chukar*)
Ostrich (*Struthio camelus*)
White stork (*Ciconia ciconia*)
Egyptian vulture (*Neophron percnopterus*)
Griffon vulture (*Gyps fulvus*)

Black vulture (*Aegypius monachus*)
Eagle (undetermined)
European sparrowhawk (*Accipiter nisus*)
or Levant sparrowhawk (*Accipiter brevipes*)
Kestrel (*Falco tinnunculus*)
Corncrake (*Crex crex*)
Coot (*Fulica atra*)
Great bustard (*Otis tarda*)
Houbara bustard (*Chlamydotis undulata*)
Cream-colored courser (*Cursorius cursor*)
Stone curlew (*Burhinus oedicnemus*)
Rock dove (*Columba livia*)
Laughing dove (*Streptopelia senegalensis*)
Crested lark (*Galerida cristata*)
Wheatear (*Oenanthe* sp.)
Corn bunting (*Emberiza calandra*)
or Rock sparrow (*Petronia petronia*)
Common starling (*Sturnus vulgaris*)
Jackdaw (*Corvus monedula*)
Raven (*Corvus corax*)
Brown-necked raven (*Corvus ruficollis*)
Common pheasant (*Phasianus colchicus*)

**Reptiles** (N = 1; 1.6%)
Tortoise (*Testudo graeca terrestris*)

**Fish** (N = 9; 14.3%)
*Freshwater Fish*
Cichlids (Cichlidae)
Catfish (Clariidae)
Carps (Cyprinidae)

*Marine Fish*
Grey mullets (Mugilidae)
Parrotfish (Scaridae)
Drums/Croakers (Sciaenidae)
Sea bream (Sparidae)
Grouper (Serranidae)
Wrasse (Labridae)

*Note:* Total N = 63. *Citations*: Dhiban (Kansa 2011:257, table 1); Hisban (Driesch and Boessneck 1995; Boessneck 1995); Karak (Brown and Rielly forthcoming, table 2); Shawbak [1986] (Brown and Rielly 2010a: 181, table 3); Shawbak [2005] (Mazza and Corbino 2007b: 75, fig. 51); Wadi Farasa (Schmid and Studer 2003: 485, fig. 32); Wu'ayra [1987] (Brown and Rielly 2010b: 127, table 1); Wu'ayra [1993] (Corbino and Mazza 2013: 160, table 1).

The cats frequenting the settlements thrived on vermin, while trained dogs assisted shepherds, provided security, and may have participated in hunting ventures.

Several wild mammals native to the steppe and woodlands were consumed periodically. As indicated in Table 4.2, these included gazelle, Nubian ibex, Syrian onager, Persian fallow deer, wild boar, and Cape hare. Among the nonfood animals were striped hyena, wild cat, and leopard, any of which may have been valued for their pelts. These species, in addition to chukar partridge and other wild fowl, would have been the object of sport hunters. Nonnative specimens of red deer, wild goat, and primate are documented.[12] Hunting birds, such as kestrels and sparrowhawks, were procured either locally or through trade.[13] Most fish were apparently imported from the Red Sea (see below). While not all cultural interactions among animal populations and the communities of the southern highlands are reflected in the faunal remains, the selective nature of such relationships is evident.

## Major Food Animal Distributions

Among the southern highland assemblages, sheep and goats figure prominently, and while these may have been significant contributors of by-products in some contexts, meat production appears to have been a common objective (see below). Cattle were consumed as adults, but a few calf remains indicate occasional consumption of veal.[14] Pigs provided only meat, and domestic offspring were certainly slaughtered before or at maximal meat weight to conserve water and fodder resources. The relative frequencies of sheep/goat, cattle, and pig shown in Table 4.3 suggest shifts in production among these major food animals. (Table 4.3 necessarily refers to all pig specimens, as elements of domesticated pig and wild boar are often indistinguishable.)

Most obviously, the data show a distinct increase in sheep/goat over time. The frequency of ovicaprids is lowest in the Crusader-/Ayyubid period due to relatively strong cattle and pig representations, which appear to reflect a fairly diverse meat diet. Relative frequencies for the Mamluk period are distinguished by a slight increase in cattle and a clear decrease in pigs.[15] The apparent expansion and intensification of agricultural activity in the thirteenth and fourteenth centuries may have increased demand for working cattle and hence its consumption.[16] The decrease in numbers of pigs signals a movement away from this meat source in the post-Crusader era, likely motivated by the heightened cultural emphasis on Islamic values that emerged within the Muslim community in response to the disruptive twelfth- to thirteenth-century European involvement in the Levant (see Elisséeff 1993: 170–71). The Ottoman assemblages from Karak and Shawbak show both an

Table 4.3. Relative frequencies of sheep/goat, cattle, and pig in Middle and Late Islamic faunal assemblages

| Site and Phase | Period | Sheep/Goat | | Cattle | | Pig | | Total |
|---|---|---|---|---|---|---|---|---|
| | | N | % | N | % | N | % | N |
| Wu'ayra, Phase 1a and 1b [1987] | Crusader | 167 | 60.5 | 54 | 19.6 | 55 | 19.9 | 276 |
| Shawbak, 6000c [2005] | Crusader | 248 | 75.8 | 61 | 18.7 | 18 | 5.5 | 327 |
| Wu'ayra, UT83 [1993] | Crusader or Ayyubid | 294 | 89.4 | 16 | 4.9 | 19 | 5.8 | 329 |
| Wadi Farasa, Cistern | Crusader or Ayyubid | 317 | 99.7 | 1 | 0.3 | 0 | 0 | 318 |
| Shawbak, Phase 1 [1986] | Ayyubid | 82 | 80.4 | 13 | 12.7 | 7 | 6.9 | 102 |
| Hisban, Stratum IV | Ayyubid | 71 | 88.8 | 9 | 11.2 | 0 | 0 | 80 |
| **Total Crusader and/or Ayyubid** (twelfth–mid-thirteenth century) (assemblages reported, N=6) | | **1,179** | **82.3%** % range, 60.5–99.7 [difference = 39.2] | **154** | **10.8%** % range, 0.3–19.6 [difference = 19.3] | **99** | **6.9%** % range, 0–19.9 [difference = 19.9] | **1,432** |
| Hisban, Strata II-III | Mamluk | 6,901 | 84.6 | 1,117 | 13.7 | 139 | 1.7 | 8,157 |
| Dhiban, Phase 2 | Mamluk | 194 | 76.8 | 45 | 17.7 | 15 | 5.9 | 254 |
| Karak, Phase 1b | Mamluk | 146 | 89.0 | 18 | 11.0 | 0 | 0 | 164 |
| Shawbak, Phase 3 [1986] | Mamluk | 99 | 98.0 | 2 | 2.0 | 0 | 0 | 101 |
| **Total Mamluk (mid-thirteenth–fifteenth century)** (assemblages reported, N=4) | | **7,340** | **84.6%** % range, 76.8–98.0 [difference = 21.2] | **1,182** | **13.6%** % range, 2.0–17.7 [difference = 15.7] | **154** | **1.8%** % range, 0–5.9 [difference = 5.9] | **8,676** |
| Karak, Phase 2 | Ottoman | 104 | 100.0 | 0 | 0 | 0 | 0 | 104 |
| Shawbak, Phase 4 [1986] | Ottoman | 80 | 93.0 | 5 | 5.8 | 1 | 1.2 | 86 |
| Hisban, Stratum I | Late Ottoman–Modern | 908 | 91.4 | 60 | 6.0 | 25 | 2.5 | 993 |
| **Total Ottoman (sixteenth–early twentieth century and later)** (assemblages reported, N=3) | | **1,092** | **92.3%** % range, 91.4–100 [difference = 8.6] | **65** | **5.5%** % range, 0–6.0 [difference = 6.0] | **26** | **2.2%** % range, 0–2.5 [difference = 2.5] | **1,183** |

*Notes:* Calculations are based on reported data. "Pig" includes both domestic and wild specimens, as they are often indistinguishable.

*Citations:* Dhiban, Kansa (2011: 257, table 1); Hisban, Driesch and Boessneck (1995: 72, table 5.9; figures are exclusive of wild boar); Karak, Brown and Rielly (forthcoming, table 3); Shawbak [1986], Brown and Rielly (2010a: 181, table 3); Shawbak [2005], Mazza and Corbino (2007b: 75, fig. 51); Wadi Farasa, Schmid and Studer (2003: 485, fig. 32); Wu'ayra [1987], Brown and Rielly (2010b: 127, table 1); Wu'ayra [1993] (Corbino and Mazza 2013: 160, table 1). *Chronology:* Crusader era (1115–1188), Ayyubid period (1174–1263), Mamluk period (1263–1516), and Ottoman period (1516–1918).

absence of pigs and a notable decrease in cattle, perhaps resulting from reduced field cultivation. With this increasing dominance of sheep and goats over time, a progressive decrease in the range of variation among relative frequencies of sheep/goat, cattle, and pig is evident (see Table 4.3). The ranges of variation in the distributions of these species are far greater for the Crusader-/Ayyubid period than the Ottoman period. This indicates increasing uniformity of meat production and consumption over the course of the Mamluk and Ottoman periods, culminating in a consistently heavy reliance on sheep/goat throughout southern Transjordan. However, as the numbers of samples decrease with each period, this apparent pattern will require further review when additional Mamluk and Ottoman assemblages become available.

The increasing reliance on ovicaprids is accompanied by a shift in the relative frequency of sheep to goats. Although the samples are small due to skeletal similarities between sheep and goats, the sequence of ratios listed in Table 4.4 indicates that goat dominance emerged during the Ayyubid period and became widespread across the southern highlands thereafter and through the Ottoman period. Driesch and Boessneck proposed that the Middle Islamic rise in goats, first observed at Hisban, may have resulted from an increasingly hotter, drier climate and a consequent shift from pasturage to weeds (1995: 72). As goats are better adapted to hot, dry environments and areas with poor-quality forage (see Redding 1984: 233), this greater emphasis may have been a necessary adaptation. Nevertheless, economic decisions to increase goat populations could have been linked to other factors, such as an expansion of grazing into more arid regions, adoption of long-term herd security strategies, or a reduction in wool production.

Some of the assemblages are markedly unique with respect to relative frequencies of major food animals, and such disparities are worthy of attention. One example is the sharp divergence between the twelfth-century sample from the principal Crusader fortress at Wu'ayra and that of the military outpost at Wadi Farasa (see Table 4.3). The Wu'ayra [1987] distribution suggests that the fortress soldiery may have experienced a varied meat diet, with relatively frequent access to pig and cattle. In contrast, Wadi Farasa shows virtually no variety, with a nearly exclusive reliance on sheep/goat. In both cases, however, fish provided a significant meat supplement.[17] If the Wadi Farasa site had been a tertiary installation within the Frankish defensive network that encompassed the Petra region, as is most likely, it would have been administratively subordinate to Wu'ayra. As storable foodstuffs were necessary, Wadi Farasa may have received only the most basic provisions of prepared and preserved meats dispensed from Wu'ayra.[18] While this scenario is conjectural, the question of food provisioning and distribution among these military sites is a rich field of inquiry.

Table 4.4. Ratios of sheep to goat in Middle and Late Islamic assemblages, with comparative data from the Byzantine and Early Islamic periods at Hisban

| Site and Phase | Period | Sheep | Goat | Ratio | Total (N) |
|---|---|---|---|---|---|
| **Byzantine and Early Islamic (fourth–tenth century)** | | | | | |
| Hisban, Strata VII–X | Byzantine | 58 | 48 | 1:0.8 | 106 |
| Hisban, Stratum VI | Umayyad | 47 | 33 | 1:0.7 | 80 |
| Hisban, Stratum V | Abbasid | 14 | 11 | 1:0.8 | 25 |
| **Crusader and/or Ayyubid (twelfth–mid-thirteenth century)** | | | | | |
| Wuʻayra, Phase 1a and 1b [1987] | Crusader | 34 | 19 | 1:0.6 | 53 |
| Shawbak, Area 6000c [2005] | Crusader | 0 | 465 | 0:465 | 465 |
| Wadi Farasa, Cistern | Crusader or Ayyubid | 13 | 5 | 1:0.4 | 18 |
| Wuʻayra, UT83 [1993] | Crusader or Ayyubid | 1 | 17 | 1:17 | 18 |
| Shawbak, Phase 1 [1986] | Ayyubid | 12 | 17 | 1:1.4 | 29 |
| Hisban, Stratum IV | Ayyubid | 4 | 6 | 1:1.5 | 10 |
| **Ayyubid/Mamluk and Mamluk (mid-thirteenth–fifteenth century)** | | | | | |
| Hisban-cistern, Strata II–IV | Ayyubid/Mamluk | 98 | 67 | 1.07 | 165 |
| Hisban, Strata II–III | Mamluk | 353 | 402 | 1:1.1 | 755 |
| Shawbak, Phase 3 [1986] | Mamluk | 8 | 10 | 1:1.3 | 18 |
| Dhiban, Phase 2 | Mamluk | 14 | 29 | 1:2.1 | 43 |
| Karak, Phase 1b | Mamluk | 14 | 25 | 1:1.8 | 39 |
| **Ottoman (sixteenth–early twentieth century and later)** | | | | | |
| Shawbak, Phase 4 [1986] | Ottoman | 9 | 11 | 1:1.2 | 20 |
| Karak, Phase 2 | Ottoman | 18 | 23 | 1:1.3 | 41 |
| Hisban, Stratum I | Late Ottoman–Modern | 36 | 52 | 1:1.4 | 88 |

*Notes:* Calculations are based on reported data. Dhiban reports a 1:1.7 sheep-goat ratio (Kansa 2011: 258), with number of total goats adjusted from 29 to 24 to reduce bias (Kansa, personal communication); the 1:2.1 ratio (cited above) is based on 29 goats, as no other raw goat counts cited above have been adjusted. The Shawbak [2005] assemblage includes 0 sheep and 465 goats, including 248 elements of a small goat species and 217 elements of a large goat species (Mazza and Corbino 2007b: 75–79).
*Citations:* Dhiban, Kansa (2011: 257, table 1); Hisban, Driesch and Boessneck (1995: 72, table 5.9; Hisban-cistern, LaBianca (1995: 50); Karak, Brown and Rielly (forthcoming table 2); Shawbak [1986], Brown and Rielly (2010a: 181, table 3); Shawbak [2005], Mazza and Corbino (2007b: 75, fig. 51; the dating of this context is apparently discussed in Corbino and Mazza 2009: 679); Wadi Farasa, Schmid and Studer (2003: 485, fig. 32); Wuʻayra [1987], Brown and Rielly (2010b: 127, table 1); Wuʻayra [1993] (Corbino and Mazza 2013: 160, table 1).
*Chronology:* Crusader era (1115–1188), Ayyubid period (1174–1263), Mamluk period (1263–1516), and Ottoman period (1516–1918).

## Demographics and Livestock Production Strategies

Demographic profiles of consumed sheep/goat are drawn from osteological indicators of age and sex. These attributes describe the specific ways that animal managers preferentially culled their stock and may offer insights regarding herd composition and livestock production strategies.[19] Although limited, the sheep/goat sex data from the southern highland assemblages are noteworthy for female predominance, for Dhiban shows a ratio of 8:1 females to males and the Hisban cistern deposit ("Hisban-cistern") shows a ratio of 32:1 females to males (Kansa 2011: 258; LaBianca 1995: 54).[20] These samples do not necessarily reflect sitewide distributions; nevertheless, they suggest two possible practices:

1. More females were retained on-site for breeding, and perhaps milk production, with periodic culling to provide meat and maintain optimal herd size. Thus females were most likely to be consumed on-site.
2. Males were heavily culled for off-site exchange, although some on-site consumption of very young males may also have occurred, leaving few remains of fragile bones. Excess males may have supplied meat for nonproducing townspeople and itinerant groups, including pilgrims, merchants, military personnel, and others traversing the *darb al-sultan* road network linking Transjordan with Palestine, Syria, Egypt, and the Hijaz.

More commonly reported are sheep-goat age distributions, as determined by mandibular wear and epiphyseal fusion of long bones with articular ends. Table 4.5 shows that sheep/goat generally survived their first year, although Dhiban may be exceptional with 50 percent mortality in this stage. The assemblages typically indicate slaughtering at or before the second year, when individuals approached or achieved maximum meat weight—a pattern often seen as evidence for an emphasis on meat production. Survival rates after the second year show a great deal of variation (see Table 4.5). Aged populations are indicated for Crusader Wu'ayra (1987) and Ayyubid Shawbak (1986), and such mature animals may have been valued for milk and/or wool; yet the data are too limited to support conclusions. Some priority on wool production may be expected for the Mamluk period, as Shawbak was famed for textile manufacture, particularly its carpet industry, and similar goods may have been fashioned at Karak (Milwright 2008: 110, 114–15; Walker 2011: 105; Walker et al. 2009: 131).

Preliminary economic interpretations based on sheep/goat demographics have been offered for the Middle Islamic village communities. Mamluk Dhiban has been proposed as a livestock-producing site (Kansa 2011: 258), while Hisban has been proposed as a livestock-consuming site during the Ayyubid and Mamluk periods, based on the Hisban-cistern assemblage (LaBianca 1995: 61). Both interpretations are phrased in reference to a market-based rural economy that would have been sustained by surplus production. Whether these assertions are justifiable with respect to the samples is open to question, particularly regarding Hisban where more males might be expected in a consuming community, yet they underscore the importance of addressing the fundamental nature of livestock production and distribution within this rural setting. While some market-driven production may have supplied meat for nonproducers, some of the livestock production undertaken by mixed farming communities may have been purposefully directed at maintaining

Table 4.5. Compiled age data for sheep/goats in Middle and Late Islamic faunal assemblages

| | | Epiphysis Fusion Stage | | | | | | | | | | |
| | | Early (juvenile) 0.5 years | | | | Intermediate (subadult) 1.5 to 2 years | | | | Late (adult) 3 to 3.5 years | | | |
| | | Fused | | Unfused | | Fused | | Unfused | | Fused | | Unfused | |
| Site and Phase | Period | N | % | N | % | N | % | N | % | N | % | N | % |
|---|---|---|---|---|---|---|---|---|---|---|---|---|---|
| Wadi Farasa, Cistern | Crusader or Ayyubid | 75% of total = culled very young at less than 2 years | | | | | | | | 25% of total = very old mandibular wear and fusion data | | | |
| **Middle Islamic (twelfth–fifteenth century)** | | | | | | | | | | | | | |
| Wu'ayra, Phase 1a and 1b [1987] | Crusader | 21 | 95.5 | 1 | 4.5 | 3 | 50.0 | 3 | 50.0 | 12 | 50.0 | 12 | 50.0 |
| Shawbak, Phase 1 [1986] | Ayyubid | 12 | 92.3 | 1 | 7.7 | 2 | 50.0 | 2 | 50.0 | 8 | 61.5 | 5 | 38.5 |
| Hisban-cistern, Strata II–III | Ayyubid and Mamluk | | | | | 12 | 48.0 | 13 | 52.0 | 46 | 34.3 | 88 | 65.7 |
| Dhiban, Phase 2 | Mamluk | >50% fused/survival up to 1 year | | | | 30% fused/survival up to 2 years | | | | 2 individuals reached maturity | | | |
| Shawbak, Phase 3 [1986] | Mamluk | 7 | 77.8 | 2 | 22.2 | 2 | 28.6 | 5 | 71.4 | 2 | 15.4 | 11 | 84.6 |
| Karak, Phase 1b | Mamluk | 19 | 73.1 | 7 | 26.9 | 1 | 12.5 | 7 | 87.5 | 3 | 12.0 | 22 | 88.0 |
| **Late Islamic (sixteenth–nineteenth century)** | | | | | | | | | | | | | |
| Shawbak, Phase 4 [1986] | Ottoman | 11 | 78.6 | 3 | 21.4 | 1 | 16.7 | 5 | 83.3 | 1 | 9.1 | 10 | 90.9 |
| Karak, Phase 2 | Ottoman | 11 | 78.6 | 3 | 21.4 | 3 | 30.0 | 7 | 70.0 | 5 | 38.5 | 8 | 61.5 |

*Notes:* Skeletal parts per epiphysis fusion stage are based on Schmid (1972: 75). The "early" group includes scapula P, humerus D, radius P, and pelvis A (fusing at 3 to 6 months of age). The "intermediate" group includes tibia D, metacarpus D, and metatarsus D (fusing at 16 to 24 months of age). The "late" group includes humerus P, ulna P, radius D, femur P and D, and tibia P (fusing at 36 to 42 months of age).

*Citations:* Dhiban, Kansa (2011: 258); Hisban-cistern (1995: 57, table 4.4); Karak, Brown and Rielly (forthcoming, table 6); Shawbak [1986], Brown and Rielly (2010a: 184, table 7); Wadi Farasa, Schmid and Studer (2003: 484); Wu'ayra [1987], Brown and Rielly (2010b: 129, table 4).

long-term, low-risk household subsistence. As multiple production strategies certainly coexisted in the Middle Islamic period, differentiating among subsistence-based, market-based, or other production schemes on the basis of faunal material poses a substantial challenge. In this light, it is important to note that culling of young animals before or at maximum meat weight is necessary to maintain any herd at an optimal size relative to the resource base, regardless of the production strategy. As such, "surplus" animals are somewhat inevitable and not necessarily indicators of market production (Sasson 2010: 8–10, 40–41). Also worthy of consideration are the intersections among livestock production and exchange systems practiced by largely sedentary, village communities and those of largely mobile communities. The interactions among these multiple spheres of livestock production and distribution represent another important topic to be further explored.

## Historical Representations of Animals

Text narratives offer exceptional insight, for discourses on cultural themes and historical events refer to animal life in ways that are scarcely reflected archaeologically. In particular, the twelfth-century memoir of Usama ibn Munqidh (d. 1188), a Syrian prince of Shayzar, and the fourteenth-century reminiscence of Abu al-Fida', the Sultan of Hama (d. 1331), describe animal involvements in social activities, state functions, and economic practices that remain invisible or poorly articulated in the faunal assemblages. Medieval historians also provide useful information. A few text examples that specifically refer to animal roles in Middle Islamic Transjordan expand our vision of the uses and values of both mundane and exotic creatures, and describe the influence of social class on animal interactions and perceptions of the natural environment.

Fish remains are of particular interest as they are archaeological descriptors of distinct but overlapping exchange systems. The wide popularity of fish meat is demonstrated by the occurrence of parrotfish and other marine varieties throughout the southern highlands, and these finds resonate with Ibn Sa'id al-Maghribi's late thirteenth-century description of Christian merchants from Karak and Shawbak receiving dried fish from the Red Sea in exchange for raisins, olives, and olive oil (in al-Bakhit 1992: 35). The distribution of marine fish clearly reflects the geography of this trade through an overland exchange network facilitating the flow of goods northward from Aqaba and the Sinai peninsula and reaching inland at least as far as Hisban. In contrast, the distribution of freshwater fish appears to reflect a local exchange mechanism. Freshwater fish are presently known only from Hisban, and these limnic species were certainly brought into this community from the nearby Jordan River system. Although fish was favored in the Middle Islamic period, its absence in Ottoman assemblages from Karak and Shawbak suggests that either access to fish or consumer interest, or both, declined or terminated after the fifteenth or sixteenth century. As the Ottoman samples are fewer and smaller than those of the Middle Islamic period, this apparent trend may be clarified when more Ottoman-era material becomes available for study.

Horses are rarely visible archaeologically, but they assume a prominent aspect when seen through narratives. Abu al-Fida' (1983) refers to an abundance of horses throughout the rural Levant, as well as large populations of mules and camels. Here, the horse economy was a substantial enterprise, with countless individuals engaged in their breeding, training, outfitting, exchange, and maintenance. Horses were not only essential to the cavalry-centric Mamluk military, but they were also held as wealth and prominently distributed through diplomatic exchanges and other gift-giving traditions. As indicated above, Mamluk sultans kept large reserve herds of horses and other livestock in southern Transjordan as a means of warehousing assets outside of the politically volatile capital of Cairo. The Mamluk state postal system depended on horses, as well as camels and carrier pigeons. Karak, Shawbak, Dhiban, and Hisban all maintained postal stations with working animals (al-Bakhit 1992: 64–68). Horses also assumed ceremonial roles, for the ethnic Turkic elites of thirteenth- and fourteenth-century Mamluk aristocracy consumed horseflesh at lavish state banquets (Stowasser 1984: 18). As Karak castle was the domain of Mamluk *amīrs* and sultans, horseflesh may have been consumed there on occasion, although there is no archaeological evidence for such.

Hunts for sport and game meat were among the pleasures of the elites. Ibn Munqidh (2008) and Abu al-Fida' (1983) provide distinct visions of animal life through princely eyes, as they observed or participated in pursuit of the swift quadrupeds of the desert steppe, woodland creatures, ground-nesting birds, and waterfowl. These narratives illustrate complex relationships, for animals were socially valued as both predators serving their hunting lords and as prey to be caught, slain, and trophied. From Shayzar, Ibn Munqidh conducted routine and highly successful sport outings with skilled assistants, saddled mounts, animal handlers, and trained raptors, dogs, cheetahs, and lynx (2008: 201–36). Consequently, the palace kitchens at Shayzar were regularly stocked with gazelle, partridge, and other game, which undoubtedly provided the bulk of meats consumed by the ruling family. Uneaten sport animals included boar, whose carcasses were abandoned. Lion was a popular challenge, but once pelts were removed, the remains were dumped in a ditch next to Shayzar castle (ibid.: 121). Similar hunting entertainments took place in southern Transjordan, where Mamluk elites found ample game. Maqrizi described the declivities around Karak as rich in birds for the hunt, and these were certainly pursued by al-Nasir Muhammad, who was seated three times as sultan between 1294 and 1340. A superb and vigorous sportsman, he relished hunts in the wadis of the Karak region and gaming expeditions with the Shaw-baki Bedouin (al-Bakhit 1992: 42; Levanoni 1995: 174). His son al-Nasir Ahmad (r. 1342) also practiced the arts of horsemanship and hunting in the Karak region.

The farming population of the southern highlands may have engaged in oc-casional hunting or trapping activities, but relatively few individuals would have had the skills, equipment, and leisure with which to pursue frequent or sophisti-cated hunts for meat. The faunal evidence indicates that game was economically insignificant to most Middle Islamic households for the assemblages generally con-tain only a few elements of gazelle and/or chukar partridge. Nevertheless, hunting practice is documented archaeologically by the remains of birds of prey, including kestrels and sparrowhawks from Mamluk Hisban (Boessneck 1995: 138, 140). As yet, there is no direct historical or archaeological indication of procurement of ani-mals specifically for pelts in the region, but it is likely that a trade in furs existed and that furriers were established in the southern highland towns, as was the case in the northern town of Ajlun during the Mamluk period (Walker 2011: 64).

Among the least visible archaeologically are exotic animals whose working as-signments were linked to a range of cultural practices and traditions. During the Middle Islamic period, African wildlife, including large mammals, primates, and birds, circulated throughout the Mediterranean and beyond as commodities and diplomatic gifts (e.g., Ibn ʿAbd al-Ẓāhir 1956: 190; Refling 2005; Rogers 1991: 71–72). Exotic specimens were popular among the Mamluk sultans, who could afford the luxury of extraordinary animals for hunting sports, exhibitions, or spectacles, and their menageries were housed in the stables at the Cairo citadel (Behrens-Abouseif 1988: 61). In 1483, Félix Fabri observed captive wild beasts and exotic ani-mal spectacles at a Cairene merchant's residence, where parrots, ostriches, monkeys, leopards, lions, and giraffes were exhibited (1975 [vol. 2]: 414–25). Exotic animals were also brought to southern Transjordan on occasion. Sultan al-Nasir Ahmad (r. 1342) sent lions, giraffes, and onagers, as well as Bactrian camels, from Cairo to Karak, thereby extending the elite appreciation of such beasts for display, ani-mal parks, or sporting events into this remote provincial setting.

A few traces of imported animals are confirmed in the faunal record, includ-ing a primate at Wuʿayra (Corbino and Mazza 2010: 160). The faunal evidence for a monkey, which certainly enhanced the social entertainments of the fortress com-munity, is particularly exceptional as nonfood animal carcasses were most likely to have been dumped at locations removed from Wuʿayra's habitation areas. This rare species provides archaeological confirmation of the movement of animals through far-reaching, intercontinental exchange networks. Although undocumented as yet, one may reasonably speculate that imported songbirds, parrots, and other remarkable cagelings once graced elite or even modest residences and gardens in the southern highlands. However rare and elusive to the archaeologist, imported animals valued as pets or exotica had very specific cultural functions and roles that lent an exceptional dimension to the spectrum of human and animal interactions during this era.

## Conclusion

Southern Transjordan was well-populated, agriculturally vibrant, and significant in interregional politics and commerce from the twelfth through the fifteenth centuries. Within the cultural and natural environments of this region, the complex ways in which humans and animals interacted are partially described by the corpus of reported faunal remains. This description is enhanced by historical literature, which lends depth to our perceptions of animal roles. The merging of information from these sources enables us to construct a fuller, blended vision of human and animal interactions that can contribute to future archaeological research questions linking faunal patterning within sites to regional trends.

As most excavations focus on specific periods at individual sites, research priorities tend to be closely tied to singular contexts. In response, this overview encourages regional approaches to faunal distributions from Levantine Islamic sites. An iterative process is suggested for the corpus of Middle Islamic data compiled here, as it may be added to, and the interpretations expanded, refined, and revised as new faunal studies emerge. Similarly, the scope of this effort will be extended considerably by forthcoming reports of Early and Late Islamic assemblages. While faunal specialists work in ways that are understandably individualistic, future research reports may contribute most effectively to a cross-site perspective by offering data in reporting formats that maximize comparability.

The questions about animal representations raised here all deserve greater attention (e.g., increasing representation of ovicaprids, increase of goats over sheep, geographic patterns of marine and freshwater fish distributions, the significance or role of game meats, and the representation of nonfood working animals). Yet the most challenging topic is that of rural production strategies, as animals were raised for different purposes, and their ante- and postmortem products were distributed in a variety of ways. It may be emphasized that risk-averse strategies for household subsistence may have been the prevailing practice, yet some entrepreneurial, market-based production dependent on surplus meat animals was likely practiced as well. These and other factors introduced above show that issues of livestock production in the southern highlands must be addressed rigorously, with targeted and research-based strategies for material collection and analysis.

Historical descriptions of animal life add to the ways archaeologists envision and study animal use by moving beyond data extracted from culinary debris. The medieval memoirs cited here offer colorful images of landscapes lush with wild animals and well traversed by costly horses and camels, as well as mules and donkeys that were also highly valued. These descriptions reflect the preoccupations of an elite social class that traveled extensively and procured and consumed large quantities of game. Naturally, they make little mention of the mundane livestock that supported the rural economy with labor, meat, and by-products. For the archaeologist, these images cast the inventories of archaeologically retrieved taxa into a much fuller arena and encourage thoughtful consideration of the roles of culturally valued species that are invisible or little represented.

Ultimately, the benefit of creating a corpus of cross-site data is to encourage and focus dialogue within the community of researchers committed to envisioning animal roles within the Levant during the Crusader, Ayyubid, Mamluk, and Ottoman periods. The crucial concept here is to add value to, and generate new knowledge from, disparate faunal reports through a comparative approach that describes relationships with animal populations in broad geographic and temporal terms. In this respect, some of the traditional and pervasive isolation of faunal studies may be reduced and greater attention afforded to integrating the many spheres of human and animal interactions within archaeological perceptions of the rural landscape.

## Notes

1. Examples of methods studies include LaBianca's taphonomic study of relationships among postdepositional context, bone preservation, and cultural patterning (1995), and Loyet's ethnographic study of butchery (1999) and investigation of the economic implications of faunal distribution variations within a single site (2000).

2. The historical periods in southern Transjordan include the Crusader or Frankish era (1115–1188) and the dynastic sultanates of the Ayyubids (1174–1263), Mamluks (1263–1516), and Ottomans (1516–1918). More broadly, the period terms Middle Islamic (1100–1516) and the Late Islamic (1516–1918) are also used.

3. A few examples of approaches to regional analyses of Islamic era settlements and ceramics in the southern Levant include Magness (2003), Kareem (2000), Brown (2000), and Walker (2009).

4. Recent and insightful approaches to cross-site faunal data from the southern Levant focus on assemblages from Bronze and Iron age sites (Lev-Tov et al. 2011; Sasson 2010: 31–61).

5. Faunal data from Khirbat Faris are excluded (Rielly 1989) as the medieval assemblage may be mixed with much earlier elements (Johns et al. 1989: 78ff). Stratigraphic issues also exclude the faunal assemblage from Lajjun (Toplyn 2006: 465, 469) and Shawbak (Corbino and Mazza 2009, 2013).

6. The Wadi Farasa and Wu'ayra regions may appear less suited to farming, yet these communities certainly obtained olives, fruits, and other crops from nearby Wadi Musa (Amr 2006: 21–24). Additionally, cultivable land exists within the Petra basin and around its drain-

age system (Russell 1995: 695–96), and pastoralism was economically significant there until recently.

7. References to cultivation and livestock production in southern Transjordan appear in medieval Latin and Arabic sources, Ottoman documents, and nineteenth-century European records (e.g., Fulcher of Chartres 1969: 146–47; William of Tyre 1943 [vol. 2]: 145, 503; Yāqūt in Marmardji 1951: 204; Abū al-Fidāʾ in Le Strange 1890: 479; Walker 2011: 154–57; 159–60; see al-Bakhit 1992: 33, 35, 39–42; Hütteroth and Abdulfattah 1977: 171–74; Tristram 1873: 82–83). For Frankish *casalia* in Transjordan, see Milwright (2008: 57–59) and Mayer (1990: 133–34).

8. Dead Sea levels show moist conditions in the late twelfth to early fourteenth centuries and early sixteenth to mid-seventeenth centuries (Klein and Flohn 1987: 153, fig. 3). The drier intervening period may have been detrimental to agriculture (Walker 2011: 225). Dendrochronological analyses indicate frequent episodic drought from the seventeenth through the twentieth centuries (Touchan and Hughes 1999: 301, fig. 6).

9. Alternatively, an assemblage may derive from a single dining event that was not representative of meat consumption practices within the setting, as suggested for a Frankish assemblage from Burj al-Ahmar, Phase C (Cartledge 1986: 178).

10. The Hisban assemblage includes the largest number of species (n=58), many of which are birds that are presently undocumented elsewhere. Most of the 343 resident and migratory bird species reported by Disi and Bouran (1987) are not represented archaeologically.

11. Water buffalo is not attested archaeologically, although it is historically indicated at Shawbak in the early fourteenth century (al-Bakhit 1992: 41).

12. The single wild goat (*Capra aegagrus*) element from Dhiban must represent an import, for this species was no longer native to southern Transjordan (Driesch and Boessneck 1995: 86).

13. Native species not represented but certainly known to inhabitants include oryx, jackal, lynx, cheetah, wolf, and Syrian bear (Mountfort 1966: 59). Native lions are undocumented in southern Transjordan in the post-Classical era (Driesch and Boessneck 1995: 86, table 5.21), but are recorded in the twelfth century in the Palestine hill country and in central Syria (Tristram 1885: 17; Ibn Munqidh 2008: 96–97, 116–19).

14. Being relatively large boned, cattle may be overrepresented (Sasson 2010: 44), whereas sheep/goat and pig younger than six months may be underrepresented due to fragile bones. The particularly large cattle bones from Ayyubid-Mamluk contexts at Hisban may represent imported zebu or *Bos primigenius f. indicus* (Driesch and Boessneck 1995: 78).

15. By comparison, Early Islamic assemblages from Tabaqat Fahl and Hisban show strong Umayyad period pig representations (53.2 percent and 12.5 percent) relative to sheep/goat and cattle, whereas Abbasid-Fatimid period pig representations (0.6 percent and 1 percent) are substantially lesser (calculated from Mairs 2002: 526, table 4; Driesch and Boessneck 1995: 72, table 5.9; Rielly 1993: 220, table 2). Crusader Palestine shows strong proportions of pig at Burj al-Ahmar (62.0 percent) and Belmont (34.8 percent), but less (5.0 percent) at Qaimun (calculated from Cartledge 1986: 177, table 12; Croft 2000: 186, table 1; Horwitz and Dahan 1996: 247, table XXII.1). Thus, the number of pigs declined with the increasing Islamization of the southern Levant but resurged among the twelfth- to thirteenth-century Frankish settlements.

16. Cattle were probably seldom raised specifically for meat and milk as this would have been a high-risk undertaking in southern Transjordan, where water and pasturage were limited (see Sasson 2010: 46).

17. Fish at Wuʿayra [1987] are 58 percent (n=378) of the total sheep/goat, cattle, pig, and fish (n=654), as calculated from Brown and Rielly (2010b: 127, table 1). Fish at Wadi Farasa are 53 percent (n=359) of the total sheep/goat, cattle, and fish (n=677), as calculated from Schmid and Studer (2003: 485, fig. 32).

18. As sheep/goat skeletal parts from Wadi Farasa indicate dining waste, slaughtering and joint preparation were accomplished elsewhere (Schmid and Studer 2003: 484).

19. Ethnographic research (e.g., Payne 1973) and pioneering zooarchaeological analyses offer important models of herd composition and livestock production strategies (Wapnish and Hesse 1988; Sasson 2010: 60–61). The ways in which such models apply to Middle Islamic Transjordan have yet to be explored.

20. LaBianca's alternative calculation based on minimum number of individuals yielded a 25:1 female to male ratio (1995: 54). Driesch and Boessneck also noted a strong dominance of females in their sample from Mamluk Hisban (1995: 79).

## Bibliography

Abū al-Fidā' 'Imad al-Dīn. 1983. *The Memoirs of a Syrian Prince: Abu'l-Fidā', Sultan of Ḥamāh (672–732/1273–1331)*, translated by Peter M. Holt. Freiburger Islamstudien 9. Wiesbaden: Steiner.

Amr, Khairieh. 2006. "Die Kreuzritter und die Oliven von les Vaux Moïses." In *Die Kreuzzüge. Petra—Eine Spurensuche*, edited by Ritterhausgesellschaft Bubikon, 6–26. Tann, Germany: Eristra.

al-Bakhīt, Muḥammad 'Adnān. 1992. *Das Königreich von al-Karak in der mamlūkischen Zeit*, translated and edited by Alexander Scheidt. Frankfurt am Main: Peter Lang.

Behrens-Abouseif, Doris. 1988. "The citadel of Cairo: stage for Mamluk ceremonial." *Annales Islamologiques* 24: 25–79.

Boessneck, Joachim. 1995. "Birds, reptiles, and amphibians." In *Faunal Remains: Taphonomical and Zooarchaeological Studies of the Animal Remains from Tell Hesban and Vicinity*, edited by Øystein Sakala LaBianca and Angela von den Driesch, 131–68. Hesban 13. Berrien Springs, MI: Andrews University.

Boessneck, Joachim, and Angela von den Driesch. 1978. "Preliminary analysis of the animal bones from Tell Hesban." *Andrews University Seminary Studies* 16(1): 259–87.

Brown, Robin M. 2000. "The distribution of 13th–15th century glazed wares in Transjordan: a case study from the Kerak Plateau." In *The Archaeology of Jordan and Beyond: Essays in Honor of James A. Sauer*, edited by Lawrence E. Stager, Joseph A. Greene, and Michael D. Coogan, 84–99. Winona Lake, IN: Eisenbrauns.

Brown, Robin M., and Kevin Rielly. 2010a. "Faunal remains from excavations in the Ayyubid palace at Shawbak Castle in southern Transjordan." *Berytus* 51–52 (2008–2009): 169–98.

———. 2010b. "A twelfth century faunal assemblage from al-Wu'ayra in the southern highlands of Jordan." *Annual of the Department of Antiquities of Jordan* 54: 121–41.

———. Forthcoming. "Faunal remains from Mamluk and Ottoman occupations in the Middle Islamic period palace at Karak Castle (Qal'at al-Karak)." *Annual of the American Schools of Oriental Research*.

Cartledge, Judith. 1986. "Faunal remains." In *The Red Tower (al-Burj al-Ahmar): Settlement in the Plain of Sharon at the Time of the Crusaders and Mamluks, A.D. 1099–1516*, edited by Denys Pringle, 176–86. British School of Archaeology in Jerusalem Monograph Series 1. London: British School of Archaeology in Jerusalem.

Corbino, Chiara A., and Paul Mazza. 2009. "How and where did the inhabitants of Shawbak Castle live? The faunal remains." *Studies in the History and Archaeology of Jordan* 10: 679–84.

———. 2013. "Faunal remains at the Castle of al-Wu'ayra, in Petra, and Shawbak (Crusader period)." *Studies in the History and Archaeology of Jordan* 11: 159–164.

Croft, Paul. 2000. "The faunal remains." In *Belmont Castle: The Excavation of a Crusader Stronghold in the Kingdom of Jerusalem*, edited by Richard P. Harper and Denys Pringle, 173–94. British Academy Monographs 10. Oxford: Oxford University.

Disi, Ahmad M., and Alia H. Bouran. 1987. *A Check-List of the Birds of the Hashemite Kingdom of Jordan: An Ecological Outlook.* Amman: University of Jordan.

Driesch, Angela von den, and Joachim Boessneck. 1995. "Final report on the zooarchaeological investigation of animal bone finds from Tell Hesban, Jordan." In *Faunal Remains: Taphonomical and Zooarchaeological Studies of the Animal Remains from Tell Hesban and Vicinity*, edited by Øystein Sakala LaBianca and Angela von den Driesch, 65–108. Hesban 13. Berrien Springs, MI: Andrews University.

al-Eisawi, Dawud M. 1985. "Vegetation in Jordan." *Studies in the History and Archaeology of Jordan* 2: 45–57.

Elisséeff, Nikita. 1993. "The reaction of the Syrian Muslims after the foundation of the first Latin kingdom of Jerusalem." In *Crusaders and Muslims in Twelfth-Century Syria*, edited by Maya Shatzmiller, 162–72. Leiden: Brill.

Fabri, Félix. 1975. *Le Voyage in Egypt de Félix Fabri, 1483*, 3 vols. Cairo: Institut Français d'Archéologie Orientale du Caire.

Fulcher of Chartres. 1969. *A History of the Expedition to Jerusalem, 1095–1127.* Translated by Frances Rila Ryan, edited by Harold S. Fink. Knoxville: University of Tennessee.

Horwitz, Liora Kolska, and Edna Dahan. 1996. "Animal husbandry practices during the historic periods." In *Yoqne'am I: The Late Periods,* edited by A. Ben-Tor, M. Avissar, and Y. Portugali, 246–55. Qedem Reports 3. Jerusalem: Institute of Archaeology, Hebrew University.

Hütteroth, Wolf-Dieter, and Kamal Abdulfattah. 1977. *Historical Geography of Palestine, Transjordan and Southern Syria in the Late 16th Century.* Erlanger geographische Arbeiten 5. Erlangen, Germany: Fränkische Geographische Gesellschaft, in Kommission bei Palm und Enke.

Ibn 'Abd al- Ẓāhir, Muḥyī al-Dīn. 1956. *Baybars I of Egypt,* edited and translated by Syedah Fatima Sadeque. Dacca: Oxford University.

Ibn Munqidh, Usāma. 2008. *The Book of Contemplation: Islam and the Crusades,* translated and introduction by Paul M. Cobb. London: Penguin.

Johns, Jeremy. 1994."The *longue durée*: state and settlement strategies in southern Transjordan across the Islamic centuries." In *Village, Steppe and State: The Social Origins of Modern Jordan*, edited by Eugene L. Rogan and Tariq Tell, 1–31. London: British Academic Press.

Johns, Jeremy, Alison McQuitty, and Robin Falkner. 1989. "The Fâris Project: preliminary report upon the 1986 and 1988 Seasons." *Levant* 21: 63–95.

Kansa, Sarah Whitcher. 2011. "Faunal evidence from Middle Islamic Dhībān: interim report on the 2005 season." Contribution in "Digging Deeper: Technical Reports from the Dhībān Excavation and Development Project (2004–2009)," Danielle Steen Fatkin, Katherine Adelsberger, Alan Farahani, et al., 256–59. *Annual of the Department of Antiquities of Jordan* 55: 249–66.

Kareem, Jum'a Mahmoud H. 2000. *The Settlement Patterns in the Jordan Valley in the Mid- to Late Islamic Period.* BAR International Series 877. Oxford: Archaeopress.

Klein, C., and H. Flohn. 1987. "Contributions to the knowledge of the fluctuations of the Dead Sea level." *Theoretical and Applied Climatology* 38: 151–56.

Kürschner, Harald. 1986. "A physiognomical-ecological classification of the vegetation of Southern Jordan." In *Contributions to the Vegetation of Southwest Asia*, edited by Harald Kürschner, 45–79. Wiesbaden: Reichert.

LaBianca, Øystein Sakala. 1995. "The effect of post-depositional contexts on the preservation and interpretation of bone samples: a case study." In *Faunal Remains: Taphonomical and*

*Zooarchaeological Studies of the Animal Remains from Tell Hesban and Vicinity*, edited by Øystein Sakala LaBianca and Angela von den Driesch, 47–63. Hesban 13. Berrien Springs, MI: Andrews University.

Le Strange, Guy. 1890. *Palestine Under the Moslems: A Description of Syria and the Holy Land from A.D. 650 to 1500*. London: Alexander P. Watt.

Lev-Tov, Justin S. E., Benjamin W. Porter, and Bruce E. Routledge. 2011. "Measuring local diversity in Early Iron Age animal economies: a view from Khirbat al-Mudayna al-'Aliya (Jordan)." *Bulletin of the American Schools of Oriental Research* 361: 67–93.

Levanoni, Amalia. 1995. *A Turning Point in Mamluk History: The Third Reign of al-Nāṣir Muḥammad ibn Qalāwun (1310–1341)*. Leiden: Brill.

Loyet, Michelle A. 1999. "Small ungulate butchery in the Islamic period (A.D. 632–1260) at Tell Tuneinir, Syria." *Journal of Near Eastern Studies* 58(1): 33–45.

———. 2000. "The potential for within-site variation of faunal remains: a case study from the Islamic period urban center of Tell Tuneinir, Syria." *Bulletin of the American Schools of Oriental Research* 320: 23–48.

Magness, Jodi. 2003. *The Archaeology of the Early Islamic Settlement in Palestine*. Winona Lake, IN: Eisenbrauns.

Mairs, Lachlan. 2002. "Archaeozoology report for an Umayyad rubbish pit in Trench XXXV.B." Contribution in "New Light on Late Antique Pella: Sydney University Excavations in Area XXXV, 1997," Kate da Costa, Margaret O'Hea, Lachlan Mairs, Rachel Sparks, and Pat Boland, 525–27. *Annual of the Department of Antiquities of Jordan* 46: 503–33.

Marmardji, A.-S. 1951. *Textes Géographiques Arabes sur la Palestine recueillis, mis en ordre alphabétique et traduits en français*. Paris: Gabalda.

Mayer, Hans Eberhard. 1990. *Die Kreuzfahrerherrschaft Montréal (Šobak): Jordanien im 12. Jahrhundert*. Abhandlungen des Deutschen Palästinavereins 14. Wiesbaden: Harrassowitz.

Mazza, Paolo, and Chiara Corbino. 2007a. "The crusader's food: faunal analyses. The faunal remains from UT 83 at Al-Wu'ayra and from Area 10000 at Shawbak Castle." In *"Medieval" Petra—Shawbak Project: Archaeological Season 2007, Field Report 2007*, edited by. Guido Vannini and Michele Nucciotti, 55–62. On file, Department of Antiquities of Jordan, Amman.

———. 2007b. "I reperti archeozoologici dell'area 6000 C." In *Archeologia dell'insediamento crociato-ayyubide in Transgiordania: Il progetto Shawbak*, edited by Guido Vannini, 75–79. Borgo San Lorenzo, Italy: All'insegna del giglio.

Milwright, Marcus. 2008. *The Fortress of the Raven: Karak in the Middle Islamic Period (1100–1650)*. Leiden: Brill.

Mountfort, Guy. 1966. *Portrait of a Desert: The Story of an Expedition to Jordan*. London: Readers Union, Collins.

Payne, Sebastian. 1973. "Kill-off patterns in sheep and goats: the mandibles from Aşvan Kale." *Anatolian Studies* 23: 281–303.

Redding, Richard W. 1984. "Theoretical determinants of a herder's decisions: modeling variation in the sheep/goat ratio." In *Animals and Archaeology*, vol. 3: *Early Herders and Their Flocks*, edited by Juliet Clutton-Brock and Caroline Grigson, 223–41. BAR International Series 202. Oxford: BAR.

Refling, Mary K. 2005. "Frederick's menagerie." Paper presented at the Second Annual Robert Dombroski Italian Conference, Storrs, CT, 17–18 September 2005.

Rielly, Kevin. 1989. "The animal bones." Contribution in "The Fâris Project: preliminary report upon the 1986 and 1988 seasons," Jeremy Johns, Alison McQuitty, and Robin Falkner, 89, 93. *Levant* 21: 63–95.

———. 1993. "The animal bones from Tell al-Ḥuṣn (Area XXXIV) and the Abbasid Complex (Area XXIX)." Contribution in "The eleventh and twelfth seasons of excavations at Pella (Ṭabaqat Faḥl) 1989–1990," Alan G. Walmsley, Phillip G. Macumber, Phillip C. Edwards,

Stephen J. Bourke, and Pamela M. Watson, 218–21. *Annual of the Department of Antiquities of Jordan* 37: 165–240.

Rogers, J. Michael. 1991. "'The Gorgeous East': trade and tribute in the Islamic Empires." In *Circa 1492: Art in the Age of Exploration*, edited by Jay A. Levenson, 69–74. Washington, DC: National Gallery of Art.

Russell, Kenneth W. 1995. "Traditional Bedouin agriculture at Petra: ethnoarchaeological insights into the evolution of food production." *Studies in the History and Archaeology of Jordan* 5: 693–705.

Sasson, Aharon. 2010. *Animal Husbandry in Ancient Israel: A Zooarchaeological Perspective on Livestock Exploitation, Herd Management and Economic Strategies*. London: Equinox.

Schmid, Elisabeth. 1972. *Atlas of Animal Bones: For Prehistorians, Archaeologists and Quaternary Geologists*. Amsterdam: Elsevier.

Schmid, Stephan G., and Jacqueline Studer. 2003. "The International Wādī Farasa Project (IWFP) preliminary report on the 2002 season." *Annual of the Department of Antiquities of Jordan* 47: 473–88.

———. 2007. "Products from the Red Sea at Petra in the medieval period." In *Natural Resources and Cultural Connections of the Red Sea*, edited by Janet Starkey, Paul Starkey, and Tony Wilkinson, 45–56. BAR International Series 1661. Oxford: Archaeopress.

Stowasser, Karl. 1984. "Manners and customs at the Mamluk Court." *Muqarnas* 2: 13–20.

Toplyn, Michael R. 2006. "Livestock and *limitanei*: the zooarchaeological evidence." In *The Roman Frontier in Central Jordan: Final Report on the Limes Arabicus Project 1980–1989*, edited by S. Thomas Parker, 463–507. Washington, DC: Dumbarton Oaks Research Library and Collection.

Touchan, Ramzi, and Malcolm K. Hughes. 1999. "Dendrochronology in Jordan." *Journal of Arid Environments* 42: 291–303.

Tristram, Henry B. 1873. *The Land of Moab: Travels and Discoveries on the East Side of the Dead Sea and the Jordan*. New York: Harper.

———. 1885. *The Survey of Western Palestine: The Fauna and Flora of Palestine*. London: Committee of the Palestine Exploration Fund.

Walker, Bethany J. 2009. "Identifying the Late Islamic period ceramically: preliminary observations on Ottoman wares from Central and Northern Jordan." In *Reflections of Empire: Archaeological and Ethnographic Studies on the Pottery of the Ottoman Levant*, edited by Bethany J. Walker, 37–65. Annual of the American Schools of Oriental Research 64. Boston: American Schools of Oriental Research.

———. 2011. *Jordan in the Late Middle Ages: Transformation of the Mamluk Frontier*. Chicago Studies on the Middle East Monograph Series. Chicago: Middle East Documentation Center, University of Chicago.

Walker, Bethany J., Francesca Dotti, and Michele Nucciotti. 2009. "Shawbak and the Mamluk Transjordan." In *Da Petra a Shawbak: Archeologia di una Frontiera,* edited by Guido Vannini and Michele Nucciotti, 127–31. Florence: Guinti.

Wapnish, Paula, and Brian Hesse. 1988. "Urbanization and the organization of animal production at Tell Jemmeh in the Middle Bronze Age Levant." *Journal of Near Eastern Studies* 47(2): 81–94.

William of Tyre. 1943. *A History of Deeds Done Beyond the Sea,* 2 vols., translated by Emily Atwater Babcock and A. C. Krey. New York: Columbia University.

# CHAPTER 5

# Zooarchaeological Perspectives on Rural Economy and Landscape Use in Eighteenth-Century Qatar

*Pernille Bangsgaard and Lisa Yeomans*

This chapter examines the relationship between the eighteenth-century urban settlement of al-Zubara in northwestern Qatar and the surrounding landscape through an examination of zooarchaeological evidence. The faunal remains from two houses form the basis of the analysis, with ethnographic evidence and historical sources providing models to examine how the rural landscape was used and inhabited and how the marine environment supplied the town with vital foods and goods.[1]

A review of early twentieth-century ethnographic sources provides evidence for the methods of fishing and herding and patterns of movement in the landscapes around al-Zubara. The aim is to begin a detailed reconstruction of dietary elements of life on the Arabian Peninsula, exploring the balance between land and marine resources. The article is also a first attempt at evaluating whether the combination of zooarchaeological data with late historical and ethnographic sources can produce new information about daily life in the Persian Gulf during this period.

## Al-Zubara

Al-Zubara in northwestern Qatar emerged as a thriving pearl fishing and trading hub during the eighteenth and nineteenth centuries. The city was established in the 1760s by the arrival of families of the 'Utub tribe from Kuwait who came to the area to exploit the rich pearling banks found nearby. They were followed by other merchants attracted by the tax-free trading (Rahman 2005; Carter 2005). This initial expansion of the city created the largest (around 110 hectares) and most important town in Qatar, but the period of prosperity was not long lived as the city was largely destroyed by forces from the Sultanate of Muscat in 1811. Subsequent rebuilding resulted in a much smaller city covering approximately a third of its earlier size and enclosed by a new town wall. The population of al-Zubara gradually started to abandon the town as other settlements rose to prominence and water shortages made occupation more and more difficult. By the early twentieth century, it was all but deserted (Richter et al. 2011).

## The Desert Hinterland and Its Resources

The environment of northwestern Qatar is not ideally suited for permanent human settlement; the peninsula consists, for the most part, of rocky, wind-beaten desert. The landscape was described by Palgrave in 1877 as "miles and miles of low barren hills, bleak and sun-scorched, with hardly a single tree to vary their dry monotonous outline" (231). There are no readily available freshwater sources in Qatar, although drinking water can be obtained from hand-dug wells (see Macumber, Chapter 2 in this volume). Fresh water forms a lens above the denser saline water and can be accessed near the coast where the water table is highest. The population of al-Zubara had to collect their water from Qala'at Murayr, which is situated approximately one-and-a-half kilometers farther inland (Macumber 2011). In such an environment, agricultural endeavors had relatively limited productivity; thus, without utilizing the additional resources of the sea, permanent settled occupation in this landscape would have been extremely difficult. This is reflected in the location of permanent settlements dispersed mainly along the coast and differs from other areas of the Persian Gulf where inland water resources could support agricultural communities. The lack of sufficient agriculturally productive settlements in Qatar made the population dependent on imports. Maritime trading provided the timber necessary for boatbuilding, and a proportion of the food was imported with al-Zubara, providing an essential nexus for exchange. The merchants of al-Zubara used the profits of pearl fishing to trade for fruit, rice, and grain to support the urban population of the town. Smaller fishing villages along the coast would have benefited from trade drawn into the area (Anscombe 1997: 9–11; Zahlan, 1979: 13–14). This is illustrated by the formation of villages along the western coast of Qatar in the 1760s (Fig. 5.1). The larger settlement of al-Zubara enticed trade into the region, and smaller settlements along the coast benefited from the increase in available commodities, making permanent settlement in coastal villages feasible.

The archaeological data is corroborated by historical evidence noting the increase in rural settlements dispersed along the coast of northwestern Qatar

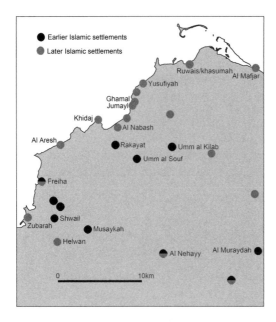

Figure 5.1 Settlements of north-western Qatar in the Early and Late Islamic period. These sites are classified according to examination of visible architectural remains and surface ceramics collected during survey (QIAH).

(Anscombe 1997: 9–11; Zahlan, 1979: 13–14). This increase in coastal settlement in the eighteenth century is comparable to the change in settlement pattern at a similar date in the United Arab Emirates that also resulted from increased trading (Carter 2005). While many of the sites in the interior of Qatar may not have been occupied year-round, it seems probable that the more extensive coastal sites of the Later Islamic period were remains of settlements occupied throughout the annual cycle. Lorimer does, however, describe part of the settled population as sometimes having camped in the interior during the winter months (1915a: 1532), indicating that the divide between settled and nomadic groups is not definite.

Animal resources were essential to human occupation in this eighteenth-century landscape inhabited by a predominantly settled population in al-Zubara and in coastal villages, along with the nomadic population who moved through the desert according to the seasons. Owing to the sparse or nonexistent vegetation, the breeding and keeping of livestock required a certain amount of movement in a constant search for sufficient fodder and water for the animals. Winter and spring were generally periods of good grazing and sufficient water, but for the rest of the year, the fodder supply was limited (Ferdinand 1993: 59).

The historical sources indicate variable seasonal movements for the different nomadic groups in Qatar. In the north, around al-Zubara, it was normal for the nomads to spend the winter in Qatar, and, upon the arrival of the hot weather of summer, part of the tribe would travel to Bahrain by boat with the livestock (Lorimer 1915a: 1532). Around fifty years later, the same al-Naʻim tribe had become partly sedentary and moved exclusively within the tribal area (Ferdinand 1993:

59). They kept a limited amount of camels but had large flocks of sheep and goats and in a few instances one or two cows (Korsholm Nielsen 2007: 16).

The nomadic al-Murra of southern Qatar had a completely different pattern of seasonal movement. In 1959, the tribe still moved large distances, with most people based in Qatar from late winter to early spring; the remainder of the year was spent in Saudi Arabia near wells with sufficient water (Ferdinand 1993: 59–60). They were still dependent on camels for transport as well as many everyday necessities, such as milk, wool, and meat. Few other livestock were kept by the al-Murra, but falcons and saluki dogs were often maintained for hunting (Korsholm Nielsen 2007: 15–18). An earlier description from the beginning of the twentieth century described the al-Murra tribe as having a similar pattern of movement, with some members of the tribe traveling as far afield as Oman (Lorimer 1915a: 1532). According to Ferdinand, the dromedary had a special position in the life and folklore of the tribe. It was the only animal milked by the men, whereas all other livestock were milked by the women (Ferdinand 1988: 130). Dromedaries were also the main animal used during the movement of the camp and for longer trips, and were most widespread in the south during Ferdinand's visit (Ferdinand 1993: 64–65).

Sources from around 1900 indicate that dromedaries were kept by both sedentary and nomadic groups. Horses were not common and were also owned by both groups, while the donkey was found in much larger numbers and was used for shorter daily transportation (Lorimer 1915b: 2335, 2342). In 1959, donkeys were still the second most important pack animal used for all kinds of local transportation by the al-Murra in the south and the al-Na'im in the north (Ferdinand 1993: 62). Cattle were mainly kept for milk and meat and were not common among the settled groups around 1900; but they were kept in slightly higher numbers by nomadic groups (Lorimer 1915b: 2345). In 1959, however, Ferdinand only found one or two among the Bedouin families he visited. At the same time, sheep and goats were the most frequent animals kept by the al-Na'im tribe and formed the basis of their livelihood. The care of the sheep and goat herds still dictated the daily activities and seasonal movement of the tribe (Ferdinand 1993: 60–62). Sheep and goats are kept by both settled and nomadic groups, but those of the settled populations would often be tended or herded by the nomadic groups (Lorimer 1915b: 2344–48). Livestock was not just an important part of daily life, providing subsistence and dictating seasonal movement; they also served as a potential source of income. Evidence suggests that flock animals, as well as camels and donkeys, were occasionally exported (Anscombe 1997: 11). In 1959, some of the al-Na'im also kept chickens and in a few instances doves—a somewhat unusual practice for a nomadic group (Ferdinand 1988: 128).

## Fishing

As the majority of the permanent settlements are located on the coast, fishing provided an essential source of food both directly and indirectly through the foddering of animals. The fishing methods used in urban and rural settlements would have been essentially the same, although local geographic features of the sea floor would have influenced the strategies employed at each settlement. The methods of procuring fish range from the simple use of hand lines and throwing and seine nets operated from the shore, to bell-shaped mesh traps (*gargurs*) set on the sea floor, to the construction of tidal traps (*hadra*). A lone fisherman could use a circular throwing net cast from the beach to catch schools of fish in the shallow waters. A net would be thrown over fish seen while wading in the water, and the weighted edges of the net would sink around the fish, trapping them. Communal effort was needed to use the larger beach seine nets that were dragged out to surround fish in the shallows. Sometimes inflated sheepskins were used to facilitate the setting of the beach seine, with the fishermen using the skins to aid in floating out into the deeper water. The technology of fishing did not change for millennia until the modern era, and the methods are well documented. Nowadays, *gargurs* are wire traps set from boats. In the past, these would have been constructed from palm leaves. Resting on the sea floor, fish enter the conical entrance and cannot escape. The bait deployed in these traps varies, but cuttlefish were frequently used, as the consumption of this animal was avoided (Bowen 1951).

Fishing was also commonly carried out using *hadra*. As with the *gargurs*, modern wire mesh has replaced the use of palm fronds for their construction. The shores of the Persian Gulf are well suited to fishing in this manner since the shallow coastal waters create a rapid change in the water level with a tidal range of one and a half meters or more. Fish are funneled into traps as the tide ebbs out and are contained in the shallow water, gradually working their way into the collection area of the trap with their escape hindered by wings projecting into this zone. The opening into the final collection pen narrows toward the base, making it even harder for the fish to get out as the water level drops (Bowen 1951).

Two basic types of *hadra* either funnel the fish into the collection area as the tides recede or direct fish swimming parallel to the shore toward the trap (Fig. 5.2). This second type is used in areas where the ebbing tide is weaker. At the head of the fish trap, the fish are funneled gradually into a collection zone, to which fishermen wade out at low tide to gather their catch (Bowen 1951). In Qatar, traps are also seen without a collection area, with the tide going out far enough that large numbers of fish are left flapping in small puddles of water where they can be picked up. This method does not seem very common across the Gulf and would only be suited to a very flat coastline with a rapid sea-level change that leaves the fish

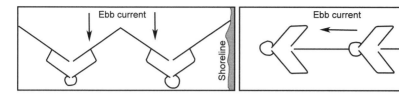

Figure 5.2 Types of intertidal fish traps built to take advantage of the differing topography of shorelines (after Bowen 1951: 389).

trapped behind stone-built enclosures. Similar ones in the United Arab Emirates have been provisionally dated to the Late Islamic period (Beech 2004).

The location of the *hadra* requires consideration of topography and tidal flows, as well as the underlying geology. The haul of fish caught in the fish traps can be considerable and often comprises smaller fish that are likely to venture into the shallowest waters. However, larger fish can be caught, and occasionally sharks as long as six feet have been recorded in these traps. Cuttlefish, commonly collected from the *hadra,* can be used as the bait in the *gargur*s (Bowen 1951). When the northern *shamal* wind blows, the catch from the *hadra* is large, but in the summer, the tidal drop of the sea is lower, making the *hadra* less effective. Many people would have been engaged in other activities at this time of year, since pearling and stone extraction from the sea had to be done in the summer months because these activities require long periods of immersion in the water. In the summer, a few people would continue to collect the small catch and keep up maintenance of the traps (Serjeant 1968).

Construction methods used for the *hadra* varied, but in many parts of the Gulf region, palm fronds were used stripped of their leaves and were either driven into the sea floor or set in place with stones. Each year these needed to be replaced, as the growth of barnacles blackened the palm fronds and frightened the fish away. Marsh reeds, where available, were used instead because they grow larger than the palm fronds (Bowen 1951; Serjeant 1968). In Qatar, the outer arms of the traps were often constructed of stone, presumably because of the lack of palm trees and the need to import much of this material. Toward the center of the traps, palm fronds provided the height necessary to catch the fish. Modern fish traps in Qatar also show this use of the two types of material, although the palm has been replaced with wire mesh held between metal stakes.

Many fish traps are visible around the coast of Qatar, and Google Earth images of the coastline show the location of such traps. Often, the form of the *hadra* can also be identified: the majority of *hadra* along the northwestern coast are of the funnel type. The dating of these structures is difficult; however, it seems likely, from the well-preserved form of the fish traps and the increase in settlement in the later Islamic period, that many of the fish traps were built as human occupation

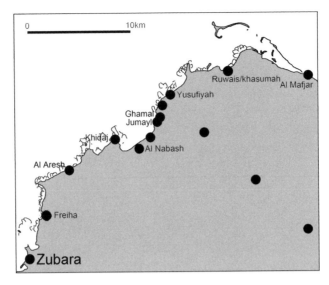

Figure 5.3 Map showing location of fish traps surrounding the Late Islamic settlements in northwestern Qatar (QIAH).

of the coastal area increased. Some fish traps are used today, but they too are probably maintained or repaired rather than newly constructed modern structures.

Figure 5.3 shows the arrangement of fish traps in the waters surrounding the later Islamic settlements. Adjacent to al-Zubara, an absence of these structures is related to the use of the bay as a harbor. *Hadra* would have hindered the passage of boats, and the deeper water that made the location suited to larger boats was not suitable for these constructions. To the south of al-Zubara, there is no evidence of fish traps for thirteen kilometers, reflecting the topography of the shoreline and settlement density.

## The al-Zubara Faunal Remains

As of now only a small percentage of the faunal collection from the al-Zubara excavations has been analyzed. Therefore, we will exclusively present the findings from two rooms in two contemporary courtyard houses, separated by an east–west aligned street and located near the seafront. Each house had a dedicated cooking room (Space 110 and Space 166), which contained various pits and numerous *tannurs* (ovens), replaced over time as occupation deposits rich in bones accumulated (Fig. 5.4). The two houses were probably constructed shortly after the arrival of the 'Utub tribe and thus belong to the al-Zubara Phase V or to the latter half of the eighteenth century (Richter et al. 2012).

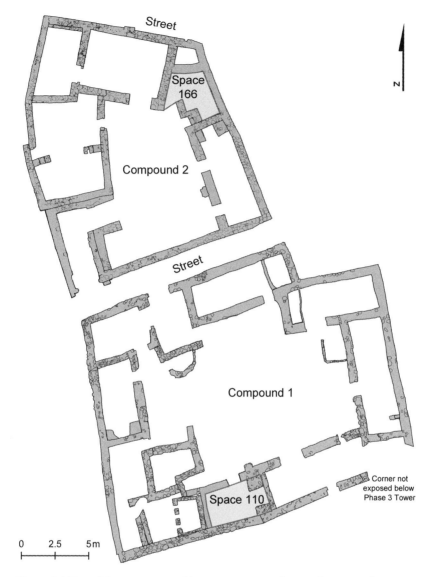

Figure 5.4 Plan of the two courtyard houses consisting of rooms for various functions surrounding a central courtyard, with the dedicated cooking rooms highlighted (QIAH).

## The Fish Fauna

Although the faunal remains studied so far derive from similar deposits and are a relatively limited contextual range of material, it is worth trying to use the available data to interpret the fishing methods that provided the town with fish. A wide range of fish species have been identified from the two cooking rooms, but a high proportion are from nine families of fish. Examining the frequency of occurrence of these fish, it is possible to start reconstructing the fishing strategies used to supply the town.

Identifying fishing methods from a zooarchaeological assemblage is difficult, and a number of factors need consideration (Coutts 1975; Colley 1987). It is important to bear in mind that the assemblage recovered may only be a selection of the types and size of fish caught. For example, the sample of material currently examined from al-Zubara is from occupation deposits and therefore will not include the fish fed to animals as fodder. So far, analysis has also concentrated on two adjacent courtyard houses from one phase of the settlement; so any patterns discussed here may be caused by differential access to resources within the settlement rather than the pattern of resource procurement across the whole town. Zooarchaeologically, there is also the problem that each fish can be caught by a number of different fishing methods, and there is a limit to the taxonomic level to which many fish bones can be identified. Even within a family of fish, differences of size and behavior can make some species more susceptible to one fishing method. Although the fish remains are well preserved, some fish, such as mullets, have thin bones that are more susceptible to destruction or at least fragmentation to the point they cannot be identified. Fish bones have only been analyzed from deposits that were sieved, but smaller species may still be underrepresented, as the flotation samples have not yet been studied. Despite these factors, the data in Table 5.1 suggest that many fish were procured from *gargur* fish traps. Fishing by *gargur*s is best indicated by the high frequency of Lethrinids, or scavengers; Serranids, or groupers; and Scarids, or parrotfish in the assemblage. Given the quantity of these fish, they are unlikely to have been taken by hand lines exclusively, and they must have been fished for on a large scale.

Evidence for the use of *hadra* is the presence of fish from the Gerridiae family, or silver biddies, and the Mugilidae family, or mullets. Other fish, such as the Siganidae or spinefoot, can be caught in *hadra,* but they are also taken by other methods, making their presence difficult to interpret. Beach seines catch similar fish to *hadra* as they obviously trap the fish venturing close to the shore; however, they require a lot more effort than the *hadra,* which yield fewer fish. Beach seines require a long net, one end of which is used to surround the fish before the net is pulled to the shore by a large group of people. Fishing weights sink the net, and although examples of these have occasionally been found in the excavations at al-Zubara, they are not common. Presumably, the fishermen of al-Zubara were using *gargur*s, nets, and hand lines, and were fishing from boats more frequently than fishermen of the rural settlements to the north, where *hadra* are found in the adjacent waters. The fishing villages expended a lot of effort in constructing the *hadra,* which are well suited to the shallow water; and occasionally, surplus fish could potentially be traded with the larger population of al-Zubara. For the most

Table 5.1. Occurrence of the main fish species identified at al-Zubara and their potential capture methods

| Family | Frequency | Fishing Methods | | | | | | |
|---|---|---|---|---|---|---|---|---|
| | | Hadra | Gargour | Set Gill Net | Drifting Gill Net | Casting Net | Handline | Beach Seine |
| Carangidae | ++ | + | + | | ++ | | + | + |
| Gerreidae | + | ++ | | | | | | ++ |
| Lethrinidae | +++ | | ++ | ++ | | | + | |
| Mugilidae | + | ++ | | | | ++ | | ++ |
| Scaridae | ++ | | ++ | | | | | |
| Scombridae | + | | | | ++ | | + | |
| Serranidae | +++ | | ++ | | | | + | |
| Siganidae | + | ++ | + | ++ | | | | ++ |
| Sparidae * | ++ | + | + | | | | | |
| Sparidae ** | +++ | | + | | | | + | |
| Sparidae *** | ++ | + | | | | | + | |

*Identification of species within the Sparidae family: \*Acanthopagrus sp., \*\*Argyrops spinifer, \*\*\*Rhabdosargus sp.*

part, the fish consumed within the town of al-Zubara seem to have been caught by the fishermen of the town, frequently using *gargur*s.

## Other Fauna

Fish are clearly the most important element of the faunal assemblage from al-Zubara, but there is also a significant terrestrial element to the collection, which includes domesticated livestock, birds, and game. Such faunal remains are well suited for studying how the inhabitants of al-Zubara, hinterland villages, and temporary camps alike interacted and used these resources.

The two cooking rooms (Spaces 110 and 166) contained approximately a thousand fragments from animals other than fish, and more than 60 percent of those were assigned to either species level or a more general category such as "small ungulate." The latter group has in the following section been distributed among the already identified species within each group in order to reach a statistically acceptable amount of fragments. See Table 5.2 for the results. Sheep and goat remains clearly dominate in both rooms, with 78 percent in Space 110 as opposed to 85 percent in Space 166. These percentages increase even further when the weight of the fragments is included: the findings are then 91 percent and 94 percent, respectively. Those fragments identified to species indicate that sheep were approximately twice as common as goats.

Mammalian long bones fuse at set intervals, allowing an estimation of the time of death (Moran and O'Connor 1994). All diagnostic sheep and goat bones are

Table 5.2. Mammalian, avian, and rodent species found at al-Zubara

| Species | Number of fragments | | Weight of fragments (in g) | |
|---|---|---|---|---|
| | Space 110 | Space 166 | Space 110 | Space 166 |
| Cattle, *Bos taurus* | 8 | 0 | 62 | 0 |
| Horse/donkey, *Equus* sp. | 0 | 5 | 0 | 84 |
| Goat/sheep, *Capra hircus/ Ovis aries* | 305 | 210 | 980 | 1571 |
| Gazelle, *Gazella* sp. | 0 | 1 | 0 | 3 |
| Bird, *Aves* sp. | 77 | 31 | 30 | 14 |
| Rodents, *Rodentia* sp. | 0 | 7 | 0 | 1 |
| Unidentified | 148 | 141 | 254 | 216 |

registered as either fused, in the process of fusing, or unfused, thus indicating if the animal at time of death was above, around, or below the indicated age. The evidence from al-Zubara suggests that the majority of sheep and goats were killed around the age of one to two years, with a few slightly older and younger individuals present. The age category of one to two years is, for both sheep and goats, the time where the optimal weight gain has been reached compared with fodder intake. It is therefore typically the time for slaughter, when no other factors, such as fodder shortage, take precedence. When age data are combined with a limited sample of sexed bones, the distribution clearly indicates that females all reached an age of one to two years, while a smaller number lived to an older age, whereas the males were killed off at a younger age. This pattern fits well with a household consumption pattern based primarily on meat, with access to an entire herd of sheep and goats. There is very limited use for adult males, whereas females are kept for breeding purposes (Marom and Bar-Oz 2009).

It is worth noting that only a single bone from a newborn or stillborn animal was found among the sheep and goat assemblage. Such a lack of material would normally suggest that the herd is not kept nearby during spring and early summer, when mortality is high, particularly without the benefits of modern veterinary medicine. But as the al-Zubara material is exclusively from kitchen spaces, the result would have to be confirmed by similar results from other areas, such as the middens. There is also limited evidence for older animals in the fusion data and a complete lack of any pathology typically caused by the presence of senile or very old animals. Such animals are rarely the meat of choice; the pattern could therefore suggest a certain subsistence surplus or unrestrained access to the livestock.

Cattle and equids are not a major component; each is only present in a single room, Space 110 for the former and Space 166 for the latter. The size and morphology of the equid bones suggest that they are from a donkey. Dromedary bones are completely lacking from both areas. There is, however, a potential uncertainty to this distribution of these species. The lack or very limited presence of all larger species of livestock could potentially be caused by the occasional cleaning of the two kitchen spaces, as such a practice would affect the presence of larger bone fragments. Therefore, the observed pattern should be confirmed by future work on assemblages from one or more of the larger middens at al-Zubara. Space 166 also included a single bone from a gazelle, the only wild species of mammal represented in the collection, but an indication that this resource of the desert hinterland was also occasionally harvested.

There is a noticeably high amount of avian fragments from both rooms. Birds are rarely a major contributor to the meat intake of any period or site, but in Spaces 110 and 166, they compose 20 percent and 13 percent, respectively, of the total number of fragments. The initial identification of species suggests that one household mainly had access to pigeons or doves, whereas the other mainly had domesticated chicken on the menu. This data could indicate a potential for distinguishing in detail specific patterns of consumption and access to animals between single households.

## Discussion and Conclusion

The evidence suggests that within the large settlement of al-Zubara, *gargurs* were frequently used for fishing and that this activity may have taken place in winter months when boats were not used for pearl diving or stone mining. Fewer of the fish consumed within the settlement were caught in the *hadra*, and these may well have been traded in from the rural settlements along the coast that are surrounded by these structures. An interesting avenue of future research would be to analyze fish bones from rural settlements along the coast to examine the difference in the fishing strategies. Overall, the trade in fish from the rural settlements to al-Zubara does not appear to have been extensive, with the city self-reliant for this type of marine resource.

Another use of fish caught at al-Zubara would have been as fodder for animals, although there is not currently any zooarchaeological evidence to support this. Sardines, caught in the winter by casting nets, are commonly left to dry in the sun and fed to livestock throughout the year (Donaldson 2000). Small fishing weights similar to ones attached to the base of casting nets have occasionally been found at al-Zubara, and fish caught could have been traded from al-Zubara to herders in the surrounding countryside.

Domesticated animals are only a small component in the diet of the two households, as the marine resources clearly dominate. Palgrave observed a similar pattern of subsistence in the two towns of Doha and Bidda during his visit there in 1866 (Palgrave 1877: 232). Sheep and goats are by far the most common domesticated animal at al-Zubara, although cattle and probably donkeys have also been identified. The presence of chickens and pigeons leaves an impression of clear household preferences, and a single gazelle bone indicates that hunting was not exclusively for the privileged few or only practiced by the nomadic desert tribes. The distribution of zooarchaeological remains display many similarities with the ethnographic and historical sources, such as the distribution of species and the importance of sheep and goats among the population of northern Qatar. It is also worth noting the lack of bones from stillborn sheep and goats, suggesting that the livestock was grazed elsewhere during the early summer months, perhaps in the care of nomadic herders.

The wider regional and seasonal movement of livestock, which both Ferdinand and Lorimer mention (1993; 1915a), is not immediately visible in the archaeological record. But the ratio of strontium isotope (Sr87/Sr86) in sheep- and goat-tooth enamel may be able to provide answers. Research into seasonal or annual movement based on the variation in geochemical factors has delivered promising results (Meiggs 2007); so a multi-isotopic approach could potentially distinguish between general areas such as Bahrain-Qatar.

The work presented here is the beginning of zooarchaeological research at al-Zubara into the use of the landscape and surrounding environments, as well as of the interaction between the town and the rural settlements. We have shown the potential of using ethnographic evidence and historical sources for fishing methods and how fish were used, in conjunction with the zooarchaeological fish bones, to understand the economy of the coastal settlements of Qatar in the eighteenth century. The use of ethnographic and historical sources as analogies for archaeological evidence have been debated, and scholars like Wylie have rightfully suggested that certain requirements should be observed, such as a high degree of similarity in living conditions, subsistence, and geographical setting (2002: 136–53). But in the case of al-Zubara, it is clear that all of these requirements can be met. The sources describe very similar living conditions in the same geographical area and are of a date similar to the archaeological remains. Likewise, the zooarchaeological evidence clearly has the potential to add to our knowledge of this formative period in the history of the modern Persian Gulf. The zooarchaeological perspective on everyday consumption and on herding and fishing delivers information of a type that is not included or not of interest to the majority of the historical sources. The literature describing the Persian Gulf in the seventeenth and eighteenth centuries is mainly historically focused, and thus describes and analyzes the economic and political development of the region (Anscombe 1997; Rahman 2005; Zahlan 1979). Although much of this work represents an important contribution to our knowledge of the area, the historical focus also means that attention to how and what everyday life was like for the general population tends to be forgotten or brushed over. The combination of the zooarchaeological data and the written sources in this context is therefore a fortunate one, and in the future may help us illuminate some very fundamental practices of daily life in the Gulf region. To date, there has been limited zooarchaeological research extending into the Islamic period (but see Beech 2004). Data from the limited number of sites do not indicate a shift in the exploitation of animal resources compared with the preceding periods of human settlement. Throughout the history of human settlement in the region, animal exploitation strategies appear to be heavily dependent on the environment and the need to provide subsistence for the population (Beech 2004). In the future, using faunal evidence from al-Zubara as well as rural settlements, we will be able to refine this broad-scale interpretation of animal exploitation and address questions of interaction between urban and rural settlements. We will also be in a position to examine other aspects of daily life, such as differential access to resources within urban centers and seasonal resource use.

## Note

1. The zooarchaeological analysis is part of the ongoing work by the Qatar Islamic Archaeology and Heritage Project, an initiative spearheaded by his Excellency Sheikh Hassan bin Mohammed al-Thani.

## Bibliography

Anscombe, Frederick J. 1997. *The Ottoman Gulf: The Creation of Kuwait, Saudi Arabia and Qatar.* New York: Columbia University Press.

Beech, Mark J. 2004. *In the Land of the Ichthyophagi: Modelling Fish Exploitation in the Arabian Gulf and Gulf of Oman from the 5th Millennium BC to the Late Islamic Period.* BAR International Series 1217. Abu Dhabi Islands Archaeological Survey. Oxford: Archaeopress.

Bowen, Richard L. Jr. 1951. "Maritime industries of Eastern Arabia." *Geographical Review* 41: 384–400.

Carter, Robert A. 2005. "History and prehistory of pearling in the Persian Gulf." *Journal of the Economic and Social History of the Orient* 48(2): 139–209.

Colley, Sarah M. 1987. "Fishing for facts: can we reconstruct fishing methods from archaeological evidence?" *Australian Archaeology* 24: 16–26.

Coutts, Peter J. F. 1975. "Marine fishing in archaeological perspective: techniques for determining fishing strategies." In *Maritime Adaptations of the Pacific,* edited by R. W. Casteel and G. I. Quimby. The Hague: Mouton.

Donaldson, William J. 2000. "Erythraean ichthyophagi: Arabian fish-eaters observed." *New Arabian Studies* 5: 7–32.

Ferdinand, Klaus. 1988. "Perlefiskere og ørkennomader." *Jordens Folk* 23(3/4): 126–33.

————. 1993. *Bedouins of Qatar*. London: Thames and Hudson.

Korsholm Nielsen, Hans Christian. 2007. *Den Danske Ekspedition til Qatar 1959*. Photographs by Jette Bang and Claus Ferdinand. Højbjerg, Denmark: Moesgaard Museum.

Lorimer, John Gordon. 1915a. *Gazetteer of the Persian Gulf, Oman and Central Arabia I Historical Part 2*. Calcutta: Superintendent Government Printing.

Lorimer, John Gordon. 1915b. *Gazetteer of the Persian Gulf, Oman and Central Arabia II B Geographical and Statistical*. Calcutta: Superintendent Government Printing.

Macumber, Phillip G. 2011. *Geomorphology, Hydrology and Occupation Across North-Eastern Qatar: Geomorphological and Geoarchaeological Results from the Third Season of the Copenhagen University Study in Northern Qatar. End of Season Report, 2011*. Qatar Islamic Archaeology and Heritage Project [unpublished report].

Marom, Nimrod, and Guy Bar-Oz. 2009. "Culling profiles: the indeterminacy of archaeozoological data to survivorship curve modeling of sheep and goat herd maintenance strategies." *Journal of Archaeological Science* 36: 1184–87.

Meiggs, David C. 2007. "Visualizing the seasonal round: a theoretical experiment with strontium isotope profiles in ovicaprine teeth." *Anthropozoologica* 42(2): 107–27.

Moran, Nuala C., and Terry P. O'Connor. 1994. "Age distribution in domestic sheep by skeletal and dental maturation: a pilot study of available sources." *International Journal of Osteoarchaeology* 4: 267–85.

Palgrave, William Gifford. 1877. *Personal Narrative of a Year's Journey Through Central and Eastern Arabia (1862–63)* II. London: Macmillan.

Rahman, Habibur. 2005. *The Emergence of Qatar*. London: Kegan Paul.

Richter, Tobias, Faisal A. al-Na'im, Lisa Yeomans, Michael House, Tom Collie, Pernille Bangsgaard Jensen, Sandra Rosendahl, Paul Wordsworth, and Alan Walmsley. 2012. "The 2010–2011 excavation season at al-Zubārah, northwest Qatar." *Proceedings of the Seminar for Arabian Studies* 42: 331–40.

Richter, Tobias, Paul Wordsworth, and Alan Walmsley. 2011. "Pearl fishers, townsfolk, Bedouins and shaykhs: economic and social relations in Islamic al-Zubārah." *Proceedings of the Seminar for Arabian Studies* 41: 1–16.

Serjeant, Robert Bertram. 1968. "Fisher-folk and fish-traps in Al-Bahrain." *Bulletin of the School of Oriental and African Studies* 31(3): 486–514.

Wylie, Alison. 2002. *Thinking from Things: Essays in the Philosophy of Archaeology*. Berkeley: University of California Press.

Zahlan, Rosemarie Said. 1979. *The Creation of Qatar*. London: Croom Helm.

*PART III*

# Landscapes of Commerce and Production

# CHAPTER 6

# Beyond Iron Age Landscapes

## Copper Mining and Smelting in Faynan in the Twelfth to Fourteenth Centuries CE

*Ian W. N. Jones*

Interest in Islamic period metal production in southern Bilad al-Sham has been marked by a somewhat unfortunate dichotomy. On the one hand, work on Early Islamic (600–1000 CE) copper production in the southern Wadi al-'Araba—primarily in southern Israel—has been quite productive. Several distinctive Early Islamic period copper smelting and mining sites have been found (Avner and Magness 1998; Rothenberg 1988; Willies 1991) that formed part of a system supplying metal to Ayla (al-'Aqaba) and that were likely linked through that city to the lucrative Red Sea trade (Whitcomb 2006; Damgaard 2009). On the other hand, little work in the southern Levant has specifically focused on metal production in the Middle Islamic period (1000–1400 CE) since Coughenour's study of iron mining in the 'Ajlun region of northern Jordan (1976). The study of mining and metallurgy can give us significant insights into local and regional economic processes, and for the Middle Islamic period, it has the potential to shed light on the history of people and places generally ignored by contemporary written sources.

With this in mind, the University of California, San Diego, Edom Lowlands Regional Archaeology Project (ELRAP) recently expanded its study of the role of mining and metallurgy in culture change over the past ten thousand years (Levy and Najjar 2007) to include an in-depth study of Islamic period copper production in the Faynan region of southern Jordan (Fig. 6.1), which presents a rather different picture from the southern Wadi al-'Araba. While limited settlement in Faynan seems to have continued into the eighth or ninth century CE, no evidence for copper production during this period has yet been found, in sharp contrast to the production system supplying Ayla. This is rather surprising and currently difficult to

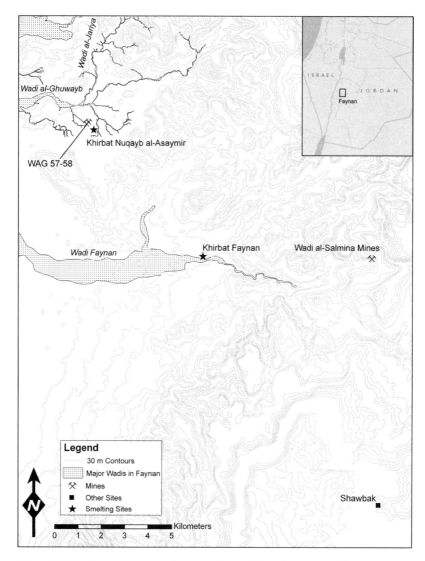

Figure 6.1 The Faynan region and areas to the south, with locations of key sites, with an inset showing the location of Faynan in the southern Levant. Contours derived from ASTER GDEM data, a product of METI and NASA. Inset map background: ©2012 Esri, DeLorme, NAVTEQ.

explain, as the nature of settlement and the economic transformations that occurred during the Late Byzantine and Early Islamic periods in Faynan are still poorly understood. Islamic period copper production only began in Faynan in the late twelfth century CE, when the small village now known as Khirbat Nuqayb al-Asaymir was founded. Khirbat Faynan, a tell in the southern part of the Faynan district with significant Roman and Byzantine occupation, was also reoccupied during the Middle Islamic period, with copper production carried out there on a smaller scale.

While other studies of copper production in the region have discussed Islamic period sites (e.g., Hauptmann 2007; Newson et al. 2007; Weisgerber 2006), none has focused on the post–eleventh century evidence or offered a truly satisfactory account of the economic or social aspects of Middle Islamic period metal production. This chapter, then, presents some preliminary insights into these issues, emerging from the 2011 excavations at Khirbat Nuqayb al-Asaymir.

## Khirbat Nuqayb al-Asaymir

Khirbat Nuqayb al-Asaymir is located to the south of the main channel of Wadi al-Ghuwayb (Fig. 6.1), about one kilometer east along the small Wadi Nuqayb al-Asaymir of the major Iron Age copper production center of Khirbat al-Nahas (see Levy et al. 2003; Levy et al. 2012a). At seven hectares, it is the largest[1] and best-preserved Islamic period copper production site in the Faynan district, yet it contains only fifteen buildings and a handful of additional, poorly preserved walls (Fig. 6.2). The site was first published by Nelson Glueck (1935) and later surveyed by teams from the Deutsches Bergbau-Museum (Hauptmann et al. 1985) and the Jabal Hamrat Fidan Project (Levy et al. 2003; Jones et al. 2012). However, before the 2011 EL-RAP investigation in Area X (Levy et al. 2012b), the site had not been excavated.

Based on available evidence, Khirbat Nuqayb al-Asaymir seems to have been founded in the late twelfth century CE, with occupation continuing at least into the mid-thirteenth century. This dating is based primarily on numismatic data collected by Kind and colleagues (2005) and my recent analyses of the ceramic material collected during the 2002 survey of Wadi al-Ghuwayb (Jones et al. 2012). Kind and colleagues' published coins provide a *terminus post quem* for the abandonment of the site, as the latest coin of the six found at the site is a half-*dirham* minted in 632 AH/1234–35 CE (2005: 179). Although the earliest coin found at the site is a *fals* minted in approximately 600 AH/1203–1204 CE (Kind et al. 2005: 179), some of the ceramics, primarily glazed stone-paste wares, suggest that the site's foundation should, in fact, be placed in the late twelfth century (Jones et al. 2012: 88). The site, then, was likely not in use for much longer than half a century and perhaps as little as thirty years.

According to Hauptmann's estimates, about a thousand tons of slag, which translates to sixty-five to a hundred tons of copper metal, were produced at Khirbat Nuqayb al-Asaymir in this short span (2007: 126, 147). While relatively small by the standards of the major contemporary European centers (Blanchard 2005: 1509) or Iron Age and Roman production in Faynan (Hauptmann 2007: 147), this is still a significant amount of copper. This, and the fact that the site was newly founded in the twelfth century, raises the question of what the copper was used for. One

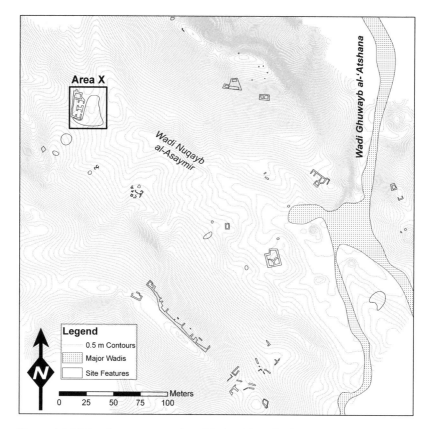

Figure 6.2 Major features mapped at Khirbat Nuqayb al-Asaymir. Contour map: Matthew Howland.

possibility is that Faynan copper in the Middle Islamic period was primarily being produced for the sugar industry. The large boiling vessels—known as *dusut* in Arabic—each required as much as 250 kilograms of copper, and as Coughenour pointed out (1976: 75), for iron production at 'Ajlun, the Catholic Church made various attempts to ban European trade with Muslims in the late twelfth and thirteenth centuries (Freidenreich 2011: 46–47; Lopez 1987: 350; Schroeder 1937). While copper had many uses beyond this, the demand for copper by the sugar industry was likely a significant factor in the twelfth-century revival of the Faynan metal industry.

## Area X

The excavations at Khirbat Nuqayb al-Asaymir in 2011 were designed to investigate Area X (formerly called Survey Building 5300; Fig. 6.3), the main locus of copper production at the site (the report of this probe appears in Levy et al. [2012b]).

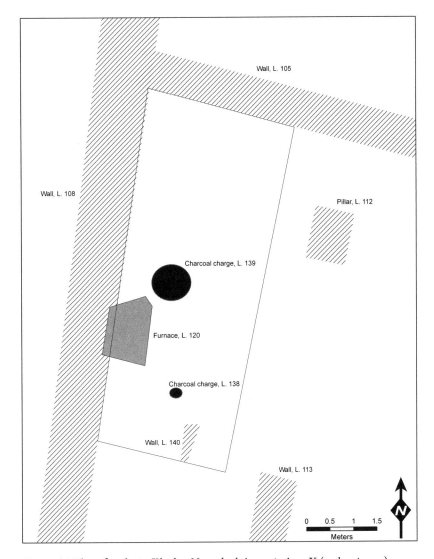

Figure 6.3 Plan of probe in Khirbat Nuqayb al-Asaymir Area X (author image).

The primary components of Area X are a five-room structure, about twenty-two by eleven meters, and associated mounds of copper slag to the east, just outside the building entrances. The walls of the building stand higher than two meters in places and are built of the shale that makes up the hills surrounding the site, with chinking stones inserted semiregularly throughout. A seven-by-three-meter test excavation, or probe,[2] was excavated in the northwestern corner of the main building and reached the foundations of the walls. Within this probe, no stratigraphic separation of levels was possible. This is almost certainly due to the unique site formation processes in this building, discussed below, and is not expected to be applicable across the entire site.

Although all sediment loci,[3] including topsoil loci, were sieved through a quarter-inch mesh screen, very few finds were recovered. Ceramic finds were quite limited but included several sherds of handmade painted ware, including a rim with a hook motif (Fig. 6.4) similar to designs on mid-twelfth-century wares from Wuʿayra (Tonghini and Desideri 2001: fig. 7a). One other significant find is a large piece of a copper-iron alloy found near the northern wall of the building. There is a significant amount of metal in this object, and it is difficult to interpret this deposit as simply a dump. Rather, it seems that it was set aside for refining following the final smelting operation in this building but was not reprocessed before the site went out of use. Beyond this, however, finds in Area X were limited to very small quantities of slag, copper ore, and glass and large quantities of charcoal, discussed below.

The most interesting feature revealed during the 2011 excavations was Locus 120, which before excavation appeared to be a collapsed, pillar-like installation. In fact, it is a well-preserved copper smelting furnace abutting the eastern wall of the Area X building (Fig. 6.5). A similar installation, about five meters south of Locus 120, is likely a second smelting furnace, although this area was not excavated. The furnace itself is about 1-by-1.6 meters, with a slag pit to the east about 0.75 meters in diameter. The western part of the furnace, like the walls of the building, is made of local shale, with a facing made of granite, now very decayed (likely due to exposure to heat), and clay. The clay portion of the facing would have been replaced with every smelting operation, whereas the granite would have been replaced less frequently. Between the shale structure and this facing is a layer of red, iron-rich, clayey loess, which seems to have been used as mortar. This mortar, too, is now heavily decayed and has run off in large quantities into the slag pit. Overall, the furnace is similar in plan to Early Islamic II (800–1000 CE) shaft furnaces

Figure 6.4 Rim of a handmade painted jar with a red hook-and-line pattern found in Area X (author image).

Figure 6.5 The furnace in Khirbat Nuqayb al-Asaymir Area X, showing the slag pit (front), as well as the replaceable facing (to left of north arrow). Photo: Thomas E. Levy (see Levy et al. 2012b).

at 'Arja in Oman, specifically those from Site 103 (Weisgerber 1987:155),[4] which suggests that this type of furnace was both widespread and long-lived in the Islamic world.

The furnace does seem unique, however, in that air was supplied in two different ways. First, a small opening is visible at the bottom of the external side of the building's western wall, in the same section of the wall as the furnace (Fig. 6.6). This would have taken advantage of the winds blowing through the site from the west along Wadi Nuqayb al-Asaymir and partially explains the location of Area X at the western margins of the site along this wadi. Second, there is some evidence that air was forced into the furnace from the opposite side with bellows. Fragments of an unfired clay bellows tube were found to the east of the furnace, and the very fragmentary textile and rope finds from nearby loci may represent the remains of cloth bellows. No fragments of *tuyères*—the nozzles of the bellows tubes—were excavated, but one example was collected from the surface of the slag mounds outside of the building.

To the east of the furnace, we also found two concentrations of wood charcoal. These piles of charcoal, along with crushed copper ore, would have formed the furnace charge. Their location in relation to the furnace suggests a workshop layout at Khirbat Nuqayb al-Asaymir similar to a fifteenth-century European workshop shown in a woodcut in Agricola (1950: 389) but on a smaller scale. Based on the lack of stratigraphy in Area X, these charcoal charges very likely represent the

Figure 6.6 Air passage on the exterior of the Area X building's western wall (L. 108). The furnace is on the opposite side of the wall, with its center just to the left of the meter stick. Photo: Thomas E. Levy.

remains of the final copper smelting event—or, at the very least, the final smelting event in this furnace in Area X. The botanical remains from these features—over twelve kilograms of charcoal, including several complete carbonized branches—will provide significant data both for radiocarbon dating the final use of Area X and for reconstructing landscape exploitation. The species of this sample has been identified[5] as white saxaul (*Haloxylon persicum*), a small tree still quite commonly found in Faynan. The significance of this identification in terms of provisioning strategies is discussed later in this paper.

Overall, the results of the Area X probe are surprising. Other than the furnace itself and finds related to the last smelting event in the building, very few artifacts were recovered. This suggests that the Area X workshop was cleaned regularly, and the material removed from the building was dumped on the slag mounds outside.

## Ore to Metal: The Production Process

One of the primary goals of the excavations at Khirbat Nuqayb al-Asaymir was to reconstruct the past activities of miners and smelters at the site. While the process of copper production in Faynan has been described for earlier periods by researchers from the Deutsches Bergbau-Museum (e.g., Hauptmann 2007) and the current project (summarized in Levy et al. 2012a), a detailed reconstruction of how copper was smelted during the Middle Islamic period has not yet been attempted. In order to establish a consistent methodology for doing this, I rely on several "middle-range" conceptual tools, key among which is the *chaîne opératoire*, first proposed by the André Leroi-Gourhan (1993), drawing on work by Mauss (1973). Constructing a *chaîne opératoire* involves determining step by step the actions performed with and on material objects in a specific technical sequence. Dobres argues that "because it is specifically designed to identify and describe the material sequence(s) of gestural acts through which natural resources were modified (and remodified) into culturally useful objects," a *chaîne opératoire* can be a useful starting point for linking the archaeological and the social (1999: 129). As such, the initial reconstructions presented here are the first step toward establishing a broader picture of how miners at Khirbat Nuqayb al-Asaymir worked and lived.

The excavations in Area X, specifically, have allowed for the reconstruction of a more detailed *chaîne opératoire* for copper production in the Middle Islamic period in Faynan (Fig. 6.7). Ore was mined primarily at two sites known as WAG 57 and 58 (Fig. 6.1), both located about two hundred meters northwest of Area X in Wadi Nuqayb al-Asaymir (Levy et al. 2003: 254, 260; Jones et al. 2012: 74). Once mined and processed ore reached Khirbat Nuqayb al-Asaymir, it likely went through another phase of processing before being brought into the Area X building itself.

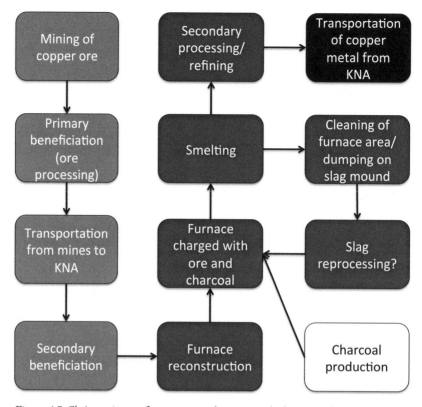

Figure 6.7 *Chaîne opératoire* for copper production at Khirbat Nuqayb al-Asaymir.

This second processing phase is indicated by small dumps of mining waste to the south of the Area X building (Jones et al. 2012: fig. 4; Hauptmann 2007: 126). Before the actual smelting, at least some of the furnace facing would need to be rebuilt. This would involve primarily replacing only the clay portion of the facing, but it is likely that the stone facing would, over time, decay due to heat exposure and require replacement as well. The processed ore would then have been added to the furnace charge, along with charcoal, which evidently was stored in the Area X building in small charge piles. Although integral to the copper production process, the *chaîne opératoire* for charcoal production is treated here as separate from copper production itself, in part because of the current difficulty of reconstructing this process. As work progresses on the botanical remains, reconstructing the process of charcoal production will become more feasible.

After the furnace was charged, the actual smelting would have occurred, separating the copper from the other minerals present in the ore and producing slag as waste. The dearth of finds, especially of metallurgical waste, in Area X—quite notable in comparison to excavations of earlier sites in Faynan (e.g., Levy et al. 2002;

Levy et al. 2012a)—indicates that the smelting workshop was cleaned regularly, with the majority of the material being taken out and dumped on the slag mound directly outside of the building. The layout of the workshop, and especially the placement of the permanent furnace inside the building, would have necessitated this step, as smelting in the workshop would quickly have become impossible if metallurgical waste were allowed to accumulate in front of the furnace. It is not entirely clear if, at this stage, the slag would have undergone further processing. Slag is commonly crushed in order to extract copper prills, and the excavations at Khirbat al-Nahas have revealed that during the Iron Age, this crushed slag was also used as a flux in the furnace charge, as a leveling material for building foundations, and as a temper in technological ceramics such as *tuyères*[6] as well as in handmade domestic pottery (Ben-Yosef 2010: 929; Smith and Levy 2008: 49, 80). Slag-crushing installations have not been found at Khirbat Nuqayb al-Asaymir, but ceramic *tuyères* collected from the surface of the slag mound do indicate the use of crushed slag as temper. Further analysis of excavated material from the site is required to determine whether crushed slag had other uses and to add more detail to this portion of the *chaîne opératoire*.

The last step of the *chaîne opératoire* involves the refining of the smelted copper. The necessity of this step is indicated by chunks of copper-iron alloy in the Area X building, noted during the Deutsches Bergbau-Museum surveys (Hauptmann 2007: 126) and confirmed by finds from the ELRAP excavations, including the large lump of this material found in the northwestern corner of the building. Hauptmann argues that the high iron content in this material calls into question whether copper or iron was the desired end product (2007: 126), although iron content in copper generally increases as smelting technology improves (Cooke and Aschenbrenner 1975; Craddock and Meeks 1987). For the technologically similar furnace at 'Arja, steps were taken to prevent the formation of copper-iron alloys (Weisgerber 1987: 160). It is possible that at Khirbat Nuqayb al-Asaymir these stages were intentionally omitted, as both metals were the desired end products after refining, but it is quite unlikely that a new settlement was founded in Faynan to produce iron rather than copper. Craddock and Meeks also discuss the intentional production of copper-iron alloys for use as currency (1987: 201–202), but it is unclear if this practice occurred in the twelfth and thirteenth centuries.[7] If the assertion by me and my colleagues (Jones et al. 2012) that Middle Islamic period copper production in Faynan primarily served to provision the sugar industry is correct, a refining stage would certainly have been necessary. The excavations at Khirbat Nuqayb al-Asaymir have not yet produced evidence of this, however, and further analysis of the metal and slag finds from the site is necessary to fill in this stage of the *chaîne opératoire*.

## Charcoal Provisioning

In order to demonstrate the difficulties currently faced trying to reconstruct the *chaîne opératoire* for charcoal production in Middle Islamic Faynan, it will be useful to summarize what is currently known about charcoal provisioning in this period. Several multiperiod studies of charcoal resources in Faynan have been published by teams from the Deutsches Bergbau-Museum (Baierle et al. 1989; Engel and Frey 1996). Although no charcoal samples were taken from Khirbat Nuqayb al-Asaymir for these studies, over three hundred samples from Middle Islamic period slag mounds at Khirbat Faynan to the south were processed. In terms of dating, the relationship of these mounds—labeled Faynan 2 and Faynan 6—to the slag mounds at Khirbat Nuqayb al-Asaymir is unclear. Hauptmann places Faynan 2 in the late thirteenth century (2007: 97), although his reasons for doing so are not entirely clear, and Faynan 6 in the fourteenth century on the basis of Bahri Mamluk coins found nearby (Kind et al. 2005: 179). Based on this numismatic data, and as I and my colleagues have suggested elsewhere (Jones et al. 2012: 88–89), the slag mounds at Khirbat Faynan are likely either broadly contemporary with a late phase of production at Khirbat Nuqayb al-Asaymir or postdate production there by several decades.

It is interesting, then, to compare the charcoal resources being exploited by copper producers at these two sites. The resources that were exploited at Khirbat Faynan in the Middle Islamic period are rather surprising. The Faynan 2 slag mound contained charcoal from only Palestine oak (*Quercus calliprinos*) and Phoenician juniper (*Juniperus phoenicea*), while the Faynan 6 slag mound included these species, as well as olive (*Olea europaea*) and small quantities of tamarisk (*Tamarix* species) (Baierle et al. 1989: 216). Oak, juniper, and olive are virtually unknown in charcoal assemblages from Faynan after the Early Bronze Age (c. 3600–2000 BC) and—with the possible exception of olive (see Hunt et al. 2007: 1325)—almost certainly had to be transported from the highland plateau into the lowlands of Faynan during the Middle Islamic period (Baierle et al. 1989: 220). The effort and coordination that this implies suggests that Weisgerber's view of Middle Islamic copper production at Khirbat Faynan as decentralized, "trial-and-error" resmelting of old slag (2006: 27)—called into question elsewhere (Jones et al. 2012: 90)—is probably incorrect for both Khirbat Nuqayb al-Asaymir and Khirbat Faynan.

What is known about charcoal use at Khirbat Nuqayb al-Asaymir is currently much more limited. Only one sample from the Area X charcoal charges has been processed, but the result is rather different from the Deutsches Bergbau-Museum results. This sample turned out to be white saxaul (*Haloxylon persicum*), a small tree common in arid and semiarid environments and still common today in Faynan. This tree was used as fuel for smelting during most periods in Faynan, forming more than half of the charcoal assemblage in the Roman period Faynan 1 slag mound, but was not present at all in the Middle Islamic period Faynan 2 and Faynan 6 mounds (Baierle et al. 1989: 216). While the conclusions that can be made on the basis of a single sample are rather weak, this result brings up further questions about the nature of charcoal provisioning at Middle Islamic Khirbat Faynan.

While saxaul charcoal was unexpected, given its complete absence in the Middle Islamic Khirbat Faynan assemblage, it also requires little explanation. As Hauptmann points out, the picture we get for charcoal provisioning in most periods is that "generally woods from the direct surrounding of the smelting sites have been used" (2007: 53). In fact, given current assumptions about the plant life of Faynan in the Middle Islamic period, it would be unsurprising if the charcoal from Khirbat Nuqayb al-Asaymir turned out to be closer to the Roman period and Iron Age assemblages, and was made up primarily of arid and semiarid species like saxaul, highlighting the Khirbat Faynan mounds as anomalous.

One possible explanation for the differences between Khirbat Nuqayb al-Asaymir and Khirbat Faynan is that the availability of wood differed between the Wadi al-Ghuwayb and Wadi Faynan systems, perhaps due to overexploitation of wood resources in preceding periods. Roman copper smelting, concentrated entirely in the area near Khirbat Faynan, would have consumed a massive amount of charcoal. Hauptmann estimates that Roman copper production required 320,000 to 560,000 tons of wood over approximately four hundred years (2007: 53). Of this, according to the percentages given by Baierle and colleagues (1989: 216), roughly 220,000 to 385,000 tons would have been saxaul.[8] It is likely that saxaul populations would have recovered in the five hundred years (if not eight hundred) that passed between the end of this production phase and the beginning of Middle Islamic copper production, but, nonetheless, this remains a possibility. Unfortunately, available environmental reconstructions (e.g., Hunt et al. 2007) do not have the temporal resolution necessary to determine the prevalence of these species in Faynan during the Middle Islamic period.

Another possibility lies in the fact that the mining feature system (on the use of this term, see Hardesty 1988) of Middle Islamic Khirbat Faynan was generally more oriented toward resources to the east of Faynan. Where mining at Khirbat Nuqayb al-Asaymir largely focused on resources in the immediate vicinity of the site, there are indications from surveys that ore was transported to Khirbat Faynan from mines in Wadi al-Salmina, a small tributary wadi roughly seven kilometers east of Khirbat Faynan (Ben-Yosef 2010: 101; Jones et al. 2012: 90). The mines in Wadi al-Salmina are located at the margins of the plateau (Fig. 6.1), and even today some plateau species, such as juniper, grow in and around the wadi. While this does not explain why plateau species were favored over plants growing in Faynan, it does at least place this shift in the context of a more general pattern of resource use near the highlands. Of course, these two explanations are not mutually exclusive, and it is possible that populations of plants useful for charcoal production in Wadi Faynan were low, while the plateau species common at Faynan 2 and Faynan 6 were located conveniently near ore sources.

## Conclusion

Many questions remain about the nature of the shift from Khirbat Nuqayb al-Asaymir to Khirbat Faynan, both in terms of the relocation of the production center and more specifically the shift in provisioning strategies. In large part, this is due to our limited understanding of the temporal relationship between the sites, especially as the dates for Khirbat Faynan are still quite uncertain. With this in mind, a small probe was made in the Faynan 6 slag mound (Khirbat Faynan Area 15 on the ELRAP grid) during the 2012 field season. The data from this probe, once analyzed and processed, will help narrow down the dating of this production phase. Likewise, further analysis of the botanical material will clarify how charcoal provisioning strategies changed as copper production shifted from Khirbat Nuqayb al-Asaymir to Khirbat Faynan.

Although it is not yet possible to comment on how the Faynan production system changed over time, data from the excavations presented above has allowed for a preliminary reconstruction of the *chaîne opératoire* of copper production and the strategies for provisioning this activity. This represents a first step toward sharpening our picture both of daily life at the site and of the nature of the copper industry during the Middle Islamic period. As work at the site progresses, it is becoming clearer that lowland southern Jordan, and Faynan specifically, was not simply a backwater worthy of little comment but was an important component—and product—of the broader economy of southern Bilad al-Sham.

## Notes

I would first like to acknowledge the Department of Antiquities of Jordan, especially Jihad Haroun, Khalil Hamdan, Qutaiba al-Dasouqi, and in particular Abdelrahim Al Dwikat, who served as the representative at Khirbat Nuqayb al-Asaymir (KNA). Special thanks are due to my advisor and ELRAP principal investigator, Professor Thomas E. Levy, without whose support—academic, logistical, and financial—the 2011 excavations at KNA would not have occurred. Additionally, I thank ELRAP co-principal investigator Dr. Mohammad Najjar, who makes our project in Faynan possible. Parts of this work were also supported financially by the National Science Foundation under IGERT Award #DGE-0966375, "Training, Research and Education in Engineering for Cultural Heritage Diagnostics." I would also like to thank the staff of the American Center of Oriental Research in Amman, especially director Dr. Barbara

Porter and associate director Dr. Christopher Tuttle, for their help and logistical support. I am also grateful to all of the 2011 ELRAP field staff, but especially Kathleen Bennallack and Aaron Gidding, who assisted with directing the excavation at KNA, as well as Sowparnika Balaswaminathan, Craig Smitheram, and Matthew Vincent, whose work in the field lab was essential, and Matthew Howland, who supervised the collection of aerial photography at KNA in 2012. Professor Dr. Erez Ben-Yosef provided much advice on the metallurgical finds during his visit to the site, and I thank him for that, as well as for many productive discussions on these subjects as he was writing up his dissertation in San Diego. I must also thank our University of California, San Diego, undergraduates and ELRAP volunteers, as well as the Bedouin workers from the ʿAzazma, ʿAmarin, and al-Manaja tribes, whose work made the excavation possible. I also thank the organizers of the Materiality of the Islamic Rural Economy workshop, Paul Wordsworth and Stephen McPhillips, for allowing me to present this work and for providing very useful feedback on the first draft of this chapter, as well as all of the participants in the workshop for their valuable comments and suggestions. All errors in the work are, of course, my own. Finally, I am grateful to the Royal Society for the Conservation of Nature in Jordan for their help and cooperation. KNA is located in the Dana UNESCO Biosphere protected area.

1. Discounting Khirbat Faynan, which is a much larger site overall, but with a fairly small Middle Islamic period occupation.

2. Initially, this probe was planned as five by two-and-a-half meters but expanded in both directions to increase coverage of specific features.

3. "Locus"—roughly equivalent to Harris's (1989) "unit of stratification" or the "context" of single-context recording—is a broad term referring to a homogeneous sediment deposit, installation, or wall.

4. There are also interesting superficial similarities to stone-built Late Bronze Age furnaces in the Wadi al-ʿAraba, at Timna Site 2 (Rothenberg 1990: 71). The dating of these furnaces is rather uncertain, and some furnaces at Site 2 have yielded Early Islamic period radiocarbon dates (Ben-Yosef 2010: 671). I thank Dr. Erez Ben-Yosef for pointing out this connection.

5. This analysis was conducted by Brita Lorentzen of Cornell University.

6. A *tuyère* is the nozzle that serves as the interface between the furnace bellows and the furnace itself.

7. Shoshan mentions accounts of debased fifteenth-century Egyptian *fulus* reputed to contain significantly more iron and lead than copper (1982: 109), but given the difficulty of casting this material (Craddock and Meeks 1987: 201), Bacharach's description (1976: 41–42) of bags of *fulus* being partially filled with scrap iron and lead to increase their weight makes more sense.

8. Ben-Yosef (2010: 935–37; Ben-Yosef et al. 2010: 732–35) argues that Hauptmann (2007) overestimates the slag content of many slag mounds, and therefore his estimates of the amount of wood required for charcoal, which are generally based on estimates of slag weight, would also be high. Nonetheless, a significant amount of wood was required during the formation of the large Faynan 1 slag mound.

# Bibliography

Agricola, Georgius. 1950. *De re metallica*, translated by Herbert Clark Hoover and Lou Henry Hoover. New York: Dover.

Avner, Uzi, and Jodi Magness. 1998. "Early Islamic settlement in the southern Negev." *Bulletin of the American Schools of Oriental Research* 310: 39–57.

Bacharach, Jere L. 1976. "Circassian monetary policy: copper." *Journal of the Economic and Social History of the Orient* 19(1): 32–47.

Baierle, Hans Ulrich, Wolfgang Frey, Christian Jagiella, and Harald Kürschner. 1989. "Die Brennstoffressourcen im Raum Fenan (Wadi Araba, Jordanien) und die bei der Kupferz- verhüttung verwendeten Brennstoffe." In *Archäometallurgie der Alten Welt: Beiträge zum In- ternationalen Symposium "Old World Archaeometallurgy," Heidelberg 1987*, edited by Andreas Hauptmann, Ernst Pernicka, and Günther A. Wagner, 213–22. Bochum: Deutsches Bergbau-Museum.

Ben-Yosef, Erez. 2010. *Technology and Social Process: Oscillations in Iron Age Copper Production and Power in Southern Jordan*. PhD dissertation, Department of Anthropology, University of California, San Diego.

Ben-Yosef, Erez, Thomas E. Levy, Thomas Higham, Mohammad Najjar, and Lisa Tauxe. 2010. "The beginning of Iron Age copper production in the southern Levant: new evidence from Khirbat al-Jariya, Faynan, Jordan." *Antiquity* 84: 724–46.

Blanchard, Ian. 2005. *Mining, Metallurgy and Minting in the Middle Ages*, vol. 3: *Continuing Afro- European Supremacy, 1250–1450 (African Gold Production and the Second and Third Euro- pean Silver Production Long-Cycles)*. Stuttgart: Franz Steiner.

Cooke, Strathmore R. B., and Stanley Aschenbrenner. 1975. "The occurrence of metallic iron in ancient copper." *Journal of Field Archaeology* 2(3): 251–66.

Coughenour, Robert A. 1976. "Preliminary report on the exploration and excavation of Mu- gharat el-Wardeh and Abu Thawab." *Annual of the Department of Antiquities of Jordan* 21: 71–78, 186–89.

Craddock, P. T., and N. D. Meeks. 1987. "Iron in ancient copper." *Archaeometry* 29(2): 187–204.

Damgaard, Kristoffer. 2009. "A Palestinian Red Sea port on the Egyptian road to Arabia: Early Islamic Aqaba and its many hinterlands." In *Connected Hinterlands: Proceedings of Red Sea Project IV*, edited by Lucy Blue, John Cooper, Ross Thomas, and Julian Whitewright, 85– 97. Oxford: Archaeopress.

Dobres, Marcia-Anne. 1999. "Technology's links and *chaînes*: the processual unfolding of tech- nique and technician." In *The Social Dynamics of Technology: Practice, Politics, and World Views*, edited by Marcia-Anne Dobres and Christopher R. Hoffman, 124–46. Washington, DC: Smithsonian Institution Press.

Engel, Thomas, and Wolfgang Frey. 1996. "Fuel resources for copper smelting in antiquity in selected woodlands in the Edom highlands to the Wadi Arabah/Jordan." *Flora* 191: 29–39.

Freidenreich, David M. 2011. "Muslims in Western canon law, 1000–1500." In *Christian-Muslim Relations: A Bibliographical History*, vol. 3: *1050–1200*, edited by David Thomas and Alex Mallett, 41–68. Leiden: Brill.

Glueck, Nelson. 1935. *Explorations in Eastern Palestine, II*. New Haven, CT: American Schools of Oriental Research.

Hardesty, Donald L. 1988. *The Archaeology of Mining and Miners: A View from the Silver State*. Pleasant Hill, CA: Society for Historical Archaeology.

Harris, Edward C. 1989. *Principles of Archaeological Stratigraphy*. 2nd ed. London: Academic Press.

Hauptmann, Andreas. 2007. *The Archaeometallurgy of Copper: Evidence from Faynan, Jordan*. New York: Springer.

Hauptmann, Andreas, Gerd Weisgerber, and Ernst Axel Knauf. 1985. "Archäometallurgische und bergbauarchäologische Untersuchungen im Gebiet von Fenan, Wadi Arabah (Jor- danien)." *Der Anschnitt* 37: 163–95.

Hunt, Chris O., David D. Gilbertson, and Hwedi A. El-Rishi. 2007. "An 8000-year history of landscape, climate, and copper exploitation in the Middle East: the Wadi Faynan and the Wadi Dana National Reserve in southern Jordan." *Journal of Archaeological Science* 34: 1306–38.

Jones, Ian W. N., Thomas E. Levy, and Mohammad Najjar. 2012. "Khirbat Nuqayb al-Asaymir and Middle Islamic metallurgy in Faynan: surveys of Wadi al-Ghuwayb and Wadi al-

Jariya in Faynan, southern Jordan." *Bulletin of the American Schools of Oriental Research* 368: 67–102.

Kind, Hans Dieter, Karl Josef Gilles, Andreas Hauptmann, and Gerd Weisgerber. 2005. "Coins from Faynan, Jordan." *Levant* 37: 169–95.

Leroi-Gourhan, André. 1993. *Gesture and Speech*, translated by Anna Bostock Berger. Cambridge, MA: MIT Press.

Levy, Thomas E., Russell B. Adams, James D. Anderson, Mohammad Najjar, Neil Smith, Yoav Arbel, Lisa Soderbaum, and Adolfo Muniz. 2003. "An Iron Age landscape in the Edomite lowlands: archaeological surveys along Wadi al-Ghuwayb and Wadi al-Jāriya, Jabal Ḥamrat Fīdān, Jordan, 2002." *Annual of the Department of Antiquities of Jordan* 47: 247–77.

Levy, Thomas E., Russell B. Adams, Andreas Hauptmann, Michael Prange, Sigrid Schmitt-Strecker, and Mohammad Najjar. 2002. "Early Bronze Age metallurgy: a newly discovered copper manufactory in southern Jordan." *Antiquity* 76: 425–37.

Levy, Thomas E., and Mohammad Najjar. 2007. "Ancient metal production and social change in southern Jordan: the Edom Lowlands Regional Archaeology Project and hope for a UNESCO World Heritage Site in Faynan." In *Crossing Jordan: North American Contributions to the Archaeology of Jordan*, edited by Thomas E. Levy, P. M. Michèle Daviau, Randall W. Younker, and May Shaer, 97–105. London: Equinox.

Levy, Thomas E., Erez Ben-Yosef, and Mohammad Najjar. 2012a. "New perspectives on Iron Age copper production and society in the Faynan region, Jordan." In *Eastern Mediterranean Metallurgy and Metalwork in the 2nd Millennium BC*, edited by V. Kassianidou and G. Papasavvas, 167–83. Oxford: Oxbow.

Levy, Thomas E., Mohammad Najjar, Aaron D. Gidding, Ian W. N. Jones, Kyle A. Knabb, Kathleen Bennallack, Matthew Vincent, Alex Novo Lamosco, Ashley Richter, Craig Smitheram, Lauren D. Hahn, and Sowparnika Balaswaminathan. 2012b. "The 2011 Edom Lowlands Regional Archaeology Project (ELRAP): excavations and surveys in the Faynan copper ore district, Jordan." *Annual of the Department of Antiquities of Jordan*.

Lopez, Robert S. 1987. "The trade of medieval Europe: the south." In *The Cambridge Economic History of Europe*, vol. 2: *Trade and Industry in the Middle Ages*, edited by M. M. Postan and Edward Miller, 306–401. Cambridge: Cambridge University Press.

Mauss, Marcel. 1973. "Techniques of the body." *Economy and Society* 2(1): 70–88.

Newson, Paul, David Mattingly, Patrick Daly, Roberta Tomber, Hwedi el-Rishi, David Gilbertson, John Grattan, Chris Hunt, Sue McLaren, and Brian Pyatt. 2007. "The Islamic and Ottoman periods." In *Archaeology and Desertification: The Wadi Faynan Landscape Survey, Southern Jordan*, edited by Graeme Barker, David Gilbertson, and David Mattingly, 349–68. Oxford: Oxbow.

Rothenberg, Beno. 1988. "Early Islamic copper smelting—and worship—at Beer Ora, southern Arabah (Israel)." *Institute for Archaeo-Metallurgical Studies Newsletter* 12: 1–4.

———. 1990. "Copper smelting furnaces, tuyeres, slags, ingot-moulds and ingots in the Arabah: the archaeological data." In *The Ancient Metallurgy of Copper*, edited by Beno Rothenberg, 1–77. London: Institute for Archaeo-Metallurgical Studies.

Schroeder, Henry J. 1937. "Medieval Sourcebook: Twelfth Ecumenical Council: Lateran IV 1215." *Internet Medieval Sourcebook*, http://www.fordham.edu/halsall/basis/lateran4.asp.

Shoshan, Boaz. 1982. "From silver to copper: monetary changes in fifteenth-century Egypt." *Studia Islamica* 56: 97–116.

Smith, Neil G., and Thomas E. Levy. 2008. "The Iron Age pottery from Khirbat en-Nahas, Jordan: a preliminary study." *Bulletin of the American Schools of Oriental Research* 352: 41–91.

Tonghini, Cristina, and Andrea Vanni Desideri. 2001. "The material evidence from al-Wuʿayra: a sample of pottery." In *Studies in the History and Archaeology of Jordan VII: Jordan by the Millenia*, edited by Khairieh ʿAmr, 707–19. Amman: Department of Antiquities of Jordan.

Weisgerber, Gerd. 1987. "Archaeological evidence of copper exploitation at 'Arja." *Journal of Oman Studies* 9: 145–238.

———. 2006. "The mineral wealth of ancient Arabia and its use. I: Copper mining and smelting at Feinan and Timna—comparison and evaluation of techniques, production, and strategies." *Arabian Archaeology and Epigraphy* 17: 1–30.

Whitcomb, Donald. 2006. "Land behind Aqaba: the Wadi Arabah during the Early Islamic period." In *Crossing the Rift: Resources, Routes, Settlement Patterns and Interactions in the Wadi Arabah*, edited by Piotr Bienkowski and Katharina Galor, 239–42. Oxford: Oxbow.

Willies, Lynn. 1991. "Ancient copper mining at Wadi Amram, Israel: an archaeological survey." *Bulletin of the Peak District Mines Historical Society* 2(3): 109–38.

# CHAPTER 7

# Ceramic Production in the Central Highlands of Yemen During the Islamic Period

*Daniel Mahoney*

Ceramic production in rural contexts of the Islamic world has been understudied. The usually unglazed products from this zone have often been overshadowed in the analyses of archaeological pottery assemblages in favor of focusing on the provenance or technology of sherds with more complex surface treatments or fabric compositions that were created in workshops associated with urban centers. As a result, knowledge of the extent and nature of this significant aspect of the rural economy is quite limited, despite research in Greater Syria and Upper Egypt demonstrating the importance of noncommercial manufacture for the economic independence of inhabitants in rural regions (Milwright 2010: 154–56). The production of local wares does not necessarily represent technological backwardness or economic destitution but rather may be a conscious choice by a rural population to maintain a self-sufficient autonomy. At the same time, while rural ceramic production may primarily serve the needs of local consumers, that does not mean the products are limited to basic handmade wares in domestic contexts. Rather, it may also include more specialized production of vessels that require the potter to have a higher level of skill and time for their manufacture. This chapter focuses on a case study of a diverse industry of pottery production that provides for the needs of a rural population located in the central highlands of Yemen.

The study of Islamic period ceramics in Yemen has largely concentrated on establishing links to other world regions in order to contextualize it within a wider global sphere of interaction. Pottery collected through survey and excavation that had demonstrably been produced in foreign centers demonstrates connections to a wide variety of locations in the Near East, East Africa, South Asia, and East

Asia. While this evidence counters the notion of Yemen's apparent isolation on the southern tip of the Arabian Peninsula, it is also a consequence of the coastal location where most archaeological research has been pursued. Beginning with a survey in 1941 of the area around the major port of Aden (Lane and Serjeant 1948), the majority of the Islamic period projects have taken place in regions along or close to the coasts of the Indian Ocean and the Red Sea, where the material remains reflect the local population's direct integration into a network of interregional commerce (Hardy-Guilbert 2005; Hardy-Guilbert and Rougeulle 1995, 1997; Keall 1983; King and Tonghini 1996; Newton 2009; Rougeulle 2005; Whitcomb 1988). While this archaeological work has succeeded in producing a valuable temporal framework of externally and locally produced glazed wares, the sampling bias created by the location of the data collection has resulted in an emphasis on pottery manufactured in foreign locations in lieu of focusing more on the local ceramic industries. Conversely, the Dhamar Plain situated in the interior highlands offers an important comparative counterpoint for a wider comprehension of the variability in the ceramic record across South Arabia as a whole. Despite its central location within Yemen, there is limited evidence for the integration of this rural area into a wider network of exchange. Instead, its pottery points to a strong regional tradition of local ceramic production that has maintained relative coherence for millennia.

## The Regional Context and Local Economies of the Dhamar Plain

At an elevation of roughly 2,300 to 2,600 meters above sea level, the Dhamar Plain is located on a plateau in the central highlands of Yemen between the Yislah and Sumara mountain passes (Fig. 7.1). Approximately 100 kilometers south of Sanaa, Dhamar, its main settlement, lies alongside a north–south transportation route that has served as a major conduit for the movement of goods and people between the southern coast and the northern highlands at least as early as the third millennium BCE (Wilkinson 2003: 163–64). During the Islamic period, the rural population of the Dhamar Plain was not politically united under an indigenous dynasty but was divided into various sedentary tribes that sought to maintain their independence from intruding states, such as the Ayyubids, Rasulids, Ottomans, and Qasimis. Textual accounts provide multiple examples of the local population's submission to these outside aggressors and their subsequent rebellion against them. The settlement record reflects this continual conflict through a variety of examples of fortified architecture, such as tower houses, walled villages, and citadels, but without clear indication of an overarching program of defense and administration

Figure 7.1 Map of the Dhamar Survey Project location (prepared by author).

created by an external power. Hence, this evidence points to a more disjointed sociopolitical landscape involving numerous factions rather than one dominated by a single center or political group. This scattered autonomy also corresponds to the diversity of the economic practices of this rural region.

Agricultural cultivation of barley, wheat, and sorghum has been the main economic activity of the population of the Dhamar Plain for millennia (Edens 2005). As a result, extensive systems of terracing, dams, cisterns, and wells cover most of the arable land in the region. Archaeological investigation of them has shown that in the pre-Islamic period, the more limited field and water management systems maintained by smaller groups have been more resilient than the systems involving monumental works sponsored by larger political entities (Gibson and Wilkinson 1995). Additionally, together with the vast plains of Sanaa and Hasi, the Dhamar Plain was a principal location in the medieval period for the breeding of horses to be exported to the south for sale. They were first sold to the Rasulid sultan who controlled the port of Aden and later to the Baniyan merchants from India (Vallet

2010: 373–78). Finally, owing to its volcanic landscape, this region is also rich in various mineral resources, including sulfur, which was mined from a mountain approximately fifteen kilometers to the east of Dhamar for use in gunpowder during the first Ottoman occupation in the seventeenth century (Luṭf Allāh 2003: 275–76).

Craft production was also an important part of the economy of the Dhamar Plain. A thirteenth-century Rasulid administrative document, called *Nūr al-maʿārif fī nuẓum wa-qawānīn wa-aʿrāf al-Yaman fī al-ʿahd al-muẓaffarī al-wārif*, contains a section describing the market of Dhamar, revealing the variety of crafts that were undertaken in and around it (Jāzim 2003: 245–47). This inventory of merchandise includes embroidered garments and curtains of various qualities, incense burners, and glass vessels. In addition, there is a reference in this document to a goldsmith in Dhamar named Muhammad b. ʿAli b. ʿAmran (Jāzim 2005: 175). Nonetheless, the craft items occurring most often by far in the list are various types of ceramic vessels along with their sizes and prices. These vessels range from small cups (*al-tāsāt*), to larger water jars (*al-kīzān*), to containers for vegetables (*al-qulaylāt*), to many other types whose identification and function remain ambiguous. While this textual description provides clear evidence for a strong local ceramic industry involving various types of standardized wares, other information, such as their physical attributes, styles, or places and types of production, is not stated. Consequently, the exploration of the archaeological record enables the investigation of these details as well as a more well-rounded understanding of the local pottery production as a whole.

## The Dhamar Survey Project Collection of Islamic Period Ceramics

From 1994 to 2008, the Dhamar Survey Project located over 400 sites from all occupation periods in an extensive regional survey, consisting of systematic field-walking in blocks adapted to the contours of the Dhamar Plain's irregular topography (Edens 1999; Gibson and Wilkinson 1995; Lewis 2005a; Wilkinson and Edens 1999; Wilkinson et al. 1997). The majority of the 191 sites containing Islamic period remains are small hamlets dispersed among the extensive agricultural systems, often on elevated locations above the arable terrain (Mahoney 2014). There are also larger villages composed of clusters of houses and sometimes a small mosque, as well as citadels and watchtowers scattered throughout the plain. Dhamar was the largest settlement of the region during the Islamic period, but its urban nature may be put into question for much of this duration. The tenth-century geographer al-Hamdani refers to it as a large village (1989: 206), and the twelfth-century geographer al-Idrisi describes it as a small settlement with a few houses and limited population (1989: 53–54). Continuing into the seventeenth century,

European travelers passing through the plain emphasize its appearance as a cluster of separate villages rather than one city (Jourdain 1906: 86–87; Middleton 1732: 270). Not until the second half of the eighteenth century does Dhamar seem to have coalesced into an integrated urban fabric with multiple neighborhoods and a university (Niebuhr 1792: 362). Thus, the local ceramic industry emerges from what seems to be a mostly (if not entirely) rural context until the later Islamic period.

I studied sherds from 101 sites or components within sites, from which solely Islamic period material was collected, and created the first typology of Islamic period ceramic forms from the central highlands of South Arabia. Consisting mostly of vessel forms for domestic use or storage, the most common types comprise such open forms as platters, shallow bowls, medium bowls, deep bowls, and globular bowls; straight-sided forms; such closed forms as slightly closed forms and hole-mouth jars; and jars with varied types of necks. There are also flat, rounded, and ring bases, as well as strap, lug, loop, and applied handles. Finally, the collection includes one folded and three circular spouts, numerous decorated sherds with a variety of surface treatments, and fragments of smoking pipes.

There are some superficial similarities with the Islamic period assemblages from other regions of South Arabia, such as wavy-line incisions and the general repertoire of vessel forms, but their rim shapes, fabric composition, and other decorative techniques are quite different. The local material in the area of Aden at the sites of al-Jebelain, al-Qaraw, Khanfar, and Kawd am-Saila (Whitcomb 1988: 206–209, 222–29) consists of red or red-brown ware with wavy-combed incisions, but the rim shapes of the bowls and jars, cream slip, and other decorative techniques of modeling, incision, excision, and stamping are different from the Dhamar Plain material. Additionally, the sites from the interior of the Hadramawt in eastern Yemen (Whitcomb 1988: 210–21, 230–41) contain some of the same basic vessel forms and wavy-line incisions, but also have unfamiliar rim shapes, decoration, cream slips, and fabrics of buff, orange, grey, and black color. The local nonglazed redware from the coastal Hadramawt region near Sharma (Rougeulle 2007) has similar wavy-combed incisions as well as vessel forms of long-necked jars, deep basins, and medium bowls, but their rim shapes, thin cream slip, and red-painted decoration do not correspond to the Dhamar Plain sherds. Finally, some of the forms of the nonglazed pottery of the ninth to eleventh century from the sites in the Tihama along the Red Sea coast (Ciuk and Keall 1996) have clear parallels, such as short-necked jars (60–63), modeled-neck jars (68–69), deep and globular bowls (80–83), and carinated vessels with lug handles (94–95), although many of the specific rim shapes, fabrics, and slips are different. From the eleventh century onward, however, much of the unglazed pottery from this region, which has a more intricate incised and excised decoration termed trackware (Mason and Keall 1988), is not found in the Dhamar material, which generally has simpler decorative designs.

The distinctiveness of the Dhamar Survey Project collection is further reflected in the small number of sherds originating from outside of the region, despite the major north–south route passing through it. These include 16 sherds of porcelain and 89 sherds of a green and gold fineware associated with coffee drinking that was produced at the site of Hays on the Red Sea coast from the sixteenth century onward (Keall 1992; Mason and Keall 1988). Additionally, 12 sherds of other glazed ware, including blue-and-white ware and turquoise slip-painted ware, compare to pottery produced in the kilns of the Tihama region (Mason 1991; Ciuk and Keall 1996). Altogether, the 117 sherds of glazed ware make up only 3 percent of the total survey collection, demonstrating their very limited presence in the region. The spatial distribution of the thirty-three single period sites with glazed wares and the twenty-five single period sites with specifically Haysi ware are fairly uniform throughout the area. However, the eight single period sites with porcelain, mostly clustered along the north–south route, may indicate its closer connection to sites associated with long-distance travel and exchange instead of settlements where it would have been utilized by the communities living in the region. A final piece of material evidence showing clear interaction with groups from outside of the area are the 14 fragments of Ottoman tobacco pipes found at eight single period sites in the southern portion of the plain. Although they are lower in quality compared to pipes found in the Tihama (Keall 1992), their presence indicates the extension of smoking culture into the region in the early seventeenth century. Nonetheless, this collection overall seems to reflect a well-delimited ceramic industry, in which the majority of the pottery was produced and consumed within the region.

Examining this regional collection, there are many similar vessel forms that are found in previous occupation periods in the plain, such as thick platters, medium bowls, and straight-sided forms, slightly closed and hole-mouth storage vessels, and thick lug and loop handles. This pattern reinforces a general trend of continuity in ceramic production extending back to the third millennium BCE, which has been discussed in previous examinations of the Dhamar Survey Project collection as a whole (Lewis 2005a, 2005b). However, there are also innovations in the pottery of the Islamic period, including the emergence of new specialized vessel forms, the more frequent application of a burnished slip, and the greater use of an abundant mixture of both chaff and mineral inclusions. There is also a wider diversity in the shapes of rims, such as rounded, pinched, flat, inverted, everted, upturned, externally thickened, internally thickened, hammerhead, side-grooved, and top-grooved, as well as a more diverse range of decorative techniques including sherds that were incised, ridged, combed, pattern burnished, notched, applied, painted, impressed, pierced, corded, and punctated.

Despite these innovations, internal periodization of the Dhamar Survey Project collection within the Islamic period continues to be difficult due to the lack of excavation of Islamic period contexts in the Dhamar Plain, which would provide a secure stratigraphic sequence or more direct methods for dating this material more precisely. Similarly, due to the inexact and minimal parallels with the ceramics from the Indian Ocean and Red Sea coastal regions, dating them through stylistic comparison is problematic. As a result, the sherds generally are interpreted as being produced, utilized, and discarded at some point between the seventh and twentieth centuries. However, for some sherds, there are indications for more precise dating within this temporal breadth. For example, some have a deep-red burnished slip similar to pottery of the pre-Islamic Himyarite period, while some have very high-fired fabrics containing pure-white mineral inclusions connected to ceramics of the Late Islamic period. Another type of very high-fired pottery of the Late Islamic period was termed purple-painted ware by the survey team and is currently still being made and sold in markets all over Yemen. A comparative assemblage of this type, presently stored in the British Museum, was collected in the southern regions of the country during the mid-twentieth century (Posey 1994). In the Dhamar Survey Project collection, this ware has a hard brown fabric with an oxidized core and abundant chaff and mineral inclusions, which occasionally consists of only white grit. Its surface is covered by a slip of buff, light-red, or orange color on which is painted a design of diagonal and horizontal bands of dark purple, brown, or black color. With internally thickened and rounded rims of fifteen to twenty centimeters in diameter, most of its forms are hole mouths or slightly closed but also include medium bowls. Finally, the local unglazed ware may be dated based on the additional presence of nonlocal ceramics, such as the aforementioned glazed wares (including Haysi ware) and Ottoman tobacco pipes, in the individual collections from specific sites. However, no clear patterns have yet emerged from this comparison, possibly owing to the long-term occupation at the sites themselves. Thus, while a more specific periodization remains elusive because of the nature of the data set, the apparent temporal consistency of many of the forms found in the collection does mirror the wider trend of continuity for the ceramic tradition of the Dhamar Plain over millennia.

## The Diversity of Ceramic Production in the Dhamar Plain

The concept of craft specialization in the Islamic period has generally been reserved for professional workshops associated with urban centers where they directly produce their wares for a particular institution or patron, or sell them to multiple consumers in a market setting. Rural areas, on the other hand, are generally associated with a lower-level domestic sphere of production. This arbitrary dichotomy, however, does not correspond to a more complex reality in which specialized production may also be part of rural craft manufacture. In this way, specialization in ceramic production is identified in the archaeological record based on more specific criteria. These include direct indications, such as the identification of workshops and their technological implements, and indirect indications, such as the standardization of the ceramics themselves based on the homogeneity of their morphological, stylistic, and compositional attributes as well as the extent of their distribution across various sites (Costin 1991, 2001).

While the thirteenth century *Nur al-ma'arif* (Jāzim 2003, 2005) and the seventeenth-century *Qānūn Sanʿā'* (Serjeant and al-Akwaʿ 1983) provide textual evidence for the specialized production of ceramics in both rural and urban contexts of Yemen, archaeological investigation has also located pottery workshops in the coastal regions of the Tihama and Hadramawt. In the Tihama, petrographic analysis of the local pottery isolated four different centers of production at sites in the vicinities of the cities of Zabid and Hays (Mason and Keall 1988). While much of the locally produced glazed ware of the later Islamic periods came from Hays, all of the nonglazed ware of the ninth to the eleventh century, comparable to the Dhamar Plain material, came from the Zabid East site, where a kiln with wasters was exposed in excavation (Mason 1991: 191–92). In the Hadramawt, a rural production center for the local redware on the Indian Ocean coast was located at the site of Yadhghat, about twelve kilometers north of the port of Sharma (Rougeulle 2007). Dated from roughly the Abbasid period to the mid-twelfth century, this site contained large piles of kiln refuse in an open area where the pottery was fired directly upon the ground, as well as a three-meter-deep shaft to the southeast crossing a layer of pure red clay that was suspected to be the source of the red paint used for the vessels' surface decoration.

When examining the ceramic collection from the Dhamar Survey Project, a complex rural industry involving different levels of production emerges. While the majority of the sherds appear to be well formed and fired at a high temperature, the wide diversity in their rim shapes, fabric composition, and decoration does not point to a uniform standardization in their production. Some of this variety is the result of a lack of strong periodization for the long breadth of time from which the assemblage comes, but some also is likely the outcome of a more geographically dispersed level of production. At the same time, however, other wares in the Dhamar Survey Project collection indicate a higher level of standardization that demands increased skill from the potter and more time for the steps of manufacture. Among them, three types in particular point to a specialized production due to the consistency of the vessel forms, surface decoration, fabric composition, and spatial distribution in the plain: they are top-grooved ware, modeled ware, and al-Lisi ware.

Top-grooved ware (Fig. 7.2 a, b) is most easily identified based on its titular incision carved into the top of the rim, but it is not a ubiquitous attribute. In the collections from the same sites, there are also grooveless sherds that have all of the other diagnostic aspects of this type. With rim diameters of fifteen to twenty-five centimeters, the most common vessel forms are hole mouths and other closed forms, but there are also jars with varying lengths of necks. The brown and red high-fired fabric with mostly oxidized cores and fair to abundant mixed mineral inclusions enable the construction of its extremely thin (usually less than one centimeter) and hard vessel walls. Its surface is often slipped or slipped and burnished, and its decoration consists of applied thin horizontal ridges with notches or impressions in addition to vertical or diagonal combed incisions. Top-grooved ware was found distributed across the plain at thirty-four single period Islamic sites. While a specific site of production has not yet been found for this ceramic type, there are two sites with exceptionally high concentrations of it that are located more than twenty kilometers, respectively, to the east and south of Dhamar, pointing to a rural context for its manufacture.

Modeled ware (Fig. 7.2 c, d), a second example of specialized ceramic production in the Dhamar Plain, is usually a straight-sided form. With a rim diameter of fifteen to thirty-five centimeters, its very specific rounded morphology consists of both internal and external thickening. Additionally, a thin horizontal ridge roughly two centimeters below the rim may also incorporate a lug handle. It is covered by a smooth brown slip, and its brown fabric, consisting of occasional fine chaff and mineral inclusions, has a reduced core. Modeled ware was found at six single period Islamic sites clustered in the southern portion of the plain over fifteen kilometers away from Dhamar, also indicating a probable rural context for its production, although a specific site has not yet been located.

Finally, al-Lisi ware (Fig. 7.2 e, f; Fig. 7.3) is the clearest example of specialized ceramic production in the Dhamar Plain. With a rim diameter of twenty-five to thirty-five centimeters, it consists of globular and carinated forms with round rims and thick walls. It often has a large, rounded horizontal ridge and occasionally a lug handle. Its decoration includes a wavy-line incision, vertical incisions, or impressions along the upper part of its body. Its thick red-slipped and burnished surface covers a red fabric with a commonly oxidized core, containing a coarse mixture of abundant chaff and mixed minerals. The site of its production is situated at the base of al-Lisi mountain, which is located fifteen kilometers east of Dhamar. Here, a great number of sherds of this type were found during the survey, along with ceramic wasters and kilns. Incidentally, at the top of the mountain, there is a large early seventeenth-century Ottoman fort, in which the previously cited sulfur-mining operation took place. There is no direct evidence that connects these two industrial work sites, but the heavy-duty nature of al-Lisi ware's fabric may

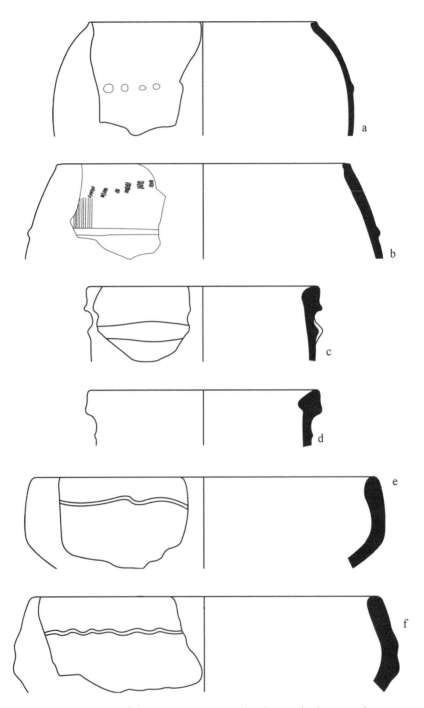

Figure 7.2 Illustrations of the ceramics mentioned in the text (author image).

Figure 7.3 Photograph of an al-Lisi ware sherd (drawing 6) (author image).

indicate an association between them. Additionally, there is a group of twelve sites in the central part of the plain close to al-Lisi mountain where sherds with similar morphological and compositional attributes may indicate its further spatial distribution. However, there is some variation both in their shapes, which have more well-formed concave walls that flare out, and in their fabrics and surfaces, which are of different colors and proportions of inclusions.

## Conclusion

The combination of both textual and material evidence for ceramic production, exchange, and consumption in the Dhamar Plain presents a composite picture of its rural economy. On the one hand, the limited amount of foreign ceramics in the survey collection demonstrates the relative economic isolation of this local population in the central highlands in contrast to the more outward-looking communities on the coasts. On the other hand, the distinct tradition of locally produced wares found in the Dhamar Plain, extending back millennia, points to the persistent economic independence of the rural population. Moreover, the variety of the regional assemblage suggests multiple levels of specialization by the local potters. This includes the production of the highly standardized wares described in the *Nur al-ma'ārif.* While their precise locales of manufacture remain unknown, pottery produced during the medieval period may be interpreted as taking place in a rural context. This well-developed local industry therefore provides a unique perspective on the rural self-sufficiency of an inland region of South Arabia.

## Note

I would like to thank many colleagues for the assistance, comments, and advice I received in the course of research and writing this chapter, including McGuire Gibson, Donald

Whitcomb, Tony Wilkinson, Krista Lewis, Lamya Khalidi, Tasha Vorderstrasse, Bethany Walker, Asa Eger, Kate Franklin, Ed Keall, Robert Mason, Ingrid Hehmeyer, Axelle Rougeulle, Claire Hardy-Guilbert, Andre Gingrich, Johann Heiss, Ali Sanabani, and Salah al-Kawmani, as well as the staffs of the General Organization of Antiquities and Museums, the Social Fund for Development, and the Dhamar Museum in Yemen. Financial support came from the American Institute of Yemeni Studies and the Austrian Science Fund (FWF) F42 "Visions of Community."

# Bibliography

Ciuk, Christopher, and Edward Keall. 1996. *Zabid Project Pottery Manual 1995: Pre-Islamic and Islamic Ceramics for the Zabid Area, North Yemen.* Oxford: Tempus Reparatum.

Costin, Cathy. 1991. "Craft specialization: issues in defining, documenting, and explaining the organization of production." In *Archaeological Method and Theory,* edited by Michael Schiffer, 1–56. Tucson: University of Arizona Press.

———. 2001. "Craft production systems." In *Archaeology at the Millennium: A Sourcebook,* edited by Gary Feinman and Douglas Price, 273–328. New York: Kluwer Academic/Plenum.

Edens, Christopher. 1999. "The Bronze Age of Highland Yemen: chronological and spatial variability of pottery and settlement." *Paléorient* 25(2): 103–26.

———. 2005. "Exploring early agriculture in the highlands of Yemen." In *Sabaean Studies: Archaeological, Epigraphical, and Historical Studies in Honour of Yusuf M. Abdullah, Alessandro De Maigret, and Christian Robin,* edited by Amida Sholan, Sabina Antonini, and Mounir Arbach, 185–211. Naples: Sanaa University.

Gibson, McGuire, and Tony Wilkinson. 1995. "The Dhamar Plain, Yemen: a preliminary study of the archaeological landscape." *Proceedings of the Seminar for Arabian Studies* 25: 159–83.

al-Hamdānī, 1989. *Ṣifat jazīrat al-ʿarab,* edited by Muḥammad al-Akwaʿ. Baghdad: Wizārat al-Thaqāfa wa-l-Iʿlām, Dār al-Shuʾūn al-Thaqāfiyya al-ʿĀmma.

Hardy-Guilbert, Claire. 2005. "The harbour of al-Shiḥr, Ḥaḍramawt, Yemen: sources and archaeological data on trade." *Proceeding of the Seminar for Arabian Studies* 35: 71–85.

Hardy-Guilbert, Claire, and Axelle Rougeulle. 1995. "Archaeological research into the Islamic period in Yemen: preliminary notes on the French Expedition, 1993." *Proceedings of the Seminar for Arabian Studies* 25: 29–44.

———. 1997. "Al-Shihr and the southern coast of the Yemen: preliminary notes on the French archaeological expedition, 1995." *Proceedings of the Seminar for Arabian Studies* 27: 129–40.

al-Idrīsī, Muḥammad. 1989. *Kitāb nuzhat al-mushtāq fī ikhtirāq al-āfāq.* 2 vols. Beirut: ʿAlam al-Kutub.

Jāzim, Muḥammad, ed. 2003. *Nūr al-maʿārif fī nuẓum wa-qawānīn wa-aʿrāf al-Yaman fī al-ʿahd al-muẓaffarī al-wārif / Lumière de la connaissance: Règles, lois et coutumes du Yémen sous le règne du sultan rasoulide al-Muẓaffar,* vol. 1. Sanaa, Yemen: Centre français d'Archéologie et de Sciences sociales de Sanaa.

———, ed. 2005. *Nūr al-maʿārif fī nuẓum wa-qawānīn wa-aʿrāf al-Yaman fī al-ʿahd al-muẓaffarī al-wārif / Lumière de la connaissance: Règles, lois et coutumes du Yémen sous le règne du sultan rasoulide al-Muẓaffar,* vol. 2. Sanaa, Yemen: Centre français d'Archéologie et de Sciences sociales de Sanaa.

Jourdain, John. 1905. *The Journal of John Jourdain, 1608–1617, Describing His Experiences in Arabia, India, and the Malay Archipelago,* edited by W. Forester. Cambridge: Hakluyt Society.

Keall, Edward. 1983. "The dynamics of Zabid and its hinterland: the survey of a town on the Tihamah Plain of North Yemen." *World Archaeology* 14(3): 378–92.

———. 1992. "Smokers' pipes and the fine pottery tradition of Hays." *Proceedings of the Seminar for Arabian Studies* 22: 29–46.

King, Geoffrey, and Cristina Tonghini. 1996. *A Survey of the Islamic Sites near Aden and in the Abyan District of Yemen.* London: School of Oriental and African Studies.

Lane, Arthur, and Robert Serjeant. 1948. "Pottery and glass fragments from the Aden littoral, with historical notes." *Journal of the Royal Asiatic Society* 80: 108–33.

Lewis, Krista. 2005a. *Space and the Spice of Life: Food, Politics, and Landscape in Ancient Yemen.* PhD dissertation, University of Chicago.

———. 2005b. "The Himyarite site of al-Adhla and its implications for the economy and chronology of Early Historic highland Yemen." *Proceedings of the Seminar for Arabian Studies* 35: 129–41.

Luṭf Allāh, ʿIsa b. 2003. *Rawḥ al-rūḥ fīmā ḥadatha baʿd al-miʾa al-tāsiʿa min al-fitan wa-l-futūḥ*, edited by Ibrāhīm al-Maqhafī. Sanaa, Yemen: Markaz Abbādī li-l-Dirāsāt wa-al-Nashr.

Mahoney, Daniel. 2014. *The Political Landscape of the Dhamar Plain in the Central Highlands of Yemen During the Late Medieval and Early Ottoman Periods.* PhD dissertation, University of Chicago.

Mason, Robert. 1991. "Petrography of Islamic ceramics." In *Recent Developments in Ceramic Petrology*, edited by Andrew Middleton and Ian Freestone, 185–210. London: British Museum.

Mason, Robert, and Edward Keall. 1988. "Provenance of local ceramic industry and the characterization of imports: petrography of pottery from medieval Yemen." *Antiquity* 62: 452–63.

Middleton, Henry. 1732. *An Account of the Captivity of Sir Henry Middleton: By the Turks at Moka or Mokha; and his Journey from thence, with thirty four Englishmen more, to the Basha at Zenan, or Sanaa: With a Description of the Country, and a Journal of their Travels to that City, and back again.* London: E. Symon.

Milwright, Marcus. 2010. *An Introduction to Islamic Archaeology.* Edinburgh: Edinburgh University Press.

Newton, Lynn. 2009. *A Landscape of Pilgrimage and Trade in Wadi Masila, Yemen: al-Qisha and Qabr Hud in the Islamic Period.* Oxford: Archaeopress.

Niebuhr, Carsten. 1792. *Travels Through Arabia and Other Countries in the East*, translated by R. Heron. 2 vols. Edinburgh: R. Morison.

Posey, Sarah. 1994. *Yemeni Pottery: The Littlewood Collection.* London: British Museum Press.

Rougeulle, Axelle. 2005. "The Šarma horizon: sgraffiato wares and other glazed ceramics of the Indian Ocean trade (c. AD 980–1140)." *Proceedings of the Seminar for Arabian Studies* 35: 223–46.

———. 2007. "Ceramic production in mediaeval Yemen: the Yaḏġaṭ kiln site." *Proceedings of the Seminar for Arabian Studies* 37: 239–52.

Serjeant, Robert, and Ismaʿil al-Akwaʿ. 1983. "The Statute of Ṣanʿāʾ (Qānūn Ṣanʿāʾ)." In *Ṣanʿāʾ: An Arabian Islamic City*, edited by Robert Serjeant and Ronald Lewcock, 179–232. London: World of Islamic Festival Trust.

Vallet, Éric. 2010. *L'Arabie Marchande: État et Commerce sous les Sultans Rasūlides du Yémen (626–858/1229–1454).* Paris: Publications de la Sorbonne.

Whitcomb, Donald. 1988. "Islamic archaeology in Aden and the Hadhramawt." In *Araby the Blest: Studies in Arabian Archaeology*, edited by Dan Potts, 177–263. Copenhagen: Museum Tusculanum Press.

Wilkinson, Tony. 2003. "The organization of settlement in highland Yemen during the Bronze and Iron Ages." *Proceedings of the Seminar for Arabian Studies* 33: 157–68.

Wilkinson, Tony, and Christopher Edens. 1999. "Survey and excavation in the Central Highlands of Yemen: results of the Dhamar Survey Project, 1996 and 1998." *Arabian Archaeology and Epigraphy* 10: 1–33.

Wilkinson, Tony, Christopher Edens, and McGuire Gibson. 1997. "The archaeology of the Yemen High Plains: a preliminary chronology." *Arabian Archaeology and Epigraphy* 8: 99–142.

# CHAPTER 8

# Harnessing Hydraulic Power in Ottoman Syria

## Water Mills and the Rural Economy of the Upper Orontes Valley

*Stephen McPhillips*

## Water Mills and the Islamic Rural World

Hydraulic networks represent one of the principal signatures of human intervention in archaeological landscapes of western Asia. Both urban water supplies and rural irrigation networks feature prominently, the latter sustaining agricultural production in areas with insufficient annual rainfall for dry farming, or permitting intensive crop growing or horticultural production in areas such as the *zur*, the valley floor gardens of western Syria.[1] Hydraulic energy was harnessed using vertical-wheeled water mills from the third century BCE in the eastern Mediterranean, greatly augmenting the capacity for processing grain and other crops grown in the region.[2] Water mills became increasingly common during the first millennium CE, linked to the expansion of irrigation systems initiated by Late Antique and Early Islamic states in (the Levant), Iraq, and Iran.[3] Few mills survive from the subsequent Abbasid to Saljuq periods (c. 750–1150 CE),[4] but an extraordinary number are known from the medieval and especially the early modern eras, representing a rich source of data for understanding the economy of the rural Islamic world.

This chapter draws on fieldwork in the Homs region of Syria in October 2010,[5] which examined eleven water mills and their associated hydraulic infrastructure in the Orontes valley. Two of the mills were documented in detail in the context of their immediate surrounds: Mill 2 (*Tahunat Umm al-Reghif*) and Mill 4 (*Tahunat al-Banjakiyya*) (Fig. 8.1). Stratigraphic architectural analysis suggests the earliest

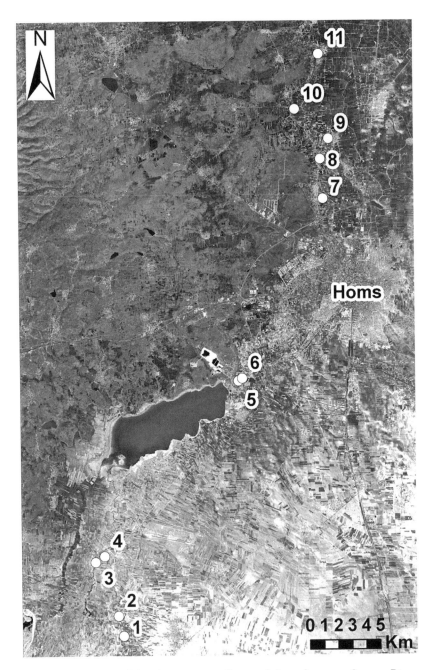

Figure 8.1 Location of the eleven water mills recorded on the upper Orontes River, numbered consecutively downstream from south to north in the surveyed zones (Image J. Bradbury and P. Wordsworth; base map: IKONOS imagery, courtesy of GeoEye, provided by Durham University).

components of one of these dates from the twelfth or thirteenth centuries, while subsequent phases of rebuilding and redevelopment continue through to the twentieth century. Highly adapted to local hydrological conditions and reflecting regional agricultural and architectural traditions, water mills are rarely isolated features in the landscape; they are grouped, often relying on a common water supply, and for the most part lie in proximity to agricultural fields and terraces. The upper Orontes water mills operate on two scales, within the *communauté hydraulique*[6] at the level of local village irrigation and agricultural networks, and as part of a much broader hydraulic landscape, referred to here as "the managed riverscape."

The mills in the study are the vertical-wheeled type, known in Syrian Arabic as *al-jaghli*, possibly because of the sound they made when in operation (Chéhadé 1973: 251–52).[7] By contrast the majority of water mills in,[8] are the much smaller horizontal-wheeled drop-tower, or penstock, mills that are well-represented in most areas where water courses run, even on limited seasonal flows.[9] In Syrian Arabic, these are known as *al-shibi*, after the vertical chute directing pressurized water onto the mill wheel (Chéhadé 1973: 248; Chanesaz 2006: 228). The Orontes water mills had an economic significance reaching beyond , highlighted by documentary evidence concentrated in the sixteenth century (see below). By the mid-nineteenth century, and most likely from a much earlier period, a level of centralization can be detected in their construction and maintenance and a transition in Syrian mill ownership takes place, from a dominance of religious endowments (*waqf*) and state parties toward individual, often local, proprietors. Although the use of hydraulic energy disappeared almost entirely from the mid-twentieth century, a small number of water mills nonetheless continued to function, and individuals who worked in mills, or remembered their operation, are still alive today (see Chéhadé 1973; and for an earlier shorter account, Thoumin 1936: 164–66). Despite this, studies of millers and milling in have been rare. In Lebanon, more than four hundred mills exist, often in association with working irrigation networks and mill leats (Chanesaz 2006). Away from the Orontes, Early Islamic mills have been documented in the Hawran and the Palmyra regions (Blanc and Genequand 2007; Genequand 2003), and potentially in the Amuq plain northeast of Antioch (Casana and Wilkinson 2005: 43, figs. 2.27–30).[10] In parts of the eastern Mediterranean, hydraulic networks have been studied extensively, perhaps most prominently in archaeological survey work in Iraq in the 1960s (Adams 1965, 1981; for further discussion, see Wilkinson and Rayne 2010), and in specific areas, water mills have also been extensively documented, particularly in Jordan, Palestine, Cyprus, and parts of Iran and Oman.[11] Less attention has been paid to the northern Levant and Turkey,[12] where the coastal mountains and medium-sized inland rivers exhibit extensive well-preserved remains of mills and related infrastructure.

## Water Mills in a Managed Riverscape

The longest inland waterway in western Syria, the Orontes was integral to the fortunes of the medieval and Ottoman Homs and Hama, whose agrarian economies were based on the surrounding rural lands. Most of the valley receives sufficient rainfall for dry farming, but the river waters have nonetheless been used to ameliorate its agricultural potential, in the process fundamentally altering its character. Unlike other rivers in western Syria, until the modern era, the Orontes had the peculiarity of maintaining regular flow over much of its length, and to a greater degree in its upper reaches, through recharge from the Lebanon, Ansariyah, and Zawiya ranges (Weulersse 1940: 38–41; Wagner 2011: 70–71).[13] As it enters Syria, the river leaves the arid northern Beqa' and passes into an alluvial plain that is bisected to the east by the two-hundred-millimeter isohyet, normally indicative of the limits of rain-fed agriculture. By the second millennium BCE, this stretch of the river had been substantially transformed by the creation of the artificial Homs lake (*Buhayrat Qattina*),[14] while the Antique or Early Islamic dam, partially preserved today to the north of the French mandate structure of 1936, still functioned until that date.[15] The dam channeled water into a major canal system, a twenty-kilometer-long channel provisioning Homs and its gardens, and two secondary channels supplying local villages. The gardens covered an area of about 1,000 hectares in the 1930s, when they were of primary significance to the economy of Homs (the gardens of Hama covered only about 260 hectares (Boissière 2005: 43–5). Water supply to the gardens and city was overseen by the head gardener, the *sheikh al-basatneh*, and distribution ensured by a network of sluice gates and conduits managed by an official referred to as the *shawi* (Boissière 2005: 83, 98–99). The upkeep of the dam can further be inferred by the remains of buttressing and repairs along its northeastern face, employing local construction techniques current in the Ottoman period that can also be observed in the watchtower built directly upon the central part of the dam wall.[16] Smaller premodern dams are located upriver of the lake at Hawsh Sayyid 'Ali and Tahunat al-'Amariyya (the location of a water mill), supplying two canal systems that irrigate large areas of fields supporting nine villages on both banks of the river (Na'aman 1951: 80–82). A separate canal system ran fourteen kilometers from the spring at 'Ayn Sakhneh at the foot of the northeastern limit of the Antilebanon (Na'aman 1951: 83–84) to feed the former gardens of the town of Qusayr before drying up completely in the 1970s.[17]

The Orontes is most commonly connected in Syrian literary and popular imagination with the *noria*, or water-lifting wheel, known especially in the city of Hama, but to the chronicler and minor notable Muhammad al-Makki (writing between 1688 and 1722), it was the water mills near his home town of Homs that exercised his civic pride. He recounts visitors to the city being taken on excursions following afternoon prayers to visit the banks of the river among the water mills (al-Makki 1987: 39; for discussion, see Guéno 2008: 28). The chronicler also provides us with several indications of the economic importance of water mills, linked financially to the major families of the city and undergoing repairs and enlargements in his lifetime (al-Makki 1987: 39, 86, 98). The vertical-wheeled mills located on the upper Orontes were on a scale and required an investment not seen elsewhere in Syria. A minimum of twenty-five of these structures are recorded on the river in mandate period maps, first occurring at al-'Amariyya, on the present Lebanese border, downstream as far as Rastan (Fig. 8.2).[18] In the 1930s, seventeen water mills were said to have been in operation on just one stretch of the river upstream from the Lake of Homs (Weulersse 1940: 59), while twenty-four were listed in the Ottoman *qada'* administration of Homs (Guéno 2008: 220–21 and n. 356), suggesting that most mills in the region were still operational at this later time. This concentration is unprecedented in and demonstrates the agricultural importance of a region that held the potential to grind more grain than could feasibly be consumed locally, even if all the mills are unlikely to have been in operation simultaneously. By 2010, the number had been substantially reduced, either through modern road expansion or lack of maintenance and flood damage. Downstream, the picture changes. As the river flows north from Homs, it is forced east by the basaltic W'ar massif and, reaching Rastan, cuts down into the underlying limestone geology of the valley. There is in this downstream region a concomitant increase in the number of noria, while by the time the river reaches Hama, water mills become considerably smaller vaulted structures usually possessing only two millstones and more frequently situated on races within the main river course. They are often associated with noria channels (e.g., Weulersse 1940: pl. IX, fig. 19) or built flush with the structure of bridges, as in the two examples at Shaizar. On the lower Orontes, after the hiatus represented by the marshy Ghab plain, water mills reappear, but they are smaller and less frequent in number on the river between Jisr al-Shughur and Antioch, where medieval sources record their presence at the village of 'Imm (Le Strange 1890: 457).

## The Orontes Vertical Water Mill: Tahunat al-Banjakiyya and Tahunat Umm al-Reghif

The character of hydraulic installations on the upper stretches of the Orontes is well illustrated by the two mills that were focused on in the 2010 fieldwork. Mill 2, *Tahunat Umm al-Reghif* (Fig. 8.3), and Mill 4, *Tahunat al-Banjakiyya* (Fig. 8.4), were chosen because of their good state of preservation and the evidence of architectural phasing suggested by initial examination of their external structures. The

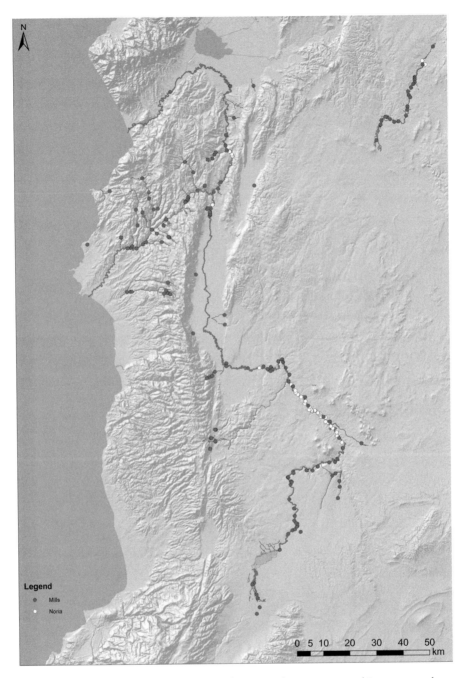

Figure 8.2 Water mills in western Syria documented using cartographic sources and satellite imagery (image: Elise Thing).

Figure 8.3 Mill 2, Umm al-Reghif, northern façade (author image).

Figure 8.4 Mill 4, al-Banjukiyya, northern façade (author image).

names of the mills are those used by the current owners of the buildings and local inhabitants and featured on the 1934 French map and in historical references.[19] Mill 2 represents a rare survival of an operational vertical-wheeled water mill. Conclusions are preliminary, but fieldwork has revealed significant new data about the mills themselves and suggests new understandings of the hydraulic networks to which they belong and their relationship to the surrounding rural landscape.[20]

The Orontes water mills in the study areas exhibit a high degree of regularity (Table 8.1). In all instances, they entirely straddle the current main channel of the river. Nine of the mills conform to approximately the same plan and, within only one to two meters of deviation, share the same dimensions. All are stone-built, using a combination of large ashlars and smaller blocks, primarily basalt, and employing lime and mud mortars and rubble interior wall packing. Larger ashlars and smaller elements in limestone were used in Mill 4, many reused from earlier structures, and sourced from the nearby classical settlement of *Laodicaea ad Libanum*.[21] Large ashlars were employed in the foundation courses of all eleven mills and formed the channels running beneath the structure and feeding the waterwheels. A head of water is collected by stone weirs in a millpond, ensuring a sufficient supply to the mill via sluice gates leading to the wheel channels (Fig. 8.5). The millponds still supply diversion channels that skirt the mill and feed local irrigation channels. All ten mills located on the Orontes were constructed with a contiguous river crossing, running above the level of the wheel channels and the weir. At Mill 4, the miller recounted that during his father's and grandfathers' custodianship, the millers themselves would plunge stakes and boards into the riverbed to control the river flow, create new channels, or block off old ones, allowing construction or restoration. The choice of mill site was dictated by environmental considerations (river gradient, flow, potential for flooding), the upper Orontes providing ideal conditions as it is subject to only minor monthly variation, reflecting increased flow in the period of snow melt in the spring months.[22] The surrounding fertile agricultural lands, proximity to concentrations of consumers in Homs, and feasible distance from other large markets also favored these locations, and the W'ar outcrop provided the basalt required for the large millstones used in the mills themselves.

The *jaghli* mills are built on three levels, comprising the lowest wheel floor, the main milling floor, and the roof terrace and roof chamber (see archaeological section-drawing through Mill 2: Fig. 8.5). The milling floor is entered through a two-meter-wide doorway in the southeastern corner and is divided in half by an elevated central platform running the width of the mill and supporting rows of stone columns carrying the central wooden roof beams. In addition to reused ashlars and column shafts, millstones and other roughly worked stone blocks are

Table 8.1. Upper Orontes water mills (numbered running downstream, south to north)

| Mill Number and Name | Condition 2010 | Length (m) | Width (m) | Raised Colonnaded Platform | Water Channels | Roof Tower Position |
|---|---|---|---|---|---|---|
| 1 al-Qantara | Half of building destroyed by road widening. Wheel pits survive. Abuts Ayyubid/Mamluk bridge | ca. 19.10 | — | Interior not preserved | 5 | — |
| 2 Umm al-Reghif | Good. Partially operational | 19.53 | 10.91 | Yes | 7 | Northeastern corner |
| 3 al-Qaddas | Ruined, building partly standing. Abandoned since 1950s | 9.82 | 8.86 | Interior collapsed | 2 | — |
| 4 al-Banjukiyya | Good, though structural damage has occurred | 22.4 | 12.15 | Yes | 6 | Northwestern corner |
| 5 al-Siddi | Reasonable. Milling floor in use as stabling. Modern house atop mill | 29.58 | 10.96 | Yes | 6 | Northwestern corner |
| 6 al-Khishani | Reasonable. Milling floor in use as cowshed. Modern house atop mill | 23.3 | 10.19 | Yes | 6 | Northwestern corner |
| 7 Tal Sheikh Muhammad (?) | Half rebuilt in cement breeze blocks. Rest in reasonable condition. Use unknown | ca. 20.20 | ca. 6.65 | No internal access | 4 visible | — |
| 8 Habub al-Rih | Structure mostly collapsed. Weir in use as pedestrian and motorbike bridge | ca. 16.35 | — | Interior collapsed | 4 | — |
| 9 Ghanto | Reasonable. Used as fodder store | 19.83 | 9.77 | Yes | 5 | — |
| 10 Unknown | Foundations of 2 piers and 1 wheel channel visible 2009. Completely destroyed 2010 | — | — | — | — | — |
| 11 Umm Sharshuh | Reasonable. Partially collapsed. | 19.42 | 10.78 | Interior collapsed | 5 | Southwestern corner |

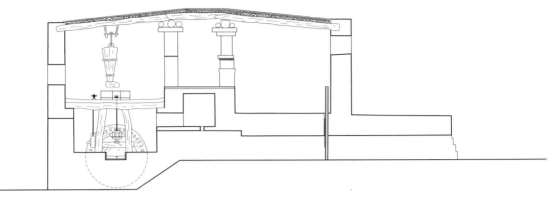

Figure 8.5 Mill 2: North–south section (drawn by Matthew Godfrey; digitized by Elise Thing).

incorporated in the structure of Mill 2, while Mill 4 features more regular, reused column shafts and capitals. The northern half of the room, the milling area, is divided into six sections separated by low concrete barriers, each of which would have housed a grinding stone (the seventh is in the eastern half of the structure added in a late phase of the mill's construction). Three millstones remain in situ in Mill 2, two used for grinding grain and one for bulgur wheat, although in October 2010, only one had the full wheel and hopper in place, with the latter suspended from the ceiling on a wooden frame. The last millstones in use were twentieth-century granite or composite stones imported from France or made in Aleppo,[23] but fragments of the earlier quarried basalt millstones can be seen in the vicinity of all eleven mills and not infrequently are incorporated within the structures. The miller knew of basalt millstones being made locally and attested to their former value; basalt millstones were similarly valued in southern and were transported from the Hawran to northern Jordan and the eastern slopes of the Antilebanon (Rogan 1995: 754; Thoumin 1936: 165). The substances ground in the miller's father's and grandfathers' time included grain for flour and fodder, maize corn, barley, bulgur wheat, chickpeas, and, on occasion, even salt. In the mid-twentieth century, all were produced locally in the intensively cultivated *zur*, or gardens, on the W'ar or in the alluvial plains to the east of the river (Na'aman 1951: 102–103). The southern half of the room allows for delivery and shipment of produce to and from the mill, a holding pen for pack animals, and access to the iron sluice gates located along the southern wall of the mill, which open and close the water channels running beneath the floor. At the eastern end of the platform, a shallow concrete-lined basin was used for soaking bulgur wheat to soften it before grinding, and a pump drew water from a channel running under the mill (see Fig. 8.5).

The wheel floor is accessed via a trapdoor into a stone-walled passage running inside the central platform of the milling floor. On its northern side, five low doorways lead to steps down onto the wheel-pit platforms. Small openings in the wall permitted surveillance of the waterwheels when they were operational to avoid close contact with the working wheels. The vertical waterwheels (three in situ at Mill 2, one at Mill 4) are of cast iron with curved, open paddles, following the design of the earlier entirely wooden wheels (corroborated by Chéhadé 1973: 252) (Fig. 8.6). The wheels are undershot (or low breastshot) and rotate on a horizontal axis. A river of the Orontes's magnitude and seasonal reliability is required for their operation, as the wheels themselves are partially submerged, requiring at least one meter in depth of fast-flowing water (Wikander 2000: 373–75). Two waterwheels were operational at Mill 2 in 2010, one running with the original wooden gearing system. This involves a wooden master face wheel mounted directly on the waterwheel,[24] meshing directly with a large cogwheel (lantern pinion) mounted on a vertical metal lay shaft, which then passes through the ceiling of the wheel pit to turn the millstones on the floor above. The pinion can be raised up and down to bring it into gear with the master face wheel and has nine teeth, while the face wheel has twenty-seven (or thirty-six), producing a gear ratio of 3:1 or 4:1, meaning that for each revolution of the waterwheel, the millstone rotates three or four times. The miller quoted production rates for each fully operational wheel reaching a hundred kilograms of ground flour per hour; with all six millstones functioning simultaneously around the clock for up to eight months of the year, overall

Figure 8.6 Mill 2, Umm al-Reghif: view of wheel floor with vertical waterwheels.

production rates were very high indeed. Somewhat smaller figures have been cited in relation to vertical water mills (which employed quite different technology) on the Zayandeh River in Isfahan, Iran (Harverson 1993: 167). The Syrian horizontal mills by comparison produced in the vicinity of four hundred to five hundred kilograms per millstone per day, around twenty kilograms per hour (Chéhadé 1973: 248; Thoumin 1936: 166). The vertical water mills also had a social resonance beyond the Orontes valley. In the mid-twentieth century, wheat, barley, bulgur wheat, and salt were transported to Mill 2 by donkey from as far as Hassiya and Tadmur (fifty and two hundred kilometers distance, respectively, to the east and southeast). Long-distance travel to mills is known in the case of Qashgai nomads in Iran, who incorporated the mills at Band-i Amir in Fars Province into their annual migrations, carrying up to a hundred kilograms of grain and flour on pack animals (Harverson 1993: 160). In Iranian Kurdistan, villagers from settlements without mills traveled long distances to locations that did possess them (Lambton 1969: 349).

The final floor of the *jaghli* mill consists of the flat roof terrace, which saw in the nineteenth century the addition of a small chamber (c. seven-by-four meters) reached by an internal staircase from the milling floor. In its initial configuration at Mill 4, this room possessed windows and may have functioned as a watchtower overlooking the Orontes bridge and the surrounding area (for examples of agricultural watchtowers in late Ottoman Palestine, see al-Houdalieh and Ghadban 2013). Periodic increases in Ottoman military presence in the Orontes valley at this time did not prevent security remaining a constant issue in the area, and it may be that the towers reflect protective measures or indeed measures taken by the Ottoman authorities to protect agricultural areas (discussed in detail by Guéno 2008: 199–203). In its final phases of use, the bridgeside windows were blocked, and this space is identified by the miller at Umm al Reghif as primarily domestic in function, a location where off-shift millworkers could rest, although guarding the mill against unspecified troublemakers remained a secondary consideration.

## Mamluk and Ottoman Water Mills on the Upper Orontes: Architectural and Documentary Evidence

Architectural and documentary evidence provide the principal components of a first attempt at addressing the chronology of water mills on the upper Orontes. Mill 4 preserves the most detailed architectural chronology, with initial analysis suggesting the existence of six distinct phases.[25] Construction techniques and materials used in its first building phase suggest a twelfth- to thirteenth-century date for the earliest preserved elements. Built in large basalt and limestone ashlars and lime mortar, probably on the same plan as the current mill, this first building is characterized by the regular lateral placement of reused column shafts in the structure and the fine masonry marks discernible on the blocks. It is likely that many of the other mills on the river also had Ayyubid, Mamluk, or even earlier antecedents, but of the eleven mills we examined in 2010, only Mill 3, Tahunat al-Qadas,[26] exhibits similar evidence of pre-Ottoman components. Located one kilometer to the southwest, on the al-Tannur tributary of the Orontes (now dry), this small mill possesses two vertical wheel channels and a large weir system, and is similar to mills in the vicinity of Hama and Shaizar. Mill 4 is alone in the group in possessing a late Mamluk or early Ottoman rebuilding phase (fifteenth to sixteenth century), characterized by the use of small blocks in the bonding and the reuse of large basalt and limestone ashlars. The final four phases identified at Mill 4 are likely to correspond to rebuilding at all the ten large mills in the nineteenth century, which saw the use of small, cut basalt blocks, rubble packing, and mud mortar. A lapse in the mill's upkeep may have caused the destructive events necessitating major rebuilding work in its northeastern corner during this time, but flash flooding was equally common and given as the reason for the collapse and subsequent rebuilding of the southern and eastern parts of Mill 2 under the father of the current miller's stewardship.

A preliminary assessment of Mill 2 has determined the existence of only three architectural phases, the first of which most likely corresponds to the final late Ottoman sequence at Mill 4. This high degree of construction standardization in the late Ottoman period (see Table 8.1) suggests that the same team of mill builders and a centralized planning process may be postulated, seen also in the addition of watchtowers and potentially in the refurbishing of *zur* irrigation canals in evidence downstream of Homs between Mills 9 and 11. When milling operations ceased after 1950, the buildings either fell into disrepair or were torn down,[27] but several gained new functions, as storehouses, farm buildings, and, in two instances, dwellings.

Historical sources do not directly discuss the presence of mills on the upper Orontes in the Mamluk period, but they do mention mills in the vicinity of Shaizar, a hundred kilometers downriver, where two smaller vertical mills survive today adjoining a stone bridge.[28] An unusual feature at Mill 4 is a large limestone ashlar lintel above the main door bearing a worn Mamluk blazon. It is reused from an earlier building, which Sauvaget connected to the Amir Sayf al-Din Manjak (d. 1375 CE), governor of Tripoli and Damascus. Sauvaget hypothesized that this once belonged to a monumental structure, a caravanserai or bridge, but then remarks that *un tel document n'est pas à sa place sur la façade d'un moulin* (1940: 9). The presence of a mill at this location up to two centuries earlier and the evidence for links to Ottoman élites less than two centuries later encourage the suggestion that such a document could indeed have had its place on the façade of a mill, possibly a mill belonging to the *waqf* of a fourteenth-century Mamluk governor.

By the sixteenth century, the upper Orontes mills were linked to the some of the wealthiest and most powerful individuals in and in some instances the imperial and provincial capitals. They featured significantly in the taxation assessments, the *tapu tahrir defter*s, although only one mill corresponds directly by name to the mills examined in the study: Mill 2, Umm al-Reghif.[29] According to this record, this mill was part of the *waqf* of the Grand Vizier Rüstem Pasha (d. 1561 CE), son-in-law of Sultan Sulayman I and one of the wealthiest individuals in the empire. The *waqf* was established to endow a *takiyya* (sufi convent) in Homs and a *khan* (caravanserai) in Hama; the record mentions five *ahjār* (millstones), and a value of 6,000 *ghurush* accorded to the mill. This does not correspond to the number of millstones of the current mill (seven), and it is unclear whether this was the first establishment of this mill or if it in fact was part of a preexisting Mamluk foundation. Earlier in the century, Murad Celebi, *defterdar* (treasurer) of the empire in Syria, endowed many mills (along with gardens, fields, norias, and urban properties) on the Orontes in both the upper and middle stretches of the river, including Umm al-Reghif, during the Ottoman administration of in the 1520s (Chéhadé 1974; Sauvan 1975). The renegotiation of this *waqf* so soon afterward to the benefit of a new governor of Syria gives an indication of the significance of its revenues. Other *waqf* endowment documents also demonstrate the close connection of mills on the river to the Ottoman ruling class: for example, the mill and village of Ghanto (Fig. 8.1: Mill 9) is included in the *waqf* of the mid-sixteenth-century governor of Syria, Lala Mustafa Pasha (d. 1580).[30] In the second half of the sixteenth century, the *waqf* of Darwish Pasha includes five mills in the Homs region, most likely in the same area, close to the modern Lebanese border.[31] Muhammad al-Makki discusses mills on the Orontes in the seventeenth and eighteenth centuries, noting the restoration and rebuilding of mills and the importance of rural land holdings and water mills to the fortunes of the principal citizens of Homs (al-Makkī 1987: 98, 197; Na'aman 1951: 91). Their increasing ownership by local notables may reflect the acquisition of rural landholdings by local officials and individuals observed elsewhere, such as in the *ghouta* (artificial oasis agricultural system) of Damascus in this period (Reilly 1992). This is seen in the nineteenth- and early twentieth-century court documents relating to the study area, which indicate the prominent role that families such as the Atasis played, buying and selling water mills on the river in tandem with large landholdings, often encompassing whole villages (Guéno 2008: 221–22).

## Water Mills and the Rural Islamic Economy

The different strands of data generated by the fieldwork and documentary investigation raise several areas of questions about rural economy of Syria through the medieval and early modern eras and highlight the particular role of the vertical-wheeled mill, or *jaghli*. The first of these concerns the chronology of milling technologies. The preliminary examination of Mill 4 suggests that this mill was built, or rebuilt, in the twelfth or thirteenth century. We were not able to determine evidence for earlier structures, although Early Islamic material culture was well represented in the neighboring alluvial plain, and historical and numismatic evidence points to the economic importance of *Jund Homs* in the Umayyad and Abbasid eras (McPhillips 2012: 695; Bone 2000: 152; Shamma 1998: 95–96). While horizontal mills appear for the first time in the late Byzantine or Umayyad period in Syria and Jordan, the vertical wheel is unlikely to have ever gone out of use in the Middle East since the Hellenistic period. An undershot wheel, as used in the Orontes mills, has been excavated at Ephesus, and this design is known from both Vitruvius[32] and in a pictorial mosaic from the Byzantine palace in Istanbul (Tölle-Kastenbein 1990: 164 and fig. 104). The only published instances of archaeological evidence are provided by Byzantine or Early Islamic vertical-wheeled mills associated with a dam near Caesarea in Palestine and a Byzantine sawmill at Jarash in Jordan (Seigne 2002: 208 and fig. 5; Ad et al. 2005).[33]

The investment required to build and maintain a large vertical-wheeled mill, and the revenues it could generate, ensured that these buildings were connected to important individuals or families, or constituted as parts of *waqf* foundations in the sixteenth century, probably reflecting a preexisting importance. A major rebuilding of the structure of Mill 4 may relate to this period, but most of the architectural evidence surviving from the other mills in the study is indicative of major building and investment under the later Ottoman Empire.

This leads us into complex questions of the relationship with nineteenth-century agrarian expansion addressed by a number of scholars in recent decades and corresponding to broader changes in the agricultural economy in nineteenth-century (Lewis 2000: 33; Quataert 1997: 843–44; Schilcher 1991: 173–78). Analysis of Ottoman and European documentary sources reveals that the Homs region was particularly significant for grain production, an activity that expanded in the later part of the nineteenth century (Guéno 2008: 218–22). This corresponded to improved security and transport links, most notably the construction of the railway through the Beqaʿ and the upper Orontes region joining Hama and the Bagdadbahn to the Damascus–Beirut line in the 1890s. Difficult negotiations took place between the Chemin de fer Damas-Hama et prolongements[34] and the Ottoman government concerning the planned route, but the company later admitted that one of its main priorities in preferring the Beqa' corridor to an alternative route to the east in the Syrian *badia* (steppe lands) was the increased flow in grain traffic to the port in Beirut that they believed it would attract (Eleftériadès 1944: 53).

As we have seen, two principal milling technologies occur in the premodern Islamic Middle East, most commonly defined as vertical and horizontal wheeled, the former exemplified by the mills presented here. Both technologies occur in the Homs region, and horizontal-wheeled mills were located on tributaries of the Orontes in the Jabal Ansariyah and to a more limited extent in the Antilebanon.[35] Horizontal tower mills still functioned here in the mid-twentieth century (Weulersse 1940: 59), including three "staircase" mills at Jusih, stacked atop each other on the same canalized stream (Thoumin 1936: 165), while several others operated on a twenty-two-kilometer-long aqueduct from the spring at Labweh to the village of Qa'a in the northeastern Beqa' (Spaven 1947: 112).[36] The horizontal-wheeled al-Asa'diyya mill, supplied by a large tank fed by canal, existed in the 1970s within the municipal boundaries of Homs (Chéhadé 1973: 251), and many others can be identified on the French mandate period maps (see Fig. 8.2).[37] The different hydraulic technologies were both successful adaptations to specific hydrological conditions. The smaller horizontal mill was directly related to village subsistence and was often situated on local irrigation systems within villages or irrigated village lands, satisfying the needs of remoter settlements for self-sufficiency in milling (Thoumin 1936: 164–66). Complex and expensive financial arrangements, often involving several parties, lay behind their establishment (see especially Rogan 1995). They were also frequently components of *waqfs* (Powers 1984; Reilly 1992; Jennings 1990), and their significance is illustrated by their role as the primary supplier of flour for Damascus, processing the grain imported from the Hawran during the French mandate (Thoumin 1936: 165). Smaller irrigation systems were managed at the village level, the *communauté hydraulique*, in the interests of local farmers and gardeners, and could encompass the networks of leats and millraces providing water to the horizontal or penstock mills (Métral and Métral 1979: 305, 1990: 395; Thoumin 1936: 165). This level of operation was well suited to the *musha'* system of agricultural land rotation, or joint ownership, that characterized many areas of inland Syria, including the Homs region (Na'aman 1951: 95–100). The requirements for establishing a vertical mill, however, and the subsequent profits that they could generate, were on another level altogether, and it is likely that the *jaghli* were part of a much broader regional hydraulic collectivity. They could not be operated without some degree of riverwide coordination, as synchronization of milling activity and water management across the twenty-five-plus large water mills in the vicinity of Homs must have been necessary for their successful installation, maintenance, and operation.[38] The strongly local character of late Ottoman mill construction in the Homs area, distinctive from those built, for example, nearer to Hama, further implies that specialist mill builders were active locally. The mills were owned by urban elites or belonged to important *waqfs*, and were often held in conjunction with large landholdings. At the same time, the local village irrigation of the *zurs* utilized associated weirs and mill-ponds, demonstrating their parallel importance to village-level hydraulic networks.

## Conclusion

The Orontes water mills represent a milling technology unique in the Levant. This was the most effective means of processing agricultural surpluses, particularly grain, before the appearance of motorized mills in the 1920s. When compared to the more common horizontal mill, their construction and maintenance required greater financial investment and concomitantly generated much larger revenues, a fact confirmed by their presence in some of the most important *waqfs* in sixteenth-century Syria. This technology can be traced in the Homs region from the twelfth or thirteenth century and raises the possibility that they had existed here since antiquity, suggesting the continuity of the region's economic significance through the Mamluk and Ottoman eras. They correlate with increased agricultural production and exportation from Syria from the late nineteenth century and the tendency toward private ownership of agricultural infrastructure in Syria. The Upper Orontes water mill is a masterly adaptation to the atypical hydrology of this river system, existing within a rural landscape characterized by an extraordinary diversity of hydraulic and irrigation technologies.

## Notes

*This project is sponsored by the Max van Berchem Foundation*

*The Max van Berchem Foundation is a scientific foundation established in Geneva, Switzerland, in memory of Max van Berchem (1863–1921), the founder of Arabic epigraphy. Its aim is to promote the study of Islamic and Arabic archaeology, history, geography, art, religion and literature.*

This chapter would not have been possible without the work of my project collaborators Marianne Boqvist (Swedish Research Institute, Istanbul), Matthew Godfrey (University of

Leicester), Cristina Tonghini (University Ca'Foscari, Venice), and Holly Parton (independent researcher). It precedes a full publication on the results of 2010 fieldwork. Thanks to all those others who have helped, either on fieldwork in Syria, or in the writing of this chapter. I would especially like to acknowledge Jalal and Ahmad Minbara, Shereen al-Fares, Lucia Khabbaz, Daniel Kassouha, Miriam Bshesh, Elise Thing, Paul Wordsworth, Robin Brown, Alison Mc-Quitty, Maher Tarboush, Ildikó Bellér-Hann, and Alex Bellem.

1. Word current in Levantine Arabic.

2. Wikander suggests a first-century BCE origin (2000: 394–400), while Lewis reexamines earlier textual sources that have survived in Arabic translation to argue convincingly for their presence in the century (Lewis 1997: 60–61).

3. Evidence for horizontal-wheeled water mills in the first millennium CE has been reported from central Syria (Schlumberger 1986: 4, pls. 10–11), the Hawran (Blanc and Genequand 2007), and the Amuq plain (Casana and Wilkinson 2005). In the southern Levant vertical-wheeled mills are attested at Jarash (Seigne 2002) and Caesarea (Ad et al. 2005), while drop-tower horizontal-wheeled examples are known from the Deh Luran plain in Iran (Neely 2011), Siraf (Wilkinson 1980: 129), and coastal Oman (Costa 1983; Wilkinson 1980). An expansion of irrigation networks is attested in parts of the Balikh and Euphrates valleys in Syria (Berthier 2001; Wilkinson and Rayne 2010).

4. Exceptions include those in the vicinity of Siraf and in Oman (Wilkinson 1980: 127–28). Textual references for water mills in this period do exist, such as the al-Faradis mill, located in Damascus near the city gate of the same name and mentioned in a *waqf* document of 1043 CE (Sourdel-Thomine and Sourdel 1972: 294).

5. The Upper Orontes Watermill Documentation Project was financed by a grant from the Max van Berchem Foundation and was a collaboration between the scholars listed in the acknowledgments and the Directorate General of Antiquities and Museums of Syria (DGAMS), Homs. The project was developed in collaboration with the University of Durham and DGAMS Survey of the Homs Region, directed by Graham Philip and the Rural Islamic Syria Project, financed by a postdoctoral grant from the Danish Humanities Research Council (Forskningsrådet for Kultur og Kommunikation) held at the Institute of Cross-Cultural and Regional Studies, University of Copenhagen. First field visits of water mills took place in 2009.

6. For discussion, see Weulersse (1946: 41) and Métral and Métral (1990).

7. The word is of Turkish origin and refers the channel leading water to a water mill (Barthélemy 1935: 114). With thanks to Marianne Boqvist and Alex Bellem for their help researching this word.

8. With the exception of a group of early twentieth-century mills in the Wadi Lejjun, central Jordan, which were built and operated by Armenian millers to supply the local Ottoman garrison (de Vries 2006).

9. Selected smaller river systems in the coastal Lebanon Mountains were visited to provide comparative data. Financed by a research grant from the Board of the Danish Institute in Damascus. Paul Wordsworth, University of Copenhagen, collaborated in this research visit. It was not possible to visit Syrian examples.

10. An ethnographic study of a water mill in the Jabal Qalamun has been published but was not available for consultation by the author (al-Maqdissi and Trak al-Maqdassi 2006).

11. For Cyprus, see in particular Given et al. (2013: 214–34); Egoumenidoul and Myrianthefs (2003); von Wartburg (2001); Lebanon: Chanesaz (2006); Jordan: Greene (1995); McQuitty (1995, 2007); Rogan (1995); Palestine: Ad et al. (2005); Avitsur (1960); Oman: Costa (1983); Wilkinson (1980); Iran: Harverson (1993).

12. For ethnographic and documentary investigations of Ottoman mills in Turkey, see Çelmeoğlu (2010); Donners et al. (2002); Yiğit (2011); and Sadler (1989).

13. Weulersse's detailed study of the river records its condition before the major dam and irrigation works of the 1930s and postindependence pumping of subsurface aquifers, resulting in a vastly changed groundwater regime (Weulersse 1940).

14. Suggested by the analysis of core samples of lake sediments, see Philip (2007: 221–23).

15. Strabo refers to a pre-Roman "Egyptian wall" in this area (Strabo XVI, 2, 19; see Dussaud 1927: 112–13). The dam has been dated broadly to the Classical or Islamic periods (Seyrig 1959: 188), but a convincing argument for an Umayyad date for the well-preserved dam at Harbaqa in central Syria (Genequand 2009: 15) adds weight to an early Islamic origin.

16. Abu-l-Fida describes two towers situated on the dam in the early fourteenth century (Le Strange 1890: 70), but the similarity in construction to late Ottoman stone buildings in Homs suggests that the current tower may have been built or rebuilt at that time. A report on the dam before its being obscured by the French construction notes multiple repairs and continued use (Brossé 1923: 237–38).

17. On the demise of the Qusayr gardens, see Boissière (2005: 21). The canal system could be followed in 2010; 'Ayn Sakhneh is now completely dry, but sections of an antique or early Islamic subsurface stone aqueduct were visible near the twentieth-century pump house.

18. Digitization by Elise Thing, University of Copenhagen. Maps: Service Géographique de l'Armée 1:50000 "Rastane-Mecherfeh" (nd); Service Géographique de l'Armée 1:50000 "Homs" (1934).

19. Ibid.

20. Subsequent fieldwork was canceled. For a more detailed presentation of the results, see McPhillips et al. (2012). The fieldwork was complementary to the Rural Islamic Syria Project (RISP), funded by a grant from the Danish Forskningsrådet for Kultur og Kommunikation, developed from an involvement since 2007 with the Settlement and Landscape Development in the Homs Region, Syria, directed by Graham Philip (University of Durham, Department of Archaeology) and run jointly by the University of Durham and the Direction générale des Antiquités et Musées syriennes.

21. Greek letters were recorded on two of the capitals in Mill 4.

22. See Weulersse (1940: 37), whose study predates modern dam and irrigation work on the river. The seasonal Wadi Rabiah could, however, provoke major flash-flooding events, and the miller described such an event in the 1960s, which caused much of Umm al-Reghif to be brought down. On the Wadi Rabiah, see Philip (2007: 220).

23. Chéhadé reports that millstones made in Aleppo were in use on the Orontes in 1973 (Chéhadé 1973: 255).

24. A space-saving technological adaptation differing from the separate pit wheel common in Europe and described in antiquity by Vitruvius (X 5.2) (see Fig. 8.6; Wikander 2000: 374, fig. 1).

25. See Tonghini in McPhillips et al. (forthcoming) for full discussion.

26. Preserving in usage the ancient name for Tell Nebi Mend, also used to refer to the lake of Homs by some medieval authors (Le Strange 1890: 60, 69–70, 468). Sauvaget incorrectly refers to Mill 4, al-Banjakkiyya, by this name (1940: 9).

27. The remains of Mill 10 were completely obliterated by road building between first recording in 2009 and a subsequent visit in 2010.

28. Referred to by Ibn Munqidh in the twelfth century (Yusuf 1985: 74).

29. Tapu Tahrir Defter 1026/1341 h., p. 39. For discussion of the Ottoman textual sources relating to the Upper Orontes mills, see Boqvist's contribution in McPhillips et al. (forthcoming). Mills were taxed according to the number of millstones and whether they operated for the whole or part of the year (Hütteroth and AbdulFattah 1977: 72).

---

30. Lala Mustafa Pasha Waqf (Mardam 1956: 92). See Boqvist in McPhillips et al. (forthcoming).

31. Vakıflar Genel Müdürlüğü, 599/36, pp. 3a, 3b–4a, 4b, 4b, 4b–5a.

32. *De Architectura* (Vitruvius 1934: vol. 2: 305–307; X.V.2).

33. These represent quite a different technology, involving small structures situated on sluices running from a dam and operating Pompeian grinding mechanisms.

34. Built by the French railway and bridge-building company, the Société de Construction des Batignolles.

35. For these regions, the study of Ottoman documentary sources is currently only at a beginning, but Ottoman tax records for elsewhere contain detailed data about the taxes levied on horizontal water mills. See Hütteroth and AbdulFattah (1977). For northern Lebanon, see Khalifé (1998). For eastern Anatolia, see Yiğit (2011).

36. The author has observed two surviving in good condition much farther south in close proximity to Ba'albak.

37. It is hoped that full study of the taxation records for western Syria will reveal more information about them.

38. An indication of a broader river management might be detected in the description of a canal supplying water to Jusih built by the Egyptian ruler of Syria Ibrahim Pasha in the early nineteenth century on the current Lebanese border (Porter 1855: 366). Ibrahim Pasha is also reported to have planned improvements of the maritime access to the Orontes below Antioch (Chesney 1838: 229).

# Bibliography

Ad, Uzi, 'Abd al-Salam Sa'id, and Rafael Frankel. 2005. "Water-mills with Pompeian-type mill-stones at Naḥal Tanninim." *Israel Exploration Journal* 55(2): 156–71.

Adams, Robert McCormick Jr. 1965. *Land Behind Baghdad*. Chicago: University of Chicago Press.

———. 1981. *Heartland of Cities: Surveys of Ancient Settlement and Land Use on the Central Floodplain of the Euphrates*. Chicago: University of Chicago Press.

Avitsur, Shmuel. 1960. "On the history of the exploitation of water power in Eretz-Israel." *Israel Exploration Journal* 10(1): 37–45.

Barthélemy, Adrien, 1935. *Dictionnaire arabe-français. Dialectes de Syrie: Alep, Damas, Liban, Jérusalem*. France, Haut-commissariat en Syrie et au Liban. Paris: Librairie orientaliste Paul Geuthner.

Berthier, Sophie. 2001. *Peuplement Rural et Aménagements Hydroagricoles dans la Moyenne Vallée de l'Euphrate, Fin VIIe–XIXe Siècle: Région de Deir ez Zor-Abu Kemal, Syrie. Mission Méso-potamie Syrienne, Archéologie Islamique, 1986–1989*. Damascus: Institut Français d'Études Arabes de Damas.

Blanc, Pierre-Marie, and Denis Genequand. 2007. "Le développement du moulin hydraulique à roue horizontale à l'époque Omeyyade: à propos d'un moulin sur l'aqueduc de Bosra (Syrie Du Sud)." *Syria* 84: 295–306.

Boissière, Thierry. 2005. *Le Jardinier et le Citadin: Ethnologie d'un Éspace Agricole Urbain dans la Vallée de l'Oronte en Syrie*. PIFD 214. Damascus: Institut Français du Proche-Orient, Direction Scientifique des Études Médiévales, Modernes et Arabes.

Bone, Harry. 2000. *The Administration of Umayyad Syria: The Evidence of the Copper Coins*. Princeton: Princeton University Press.

Brossé, Léonce. 1923. "La Digue du Lac de Homs." *Syria*: 234–40.

Casana, Jesse, and Tony. J. Wilkinson. 2005. "Settlement and landscapes in the Amuq region." In *The Amuq Valley Regional Projects* 1: 1995–2002, edited by K. Aslıhan Yener. Chicago: Oriental Institute of the University of Chicago.

Çelmeoğlu, Nurettin. 2010. "The historical anthroscape of Adana and the fertile lands." In *Sustainable Land Management*, edited by Selim Kapur, Hari Eswaran, and Winfried E. H. Blum, 259–84. Berlin: Springer.

Chanesaz, Moheb. 2006. *Le Matruf, le Madras et le Bequf: La Fabrication de l'Huile d'Olive au Liban—Essai d'Anthropologie des Techniques.* Lyons: Maison de l'Orient et de la Méditerranée.

Chéhadé, Kamal. 1973. "L'histoire du moulin comme institution économique, 1er Partie (in Arabic)." *Annales Archéologiques Arabes Syriennes* 23: 242–73.

———. 1974. "L'histoire du moulin comme institution économique, 2e Partie (in Arabic)." *Annales Archéologiques Arabes Syriennes* 24: 109–23.

Chesney (Lieutenant-Colonel). 1838. "On the Bay of Antioch, and the ruins of Seleucia Pieria." *Journal of the Royal Geographical Society of London* 8: 228–34.

Costa, Paolo M. 1983. "Notes on traditional hydraulics and agriculture in Oman." *World Archaeology* 14(3): 273–95.

Donners, K., M. Waelkens, and J. Deckers. 2002. "Water mills in the area of Sagalassos: a disappearing ancient technology source." *Anatolian Studies* 52: 1–17.

Dussaud, René. 1927. *Topographie Historique de la Syrie Antique et Médiévale.* Paris: Geuthner.

Egoumenidoul, Euphrosyne, and Diomedes Myrianthefs. 2003. "Trade and use of millstones in Cyprus during the recent past (18th–20th century)." In *Meules à Grains: Actes du Colloque International de La Ferté-sous-Jouarre, 16–19 Mai 2002*, 175. Paris: Editions de la MSH.

Eleftériadès, Eleuthère. 1944. *Les Chemins de Fer en Syrie et au Liban: Étude Historique, Financière et Économique.* Beirut: Presses de l'Imprimerie catholique.

Genequand, Denis. 2003. "Rapport préliminaire de la campagne de fouille 2002 à Qasr al-Hayr al-Sharqi (Syrie)." In *Schweizerisch-Liechtensteinische Stiftung für Archäologische Forschungen im Ausland. Jahresbericht 2002*, 69–96.

———. 2009. "Économie de production, affirmation du pouvoir et dolce vita: aspects de la politique de l'eau sous les Omeyyades au Bilad al-Sham." In *Stratégies d'Acquisition de l'Eau et Société au Moyen-Orient depuis l'Antiquité*, edited by Mohamed Al-Dbiyat et Michel Mouton. Bibliothèque Archéologique et Historique 186: 157–77. Beirut: Presses de l'IFPO.

Given, Michael A. Bernard Knapp, Jay Noller, Luke Sollars, and Vasiliki Kassianidou. 2013. *Landscape and Interaction: The Troodos Archaeological and Environmental Survey Project, Cyprus*, vol. 1: *Methodology, Analysis and Interpretation.* London: Council for British Research in the Levant.

Greene, Joseph A. 1995. "The water mills of the 'Ajlun-Kufranja Valley: the relationship of technology, society and settlement." *Studies in the History and Archaeology of Jordan* 5: 757–65.

Guéno, Vanessa. 2008. "Homs durant les dernières décennies Ottomanes: les relations ville-campagne à travers les archives locales." Unpublished dissertation. Aix-en-Provence: University of Provence.

Harverson, Michael. 1993. "Watermills in Iran." *Iran* 31: 149–77.

al-Houdalieh, Salah Hussein, and Shadi Sami Ghadban. 2013. "Agricultural watchtowers in Al-Tireh Quarter and 'Ain Qinia Village, Ramallah, Palestine." *International Journal of Architectural Heritage* 7(5): 509–35.

Hütteroth, Wolf Dieter, and Kamal AbdulFattah. 1977. *Historical Geography of Palestine, Trans-Jordan and South Syria in the Late 16th Century.* Erlangen, Germany: Frankische Geographische.

Jennings, Ronald C. 1990. "Pious foundations in the society and economy of Ottoman Trabzon, 1565–1640: a study based on the judicial registers (şer'i Mahkeme Sicilleri) of Trabzon." *Journal of the Economic and Social History of the Orient* 33: 271–336.

Khalifé, Isaam. 1998. "Les moulins, les pressoirs d'huile et de raisin et les roues à soie dans la Nawâii du nord du Liban au XVIème siècle." *ARAM Periodical* 10(1–2): 377–418.

Lambton, Ann K. S. 1969. *Landlord and Peasant in Persia: A Study of Land Tenure and Land Revenue Administration.* Oxford: Oxford University Press.

Le Strange, Guy. 1890. *Palestine Under the Moslems: A Description of Syria and the Holy Land from A.D. 650 to 1500.* Boston: Houghton Mifflin.

Lewis, M. J. T. 1997. *Millstone and Hammer: The Origins of Water Power.* Hull, U.K.: University of Hull.

Lewis, Norman. 2000. "The Syrian steppe during the last century of Ottoman rule: Hawran and Palmyrena." In *The Transformation of Nomadic Society in the Arab East*, edited by Martha Mundy and Basim Musallam, 33–43. Cambridge: Cambridge University Press.

al-Makkī, Muḥammad. 1987. *Homs de 1688 à 1722: Journal de Muḥammad al-Makkī.* Damascus: Institut Français de Damas.

al-Maqdissi, Michel, and J. Trak al-Maqdassi. 2006. "Une mission ethnoarchéologique dans le Qalamoun: le moulin à eau M2 de Yabroud." In *Mémorial Monseigneur Joseph Nasrallah*, edited by P. Canivet and J. P. Rey-Coquais, 23–36. Damascus: Institut français du Proche-Orient.

Mardam Bek, Khalil, 1956. *Firmân liwâlî Saidâ wa Shâm bi khusûs waqf Lâlâ Muṣṭafâ bâshâ wa zawjatuhu Fâṭima Khâṭûn bint sulṭân al-Ghûr.* Damascus: Waqf Directorate.

McPhillips, Stephen. 2012. "Islamic settlement in the Upper Orontes Valley, Syria: recent fieldwork (2009)." In *Proceedings of the 7th International Congress on the Archaeology of the Ancient Near East, 12 April–16 April 2010, the British Museum and UCL, London*, edited by Roger Matthews and John Curtis, vol. 2: *Ancient and Modern Issues in Cultural Heritage; Colour and Light in Architecture; Art and Material Culture Islamic Archaeology*, 691–710. Wiesbaden, Germany: Harrassowitz.

McPhillips, Stephen, Marianne Boqvist, Matthew Godfrey, Holly Parton, and Cristina Tonghini. Forthcoming. "Hydraulic Landscapes in Syria: Archaeological and Ethnographic approaches to watermilling in the Orontes Valley."

McQuitty, Alison. 1995. "Water-mills in Jordan: technology, typology dating and development." *Studies in the History and Archaeology of Jordan* 5: 745–51.

———. 2007. "Harnessing the power of water: watermills in Jordan." In *Men of Dikes and Canals: The Archaeology of Water in the Middle East*, edited by Hans-Dieter Bienert and Jutta Häser, Orient-Archäologie Band 13: 261–72. Rahden, Germany: Marie Leidorf.Métral, Françoise, and Jean Métral. 1979. "Maîtrise de l'eau et société dans la Plaine du Ghab." *Revue de Géographie de Lyon* 54(3): 305–25.

———. 1990. "Irrigations sur l'Oronte à la veille de la motorisation." In *Techniques et Pratiques Hydro-agricoles traditionnelles en Domaine irrigué: Approche Pluridisciplinaire des Modes de Culture Avant la Motorisation en Syrie: Actes du Colloque de Damas 27 juin–1er juillet 1987*, vol. 2, 395–418. Paris: IFAPO.

Na'aman, Anoir. 1951. *Le Pays de Homs (Syrie Centrale): Étude de Régime agraire et d'Économie rurale*, vols. 1–2. Paris: Sorbonne.

Neely, James A. 2011. "Sasanian period drop-tower gristmills on the Deh Luran Plain, southwestern Iran." *Journal of Field Archaeology* 36(3): 232–54.

Philip, Graham. 2007. "Natural and cultural aspects of the development of the marl landscape east of Lake Qatina during the Bronze and Iron Ages." In *Urban and Natural Landscapes of an Ancient Syrian Capital: Settlement and Environment at Tell Mishrifeh/Qatna and in Central-western Syria*, edited by Daniel Morandi Bonacossi. Studi Archeologici Su Qatna,233–42. Udine, Italy: Forum.

Porter, Josias Leslie. 1855. *Five Years in Damascus*. London: J. Murray.

Powers, David S. 1984. "Revenues of public waqfs in sixteenth century Jerusalem." *Archivum Ottomanicum* 9: 163–202.

Quataert, Donald. 1997. "The Age of Reforms, 1812–1914 (Part IV)." In *An Economic and Social History of the Ottoman Empire*, vol. 2: *1600–1914*, edited by Halil İnalcık, Donald Quataert, Suraiya Faroqhi, Bruce McGowan, and Şevket Pamuk, 759–943. Cambridge: Cambridge University Press.

Reilly, James A. 1992. "Property, status, and class in Ottoman Damascus: case studies from the nineteenth century." *Journal of the American Oriental Society* 112(1): 9–21.

Rogan, Eugene L. 1995. "Reconstructing water mills in late Ottoman Transjordan." *Studies in the History and Archaeology of Jordan* 5: 753–56.

Sadler, Serge. 1989. "Le moulin hydraulique à conduites forcées de Karapinar (Turquie)." *Techniques and Culture: Revue Semestrielle d'Anthropologie des Techniques* 12: 121–49.

Sauvaget, Jean. 1940. "Caravansérails Syriens du moyen-âge: II. Caravansérails Mamelouks." *Ars Islamica* 7(1): 1–19.

Sauvan, Yvette. 1975. "Une liste de fondations pieuses (waqfiyya) au temps de Sélim II." *Bulletin d'Études Orientales* 28: 231–57.

Schilcher, Linda. 1991. "The grain economy of late Ottoman Syria and the issue of large-scale commercialization." In *Landholding and Commercial Agriculture in the Middle East*, edited by Keyder Çağlar and Tabak Faruk, 173–98. Albany: State University of New York Press.

Schlumberger, Daniel. 1986. *Qasr el-Heir el Gharbi: textes et planches*. Paris: Librairie Orientaliste Paul Geuthner.

Seigne, Jacques. 2002. "A sixth century water-powered sawmill at Jarash." *Annual of the Department of Antiquities of Jordan* 46: 205–15.

Seyrig, Henri. 1959. "Antiquités Syriennes: 76. Caractères de l'histoire d'Émèse." *Syria* 36(3–4): 184–92.

Shamma, Samir. 1998. *A Catalogue of Abbasid Copper Coins*. London: Al-Rafid.

Sourdel-Thomine, Janine, and Dominique Sourdel. 1972. "Biens fonciers constitués waqf en Syrie Fatimide pour une famille de Šarīfs Damascains." *Journal of the Economic and Social History of the Orient* 15(3): 269–96.

Spaven, F. D. N. 1947. "The landscape of Northern Beqā', Lebanon." *Scottish Geographical Magazine* 63(3): 108–15.

Thoumin, Richard Lodoïs. 1936. *Géographie Humaine de la Syrie Centrale*. Tours, France: Arrault.

Tölle-Kastenbein, Renate. 1990. *Antike Wasserkultur*. Munich: Beck.

Vitruvius. 1934. *On Architecture*, edited by Frank Granger, vol. 2. London: Heinemann.

De Vries, Bert. 2006. "The water mills in Wadi el-Lejjun." In *The Roman Frontier in Central Jordan: Final Report on the Limes Arabicus Project, 1980–1989*, edited by Samuel Thomas Parker and John Wilson Betlyon, 271–74. Washington, DC: Dumbarton Oaks Research Library and Collection.

Wagner, Wolfgang. 2011. *Groundwater in the Arab Middle East*, 63–137. Berlin: Springer.

von Wartburg, Marie-Louise. 2001. "The archaeology of cane sugar production: a survey of twenty years of research in Cyprus." *Antiquaries Journal* 81: 305–35.

Weulersse, Jacques. 1940. *L'Oronte: Étude de Fleuve*. Tours, France: Arrault.

———. 1946. *Paysans de Syrie et du Proche-Orient*. Paris: Gallimard.

Wikander, Örjan. 2000. *Handbook of Ancient Water Technology*. Leiden: Brill.

Wilkinson, Tony James. 1980. "Water mills of the Batinah Coast of Oman." *Proceedings of the Seminar for Arabian Studies* 10: 127–32.

Wilkinson, Tony James, and Louise Rayne. 2010. "Hydraulic landscapes and imperial power in the Near East." *Water History* 2: 115–44.

Yiğit, Ahmed. 2011. "XIV–XVI. Yüzyıllarda Menteşe Livasında Değirmenler." *Sosyal Bilimler Ensitüsü Degirsi* 1(18): 97–155.

Yusuf, Muhsin D. 1985. *Economic Survey of Syria During the Tenth and Eleventh Centuries*. Berlin: Schwarz.

# PART IV

# Transience and Permanence

Movement and Memory in the Landscape

# CHAPTER 9

# The Architectural Legacy of the Seasonally Nomadic Ghurids

*David C. Thomas and Alison L. Gascoigne*

The positive role of nomads, in their multiple guises, in premodern Islamic Central Asia has often been overlooked amid the devastation associated with the Mongol campaigns and other nomad invasions. Accounts found in historical sources, which are largely from the perspective of urban-based chroniclers, ignore or downplay the significant contributions nomads made to rural and urban life and economic activity (Rosen 2008: 117; Wheatley 2001: 73). This "invisibility" is compounded by the fact that their archaeological imprint is often ephemeral: nomads are not generally known for their built structures, and the transitory nature of their campsites means that such remains are less likely to be preserved, identified, and excavated while more obvious and impressive urban sites are in abundance (Hole 2004: 67). The limited and portable nature of their material culture further compounds the difficulties in recognizing and dating nomad sites, while ethnographic studies of nomads highlight their complex and variable socioeconomic structures (Glatzer and Casimir 1983: 307) and, therefore, the perils of attempting to retroject simplified and generalized analogies onto the past.

The Shansabanid dynasty of central Afghanistan (c. 543–612 AH/1148–1215 CE), better known by its toponym, the Ghurids, is characterized as ruling over a seasonally nomadic society. The contemporary Ghurid historian, al-Juzjani (1970 [1881] I: 386), informs us that the royal court, and presumably a sizable proportion of their subjects, migrated annually between the lower overwintering region of Zamin-Dawar, "a prosperous district on the frontier between Ghur and Bust" (according to the anonymous author of the tenth-century work *Ḥudud al-ʿĀlam*, tr. Minorsky 1970 [1937]: 111) and its upland summer "capital" at Firuzkuh. This sort of seasonal migration was a common feature of royal courts in the broader

Iranian world, although Melville (1990: 55) emphasizes that for the Ilkhanids, it was "essentially an economic activity within the sphere of transhumant pastoralism," distinct from other seasonally mobile royal courts such as those of the Achaemenians and Parthians. It is notable, however, that the Ghurid elite appear to have had a more limited itinerary than the Ilkhanid Sultan Öljeitü, although the available historical data for the Ghurids is much more limited.

Firuzkuh is thought to be modern Jam, Afghanistan's first World Heritage Site and the location of the second tallest premodern minaret in the world (Fig. 9.1; Maricq and Wiet 1959; Pinder-Wilson 2001: 166–67; Sourdel-Thomine 2004). The sixty-five-meter-high minaret exemplifies the problem archaeologists have investigating Ghurid society: scholars have, until recently, had little other than ruined mountain fortifications and magnificent religious monuments to study. These structures, which were largely commissioned by the Ghurid elite, provide a somewhat incongruous and arguably unrepresentative data set for a supposedly seasonally nomadic society. Many of these structures, however, appear to be isolated, dotted around the mountainous landscape of central Afghanistan, rather than located in urban centers, thus signifying the inherently rural and mobile basis of Ghurid society as a whole (Ball 2002: 43–44).

In this chapter, we will consider the background to our understanding of nomadic societies in general before analyzing the Ghurids' architectural remains and the insights these provide into their society. We will then focus on the results of

Figure 9.1 The minaret and archaeological remains at Jam (photograph: Thomas 2005).

two seasons of fieldwork at Jam and illustrate how the material culture at the site has illuminated our understanding of Ghurid society in terms of mobility, the built environment, and supply networks in the hinterland and beyond.

## Nomads and Mobile Courts

The study of nomads has been dominated until relatively recently by isolated ethnographic descriptions, with few comparative studies considering the broader theoretical aspects of the phenomenon (Ingold 1985: 384) and their archaeological manifestations. Nomads should not, however, be dismissed as literally and metaphorically peripheral to past societies and economies (Rowton 1973: 203). In the mid-tenth century, the nomadic population of Iran reportedly numbered roughly half a million tents (al-Istakhri, cited in Rowton 1973: 205). Given their prevalence, it is likely that nomads were an integral part of the socioeconomic structure of the region (Lambton 1973: 107–110, 124), as they were until recently in Afghanistan (Rowton 1973: 204). Despite the lack of census data, nomads are thought to have numbered around two million, or 17 percent of the total population of Afghanistan in the 1950s (Michel 1960: 362 n. 7).

As with so many typological terms, the label "nomad" covers a multitude of flexible mobile and semimobile subsistence strategies and lifestyles (Cribb 2004: 15–22; Hole 1978: 130). The dichotomies between nomad and sedentist, agriculturalist and pastoralist, however, are misleading: these commonly used socioeconomic categories are rare in their pure form and should be thought of as opposing ends of fluid continua (Gilbert 1983: 106; Lucke et al. 2012: 122; Mohammed 1973; Rosen 2008: 118). Similarly, the intermediate term "semi-nomadic" is ill defined and overused (Cribb 2004: 19).

Cribb argues that nomadic tendencies are "manifested in varying degrees in a wide range of societies and communities" (2004:16). Consequently, he proposes a broad definition: "Essentially nomadism involves the regular migration of a community together with much of *its productive base* within a single ecological niche. This may occur between different environmental zones or within a single zone" (20, italics in the original). It is worth noting, however, that mountain, steppe, and desert nomads inevitably practice different lifestyles and employ a variety of strategies, as do those herding different types of domesticates: Hole (1992), for example, criticized Cribb's work (originally published in 1991) for focusing on sheep and goat herders practicing vertical transhumance in Anatolia and Iran, while largely ignoring the camel- and horse-herding Bedouin of the deserts and steppes. Nomads operating in close proximity to urban civilization also differ from those more separate from urban centers, and their characteristics and relationships with more sedentary societies are prone to change markedly over time, as may their material culture (Rosen 2008: 128–30).

The plurality inherent within the umbrella term "nomads," and the region's fluid ethnic composition, are evident in Ghurid military history—nomad (in this case, Ghuzz) desertions contributed to the Ghurids' defeat at the hands of the Saljuq sultan Sanjar in 547 AH/1152 CE (al-Juzjani 1970 [1881] I: 359), but the Ghuzz's presence in the Ghazni region in the following decades provided useful recruits and horses for the subsequent Ghurid campaigns in the northern Indian subcontinent (Wink 1991: 137). This fundamental change in the composition of the Ghurids' armies from a predominance of local foot soldiers, practiced in sieges of hilltop fortresses, to Turk cavalry regiments, better suited to engagements on the plains, was key to their military successes in the second half of the twelfth century (137–39).

During their ascendency in the mid-twelfth century, the Ghurids appear to have employed a variety of flexible nomadic strategies based around a mixed economy, seasonal mobility, and periodic campaigning in Khurasan and the northern Indian subcontinent. Unfortunately, most of what we know about Ghurid society relates to their elite. It is clear from architectural remains, for example, that Sultan Ghiyath al-Din (r. 558–599/1163–1203), and his brother Mu'izz al-Din, patronized the established urban centers of Harat, Ghazni, and Lashkar-i Bazar/Bust, despite the fact that their predecessors had sacked the latter two sites in 545 AH/1150–51 CE (Bosworth 1977: 115–18). The Ghurid elite, however, also appears to have retained a transitory lifestyle, moving between their summer and winter "capitals" rather than becoming fully urbanized.[1] It is notable that during the short reigns of King Shah Shuja' (r. 1803–1809, 1839–1842 CE), the Afghan royal court relocated from Kabul to Jalalabad during the cold season (Pishawar had been the traditional winter capital of the Durranis but was no longer under their control; Dalrymple 2013: 17, 216, 258). Even during recent times in Ghur province, the governmental center of Shahrak district moved to Kaminj (near Jam) in the winter (Kohzad 1954: 16). Other examples of mobile courts include the medieval "wandering capitals" in Ethiopia (Fletcher 1991), the Mongol court of Sultan Öljeitü in Iran (Melville 1990), the Umayyads in Syria (Borrut 2011), and the Mughals (Sinopoli 1994). Mobile rulership can thus be seen to be a feature of some dynasties across time and space in the premodern world.

## The Contribution of Nomads in Premodern Societies

As mentioned above, contemporary chroniclers largely ignore nomads (Lambton 1973: 107–109). A notable exception is the correspondence from the twelfth-century

Saljuq sultan Sanjar's *diwan* (administrative office), which refers to the people of the deserts and steppe as being the "most deserving of compassion and mercy" and states that their "trade and occupation result in an increase in prosperity and well-being, and bring benefit and riches to the people" (cited in Lambton 1973: 109). While the nomad origins of the Saljuqs may have contributed to this sympathetic attitude, the correspondence provides a rare appreciation of the importance of nomads to the urban and regional economy, and the symbiotic, if not always harmonious, relationship between the different sectors of premodern societies in Central Asia (Hole 1978: 134; Mohammed 1973: 98).

Nomads supplied essential foodstuffs and raw materials for the manufacture of clothing, as well as horses for the armies and slaves for the elite and the military (Lambton 1973: 124; Sinor 1990: 7–11; Szynkiewicz 1989: 155). In return, they received agricultural and industrial products (particularly metal objects), the manufacture of which was often but not always beyond their knowledge or capacity (Hole 1978: 147–48). Their flocks could manure agriculturalists' fallow fields (Johnson 1990: 281; Thesiger 1955: 317; *inter alia*), while on the broader scale, nomads could add significantly to a region's economic output by exploiting rough pasture and marginal lands that otherwise yielded little (Banning 1986: 29; Lambton 1973: 124).

In this respect, the apparently barren mountainous landscape of the Ghurid heartland had much to offer. Although the mountains lack extensive flat land suitable for cultivation, they provide elevated grazing lands and reliable water sources for horses, sheep, and goats and valuable mineral resources (particularly iron ore, lead, and antimony—Hafiz-i Abru, cited in Pinder-Wilson 2001: 177), allowing for the manufacture of the much-prized armor of the region (Bosworth 1961: 120).

## Nomad Archaeological Remains

The problematic nature of the archaeological study of nomads and pastoralists is well established; with the exception of their *tumuli* or *kurgans*, nomad sites are notoriously ephemeral, due to the short duration of occupation (Childe 1965: 81; Gilbert 1983: 107–108). When a campsite is found, the periodic reuse of the site often results in a complex taphonomy.

Hole (1978) and Cribb (2004), however, have done much to demonstrate that nomads do leave archaeological remains, if archaeologists have the skills to recognize them. This is exemplified by the results of fieldwork conducted by Sören Stark and his team in the upper Argly valley system, Ustrushana, in northern Tajikistan, a comparable environment to the Ghurid heartland (Stark 2005; 2006a; 2006b). The nomads' campsites identified by Stark differ from the permanently occupied settlements and associated cemeteries in the neighboring Aktangi valley system, in part because of the latter's association with high-quality glazed ceramic wares and slag and because the sedentists' sites are less isolated and better watered. The sedentists' sites appear to have been occupied during the late Samanid or early Qarakhanid periods (tenth century) to exploit local iron-ore sources. The devastation of the nearby Shahristan oasis by the Khwarazm-Shah (c. 609 AH/1212–13 CE) or the Mongols (c. 617/1220), significantly reduced demand for iron in the region and thus prompted the abandonment of the sedentists' sites, although more mobile subsistence strategies continued as is clear from the ongoing use of the campsites (Stark 2005).

## The Archaeological Remains of the Seasonally Nomadic Ghurids

In the eleventh century, Ghur was "a land of local chieftains" prone to internecine squabbles (Bosworth 1961: 119; 1977: 7). The highly fragmented landscape and society is reflected in the military-style architecture that dominates the documented archaeological sites in the Ghurid heartland and that forms what Holly Edwards terms the "fortified domesticity . . . characteristic of Ghurid culture" (1991: 90) (Fig. 9.2; Table 9.1).

Most fortified sites consist of dried-brick superstructures on stone foundations of varying height (Herberg 1982: 75; Lee 2006: 250). The stone foundations are often roughly laid, with twigs protruding in places. Despite their rather ramshackle appearance, particularly after centuries of neglect and exposure to the elements, many walls survive to over ten meters in height, and those of Kafir Qal'a in the Ahangaran (lit. iron worker) valley, northeast of Bamiyan, exceed nineteen meters (Le Berre 1987: 56–58, pl. 63). Few of these sites, however, have been excavated or securely dated; the unsystematic surface collection of ceramics at several sites, particularly in the Bamiyan region, suggests that they were founded long before the twelfth century and continued in use until the Mongol invasions (Le Berre et al. 1987: 782; Marchal in Le Berre 1987: 10).

Several scholars have argued that the lack of distinct local styles in these widespread fortifications implies a coordinated building program (Ball 2002: 42; Herberg 1982: 83). Many of these sites may thus reflect the construction of numerous *qusur* (fortresses) and fortlike villages during the first half of the twelfth century, attested to in al-Juzjani's *Ṭabaqāt-i Nāṣirī* (1970 [1881] I: 318, 331, 341).

The purposes of the complexes are equally uncertain. Defensive structures line several key valleys in central Ghur (Ball 2002: 22, fig. 2.1), with Kohzad (1953: 62) noting that such "strong points" were constructed at regular intervals between

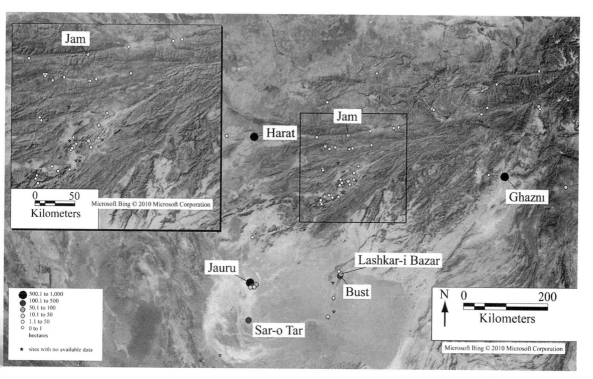

Figure 9.2 Distribution of Ghurid-period sites in Afghanistan (satellite image courtesy of Google Earth/Landsat U.S. Department of State Geographer; image date: October 4, 2013).

Taiwara and Ahangaran in Ghur province, possibly to protect the ancestral seat of the Shansabanids. Ball suggests that the homogenous nature and geographic distribution of the defensive structures imply that they were not built by localized chieftains to defend "individual valleys . . . against each other" (2002: 44). He notes the "lack of urban remains in *all* localities" in Ghur (2002: 42–43, italics in the original) and suggests that the "part-nomadic" nature of Ghurid society may explain the presence of fortifications in areas apparently lacking anything to defend: they may have formed a type of territorial marker and a means of legitimizing ancestral claims to land. Herberg, however, struggles to identify an overarching pattern or purpose to the distribution of these sites and concludes that they are the more or less organized reaction of individual family groups to unspecified external menaces (1982: 80–83).

Attempts to find a unicausal explanation for the distribution of the fortifications are likely to prove futile, particularly when the data set is obviously a complex and only partly known palimpsest. That said, the seasonally nomadic nature of Ghurid society seems to be key to explaining the location and purpose of many of the structures that, in the absence of "urban" remains, appear to reflect a concern

Table 9.1. Characterization and dates of the 91 Ghurid-period sites (data sources: Ball 1982; Lee 2006; Wannell 2002)

| Site Type | Pre+Ghurid | Ghurid | Pre+Ghurid+Post | Ghurid+Post | Total |
|---|---|---|---|---|---|
| Fort/fortress | 8 | 23 | | 1 | 32 |
| Tower | | 14 | | | 14 |
| Tepe | 2 | 7 | | | 9 |
| Isolated structure | | 8 | | | 8 |
| Unwalled town/village | 2 | 3 | 1 | 2 | 8 |
| Walled town/village | 6 | 1 | 1 | | 8 |
| Fortifications | 1 | 6 | | | 7 |
| Other | 2 | 3 | | | 5 |
| Total | 21 | 65 | 2 | 3 | 91 |

with protecting strategic routes through the landscape and grazing lands. The later, isolated monumental structures that members of the Ghurid elite commissioned are a different phenomenon but equally indicative of the state of their polity in the second half of the twelfth century.

## Monumental Architecture

The nature of Ghurid architectural remains changes markedly with the rise of the polity in the second half of the twelfth century to include "a remarkable range of civil, religious, and commemorative architecture" (Blair 1985: 83). Many of these monuments in Afghanistan are situated in isolated locations with few obvious associated archaeological remains. The example par excellence of such sites is the minaret at Jam, but other ornately decorated monuments indicative of significant investment in religious structures and institutions include two domed religious buildings at the important Sufi center of Chisht-i Sharif (Fig. 9.3; Wiet 1959) and a similar domed, octagonal structure fifteen kilometers away (the Gumbad-i Shuhada' monument; Franke and Urban 2006), the madrasa at Shah-i Mashhad (Casimir and Glatzer 1971; Glatzer 1973), and the small mosque of Masjid-i Sangi in Larwand (Scarcia and Taddei 1973). The Masjid-i Sangi is particularly unusual with its array of Indic decorative features, including lotus buds and vines, birds, and projecting lion heads (Flood 2009: 204–207). It is thought to have been part of a pilgrimage route followed by Ghurid sovereigns (Scarcia and Taddei 1973: 96) and may have been close to summer grazing or hunting grounds (Ball 1990: 109).

Figure 9.3 One of the domed religious buildings at Chisht-i Sharif (photograph: Thomas 2003).

## Jam

Archaeological data gathered by the Minaret of Jam Archaeological Project provide an interesting counterpoint to the monumental architectural evidence from the period and have considerably altered our understanding of the Ghurids' summer capital. The magnificent minaret is not an isolated monument, as some scholars previously thought, but the best-preserved structure in a sizable urban center. New data from a combination of field survey and detailed analysis of high-resolution satellite images have demonstrated the existence of a settlement of about nineteen hectares around the minaret, with significant areas of terraced domestic and civic structures, now largely buried beneath scree deposits, alluvium, and the debris from over 1,100 robber holes (Thomas 2013). The repeated plastering of the domestic structures and use of a wide range of colors on the walls indicate a hitherto unexpected concern for and investment in the aesthetics of more mundane built structures at the site (Thomas 2007: 134). The size of the site implies a population of several thousand people. Even if such a population occupied the site for only part of the year, it would still have exceeded the natural carrying capacity of the surrounding landscape, which has little agrarian potential. Consequently, the remainder of this chapter will focus on how the population was sustained by summarizing the material evidence for the site's relationship with its hinterland and broader trade networks.[2] The evidence from Jam serves to illustrate to some extent the relationship between the seasonally nomadic Ghurid elite (and their extended "households") and the wider economic networks of rural and urban Afghanistan and beyond.

Archaeobotanical analysis of flotation samples extracted from exposed sections in robber holes has confirmed the presence of thirty different identifiable plant types at Jam (Hald, in Thomas et al. 2006: 263–67). Although some of the samples may be derived from animal fodder and bedding rather than produce destined for human consumption, they include a wider than expected variety of crops, wild taxa, and fruits at the site, given its altitude 1,900 meters above sea level. In addition to the widely used cereal grains and chaffs, smaller quantities of pulses and a variety of fruits, including grape (*Vitis vinifera*), fig (*Ficus* sp.), apple and pear (*Malus* sp./ *Pyrus* sp.), oil seeds (possibly flax, *Linum* sp., or sesame, *Sesamum* sp.), and pistachio (*Pistacia* sp.) were found. Although comparable crops are mentioned in an eleventh-century legal document from Bamiyan (Scarcia 1963), it seems unlikely that the botanical remains found at Jam were all grown locally, if only because of the limited available cultivable land. Contemporary medieval travelers and historians frequently remark on the fertility of the lowlands around the mountains of central Afghanistan, which were renowned for their wheat and rice, grapes, pomegranates, melons, apricots, and pistachios (Bulliet 1994: 103; Le Strange 1976 [1905]: 410–16). Food surpluses, therefore, were seasonally available relatively close to Jam, if the Ghurids had the financial, political, or military means to acquire them.

Archaeozoological remains were also retrieved from the flotation samples (Holmes, in Thomas et al. 2006: 258–63). The assemblage, which consists of 1,426 bones (49 percent identifiable to species), is dominated by the remains of sheep or goats, with only a couple of identifiable bones originating from deer, gazelle, and hare. The sheep and goat kill-off patterns indicate a market or tax economy that was not self-sufficient. As with the archaeobotanical remains, Jam appears to have been a "consumer" site: its inhabitants butchered animals surplus to requirements at "producer" sites where secondary products were important. These were probably seasonally nomadic campsites similar to those found in the region today (Glatzer and Casimir 1983; Hole 2004).

The absence thus far of "exotic" foodstuffs or wooden materials imported from significantly different or distant environmental zones contrasts with the clear evidence for imported ceramics in the Ghurid material culture and the references to loot flowing into the royal court in al-Juzjani's *Ṭabaqāt-i Nāṣirī* (1970 [1881] I: 405–406, 430, 487–88). This partly reflects the (literal) consumption of foodstuffs as opposed to the less destructive use of artifacts, and the different degrees of perishability, preservation, bulk, and value of imported artifacts.

The high-status imported sherds among the ceramic assemblage—*mina'i* ware from Kashan, celadon from China, lusterwares and molded wares from Khurasan (Gascoigne 2010)—indicate that Jam was integrated into long- and medium-range exchange systems in the region, despite its remote location. The ceramics corroborate to a certain extent al-Juzjani's account of loot flowing into the capital from the Ghurids' campaigns, although none of the material could be identified as having come from the northern Indian subcontinent. The presence of a small Jewish community, which included a trader, a goldsmith, and a damask weaver, likewise indicates participation in the economic networks of the region (Hunter 2010: 75; Lintz 2008: 341–43; Rapp 1971: 92, 102).

## Conclusion

The monumental and extensive domestic architecture and evidence of widespread comfortable, if not luxurious, lifestyles found at Jam are the expression of the Ghurids' short-lived imperial success. The limited agricultural potential of Jam's hinterland and the estimated size of its presumably largely seasonal population imply a considerable degree of short- to mid-range importation of perishable and consumable agricultural produce. This produce was either tribute (from local Ghurid chieftains or client states in nearby Khurasan and Sistan) or paid for by tribute from around the Ghurid polity, or looted wealth acquired during their military campaigns. This inflow of tribute and booty was the life-blood of Firuzkuh and Ghurid society, enabling the elite to develop and patronize court life, enjoy a more sedentary summer lifestyle along with a sizable number of their subjects, and aggrandize key places across the rural landscape with monumental architecture.

As the Ghurids' military ascendancy started to wane, their access to external sources of wealth dwindled, and the agricultural production of the surrounding region was depleted by successive invasions and warfare. "Urban" life at Jam became untenable. The Ghurid elite, therefore, had little option other than to relocate their capital beyond the Mongol realm (as their Mamluks did in establishing the Delhi Sultanate [Kumar 2007]) or to disperse and revert to their previous seasonally nomadic lifestyle, centered on the small, autonomous fortresses scattered across Ghur. Their "urban experiment," however, and significant investment in both the construction and elaboration of monumental and more mundane structures at Jam and elsewhere challenge long-established assumptions about nomads' attitudes toward the built environment and the polar opposition of "rural" and "urban."

## Notes

1. Toward the end of his reign, however, Ghiyath al-Din appears to have favored Harat over his summer capital, Firuzkuh: he renovated the Friday Mosque, using funds from "the privy purse rather than the state treasury" (Flood 2009: 105) and was buried in a tomb adjoining the north side of the mosque (Hillenbrand 2002).

2. See Thomas (2007) for a broader discussion of the nature of the site itself.

## Bibliography

Ball, Warwick. 1982. *Archaeological Gazetteer of Afghanistan.* Paris: Editions Recherche sur les Civilisations.

———. 1990. "Some notes on the Masjid-i Sangi at Larwand in central Afghanistan." *South Asian Studies* 6: 105–10.

———. 2002. "The towers of Ghur: a Ghurid Maginot line?" In *Cairo to Kabul: Afghan and Islamic Studies Presented to Ralph Pinder-Wilson*, edited by Warwick Ball and Leonard Harrow, 21–45. London: Melisende.

Banning, Edward. 1986. "Peasants, pastoralists and 'Pax Romana': mutualism in the Southern Highlands of Jordan." *Bulletin of the American Schools of Oriental Research* 261(Feb.): 25–50.

Blair, Sheila. 1985. "The madrasa at Zuzan: Islamic architecture in Eastern Iran on the eve of the Mongol invasions." *Muqarnas* 3: 75–91.

Borrut, Antoine. 2011. *Entre mémoire et pouvoir: l'espace syrien sous les derniers Omeyyades et les premiers Abbassides (v. 72–193/692–809).* Islamic History and Civilization: Studies and Texts, vol. 81. Leiden: Brill.

Bosworth, Clifford. 1961. "The Early Islamic history of Ghur." *Central Asiatic Journal* 5: 116–33.

———. 1977. *The Later Ghaznavids: Splendour and Decay: The Dynasty in Afghanistan and Northern India 1040–1186.* Edinburgh: Edinburgh University Press.

Bulliet, Richard. 1994. *Islam: The View from the Edge.* New York: Columbia University Press.

Casimir, Michael, and Bernt Glatzer. 1971. "Šāh-i Mašhad, a recently discovered madrasah of the Ghurid period in Ġarġistān (Afghanistan)." *East and West* n.s. 21: 53–67.

Childe, Vere Gordon. 1965 [1936]. *Man Makes Himself.* 4th ed. London: Watts.

Cribb, Roger. 2004. *Nomads in Archaeology.* Cambridge: Cambridge University Press.

Dalrymple, William. 2013. *Return of a King: The Battle for Afghanistan.* London: Bloomsbury.

Edwards, Holly. 1991. "The ribāṭ of ʿAlī b. Karmākh." *Iran* 29: 85–94.

Fletcher, Roland. 1991. "Very large mobile communities: interaction stress and residential dispersal." In *Ethnoarchaeological Approaches to Mobile Campsites: Hunter-Gatherer and Pastoralist Case Studies*, edited by Clive Gamble and William Boismier, 395–420. Ann Arbor, MI: International Monographs in Prehistory.

Flood, Finbarr. 2009. *Objects of Translation: Artifacts, Elites and Medieval Hindu-Muslim Encounters.* Princeton: Princeton University Press.

Franke, Ute, and Thomas Urban. 2006. *Areia Antiqua—Ancient Herat. Summary of the Work Carried Out by the DAI-Mission in Collaboration with the Institute of Archaeology, Ministry of Information and Culture, Kabul, August–September 2006.* Berlin: German Archaeological Institute.

Gascoigne, Alison. 2010. "Pottery from Jām: a mediaeval ceramic corpus from Afghanistan." *Iran* 48: 107–51.

Gilbert, Allan. 1983. "On the origins of specialized nomadic pastoralism in western Iran." *World Archaeology* 15(1): 105–19.

Glatzer, Bernt. 1973. "The madrasah of Shah-i-Mashhad in Bagdis." *Afghanistan* 25(4): 46–68.

Glatzer, Bernt, and Michael J. Casimir. 1983. "Herds and households among Pashtun pastoral nomads: limits of growth." *Ethnology* 22(4): 307–325.

Herberg, Werner. 1982. "Die Wehrbauten von Ghor (Afghanistan): Zusammenfassende Dokumentation der Bestandsaufnahmen von 1975, 1977 und 1978." *Die Welt des Islams* n.s. 22(1/4): 67–84.

Hillenbrand, Robert. 2002. "The Ghurid tomb at Herat." In *Cairo to Kabul: Afghan and Islamic Studies Presented to Ralph Pinder-Wilson*, edited by Warwick Ball and Leonard Harrow, 123–43. London: Melisende.

Hole, Frank. 1978. "Pastoral nomadism in western Iran." In *Explorations in Ethno-archaeology*, edited by Richard Gould, 127–67. Albuquerque: University of New Mexico Press.

———. 1992. "Review of 'Nomads in archaeology' by Roger Cribb." *American Anthropologist* n.s. 94(4): 1013.

———. 2004. "Campsites of the seasonally mobile in western Iran." In *From Handaxe to Khan: Essays Presented to Peder Mortensen on the Occasion of His 70th Birthday*, edited by Kjeld von Folsach, Henrik Thrane, and Ingolf Thuesen, 67–85. Aarhus, Denmark: Aarhus University Press.

*Hudud al-'Alam*. 1970. *"The Regions of the World": A Persian Geography 372 A.H.–982 A.D.*, translated and edited by Vladimir Minorsky. London: Messrs. Luzac.

Hunter, Erica. 2010. "Hebrew-script tombstones from Jām, Afghanistan." *Journal of Jewish Studies* 61(1): 72–87.

Ingold, Tim. 1985. "Khazanov on nomads." *Current Anthropology* 26(3): 384–87.

Johnson, Douglas. 1990. "The mountain nomads of Iran: Basseri and Bakhtiari." In *The Improvement of Tropical and Subtropical Rangelands*, edited by Cyrus McKell, 275–87. Washington DC: National Academic Press.

Al-Juzjani, *Ṭabaqāt-i Nāṣirī*. trans. and ed. Henry Raverty. 1970 [1881]. *Tabakāt-i-Nāṣirī: A General History of the Muhammadan Dynasties of Asia, Including Hindustan; From A.H. 194 (810 A.D.) to A.H. 658 (1260 A.D.) and the Irruption of the Infidel Mughals into Islam, by Minhāj-ud-Dīn Abū-'Umar-i-'Usmān Maulānā Juzjani*. New Delhi: Oriental Books Reprint Corporation.

Kohzad, Ali. 1953. "Along the Koh-i-Baba and Hari-rud. Part IV." *Afghanistan* 8(4): 54–65.

———. 1954. "Along the Koh-i-Baba and Hari-rud. Part VI." *Afghanistan* 9(2): 1–21.

Kumar, Sunil. 2007. *The Emergence of the Delhi Sultanate, 1192–1286*. Ranikhet, India: Permanent Black.

Lambton, Ann. 1973. "Aspects of Saljūq-Ghuzz settlement in Persia." In *Islamic Civilisation, 950–1150: A Colloquium Published Under the Auspices of the Near Eastern History Group, Oxford, the Near East Center, University of Pennsylvania*, edited by Donald Richards, 105–25. Oxford: Cassirer.

Le Berre, Marc. 1987. *Monuments pré-Islamiques de l'Hindukush Central*. Paris: Éditions Recherche sur les Civilisations.

Le Berre, Marc, Jean-Claude. Gardin, and Bertille Lyonnet. 1987. "Données archéologiques inédites sur l'histoire de Bamiyan (Afghanistan)." In *Orientalia Iosephi Tucci memoriae dicata*, edited by Gherardo Gnoli and Lionello Lanciotti, 775–85. Rome: Istituto italiano per il Medio ed Estremo Oriente.

Le Strange, Guy. 1976 [1905]. *The Lands of the Eastern Caliphate: Mesopotamia, Persia and Central Asia from the Moslem Conquest to the Time of Timur*. New York: AMS.

Lee, Jonathan. 2006. "Monuments of Bamiyan Province, Afghanistan." *Iran* 44: 229–52.

Lintz, Ulrike-Christiane. 2008. "Persisch-hebräische Inschriften aus Afghanistan." *Judaica* 64(4): 333–58.

Lucke, Bernhard, Mohammed Shunnaq, Bethany Walker, Atef Shiyab, Zeidoun al-Muheisen, Hussein al-Sababha, Rupert Bäumler, and Michael Schmidt. 2012. "Questioning Transjordan's historic desertification: a critical review of the paradigm of 'empty lands.'" *Levant* 44(1): 101–26.

Maricq, André, and Gaston Wiet. 1959. *Le minaret de Djam: la découverte de la capitale des Sultans Ghurides (XIIe–XIIIe siècles)*. Paris: Mémoires de la Délégation Archéologique Française en Afghanistan.

Melville, Charles. 1990. "The itineraries of Sultan Öljeitü, 1304–16." *Iran* 28: 55–70.

Michel, Aloys. 1960. "On writing the geography of strange lands and faraway places—Afghanistan, for example: a review article." *Economic Geography* 36(4): 355–68.

Mohammed, Abbas. 1973. "The nomadic and the sedentary: polar complementaries—not polar opposites." In *The Desert and the Sown: Nomads in the Wider Society. Papers Presented at a Conference Held in March 1972 at the American University in Cairo*, edited by Cynthia Nelson, 97–112. Berkeley: Institute of International Studies, University of California.

Pinder-Wilson, Ralph. 2001. "Ghaznavid and Ghurid minarets." *Iran* 39: 155–86.

Rapp, Eugen. 1971. "Die persisch-hebräischen Inschriften Afghanestans aus dem 11. bis 13. Jahrhundert." *Jahrbuch der Vereinigung "Freunde der Universität Mainz"* 1–53.

Rosen, Steven. 2008. "Desert pastoral nomadism in the *Longue Durée*." In *The Archaeology of Mobility: Old World and New World Nomadism*, edited by Hans Barnard and Willeke Wendrich, 115–40. Los Angeles: Cotsen Institute of Archaeology, UCLA.

Rowton, Michael. 1973. "Urban autonomy in a nomadic environment." *Journal of Near Eastern Studies* 32(1/2): 201–15.

Scarcia, Gianroberto. 1963. "A preliminary report on a Persian legal document of 470–1078 found at Bamiyan." *East and West* n.s. 14: 73–85.

Scarcia, Gianroberto, and Maurizio Taddei. 1973. "The Masǧid-i Sangī of Larvand." *East and West* n.s. 23: 89–108.

Sinopoli, Carla. 1994. "Monumentality and mobility in Mughal capitals." *Asian Perspectives* 33: 293–308.

Sinor, Denis. 1990. "The establishment and dissolution of the Türk empire." In *The Cambridge History of Early Inner Asia*, edited by Denis Sinor, 285–316. Cambridge: Cambridge University Press.

Sourdel-Thomine, Janine. 2004. *Le minaret Ghouride de Jām: un chef d'œuvre du XIIe siècle*. Paris: Diffusion de Boccard.

Stark, Sören. 2005. *Archaeological Prospections in the Aktangi Valley System (Northern Tadjikistan) in 2005*, http://www.orientarch.uni-halle.de/sfb586/c5/2005/index.htm (accessed August 21, 2011).

———. 2006a. *Archaeological Prospections in the Argly Valley System (Northern Tadjikistan) in 2006 (1)*, http://www.orientarch.uni-halle.de/sfb586/c5/2006/index.htm (accessed August 21, 2011).

———. 2006b. *Archaeological Prospections in the Argly Valley System (Northern Tadjikistan) in 2006 (2)*, http://www.orientarch.uni-halle.de/sfb586/c5/2006/2006b.htm (accessed August 21, 2011).

Szynkiewicz, Slawoj. 1989. "Interactions between the nomadic cultures of central Asia and China in the Middle Ages." In *Centre and Periphery: Comparative Studies in Archaeology*, edited by Tim Champion, 151–58. London: Routledge.

Thesiger, Wilfred. 1955. "The Hazaras of Central Afghanistan." *Geographical Journal* 121(3): 312–19.

Thomas, David. 2007. "Firuzkuh: the summer capital of the Ghurids." In *Cities in the Pre-Modern Islamic World: The Urban Impact of Religion, State and Society*, edited by Amira Bennison and Alison Gascoigne, 115–44. London: SOAS/Routledge Studies on the Middle East.

———. 2013. "Fudging maps at Jam." In *Proceedings of the Geospatial Science Research Symposium GSR2, December 2012, Melbourne*, http://latrobe.academia.edu/DavidThomas (accessed July 8, 2013).

Thomas, David, Katleen Deckers, Mette Marie Hald, Matilda Holmes, Marco Madella, and Kevin White. 2006. "Environmental evidence from the minaret of Jam Archaeological Project, Afghanistan." *Iran* 44: 253–76.

Wannell, Bruce. 2002. "Echoes in a landscape—Western Afghanistan in 1989." In *Cairo to Kabul: Afghan and Islamic Studies Presented to Ralph Pinder-Wilson*, edited by Warwick Ball and Len Harrow, 236–47. London: Melisende.

Wheatley, Paul. 2001. *The Places Where Men Pray Together: Cities in Islamic Lands*. Chicago: University of Chicago.

Wiet, Gaston. 1959. "Appendice 1. Les Coupoles de Tshisht." In *Le minaret de Djam: La découverte de la capitale des Sultans Ghurides (XIIe–XIIIe siècles)*, edited by André Maricq and Gaston Wiet, 69–70. Paris: Mémoires de la délégation archéologique française en Afghanistan.

Wink, André. 1991. *Al-Hind: The Making of the Indo-Islamic World*, vol. 2: *The Slave Kings and the Islamic Conquest, 11th–13th Centuries*. Leiden: Brill.

# CHAPTER 10

# The Northern Jordan Project and the "Liquid Landscapes" of Late Islamic Bilad al-Sham

*Bethany J. Walker*

The widespread abandonment of villages from the late Mamluk period and the demographic shifts that followed combine to form one of the most important cultural phenomena of Late Islamic[1] Jordan suggested by archaeological surveys and noted by contemporary historians.[2] The extent of the settlements' shifts, the factors behind them, and their long-term legacy, however, are not understood. Moreover, in some cases, full-scale "migration" may be confused, in the interpretation of the archaeological record, with the "mobility" of rural communities characteristic of the period, exaggerating the extent and scale of these demographic trends.

The following chapter explores this phenomenon of human migration in rural Bilad al-Sham in the late medieval era against the backdrop of changes in land use, land tenure, and climate and the traditional mobility of peasant society, highlighting in the process lessons learned after four seasons of survey and excavation by the Northern Jordan Project.

## Assessing Settlement Decline in the Late Mamluk and Early Ottoman Periods

The mantra of the decline of rural Syria with the waning of the Mamluk state has been repeated with textbook frequency for many years in both archaeological and historical literature. While the perspective of Mamlukists echoes the fear of rural chaos that obsessed urban-based contemporaries, who were affected most directly by the collapse of Mamluk rule, archaeologists of the later Islamic periods have focused on disruptions in settlement during the transition from the Middle Islamic (Mamluk: thirteen to sixteenth centuries CE) to Late Islamic (Ottoman: sixteenth to nineteenth centuries CE) periods, as reflected in the survey record. In the Transjordan (hereafter simply Jordan) these changes are characterized by the abandonment of the majority of the large villages and towns for year-round settlement and subsequent resettlement in new ecological zones. The new sites are more ephemeral in their physical construction and smaller in scale, and appear to be associated with different patterns of land use. The extent of such settlement shifts differs from one region to the next, and it is not clear at this point to what degree they hold true for the Levant as a whole. The published archaeological literature on the topic from the last two decades has been reviewed in detail elsewhere (Walker 2011: 211–32) but can be summarized as follows.

*Archaeological Survey*

The more arid regions of southern Jordan, though comparatively lightly settled through the Middle Islamic period, appear to have lost population by the early Ottoman era. In the southern Ghur (Jordan River Valley) and northeastern Araba, archaeological surveys have documented twelve Mamluk sites, while Ottoman sites consist of only a few sherd scatters (associated with campsites and cemeteries). The walled villages of the highland plateau (such as at Tafila and Busayra) were abandoned, and settlement shifted to the wadis. In the Wadi Hasa, of the seventy-three Ottoman sites identified, only five were occupied in the Ayyubid-Mamluk period. The remaining sites were temporal and small (described in the survey reports as animal pens, caves, tombs, road stops, and campsites).

Changes in settlement intensity and distribution are most marked in the highland plateaus of central Jordan, where annual rainfall was sufficient for market-scale grain production. On the Karak Plateau, an estimated 87.5 percent of all Mamluk-era sites were abandoned; these were once substantial villages. Twenty-three percent of the Ottoman sites identified were newly occupied and consisted of isolated structures (such as watchtowers) and relatively isolated farmsteads. As in the southern plains, there was a general shift in settlement from the open plateaus for the wadis. Further north, on the Madaba Plains, 35 percent of all sites surveyed by the Madaba Plains Project were occupied in the Ayyubid-Mamluk period; by comparison, only 7 percent were identified as Ottoman in date.

The agriculturally rich Ghur was, ironically, affected the most heavily by these settlement shifts, with an estimated 78 to 86 percent decrease in the number of sites in the post-Mamluk period. What relationship this has with the collapse of the local sugar industry is not clear at this point.

The settlement of the well-watered northern highlands presents a stark contrast. The larger villages of northern Jordan generally continued to be occupied after the transition to Ottoman rule, albeit on a smaller scale. Recent regional surveys have documented a more or less continuous "carpet" of Late Islamic sherd scatters among these villages and between them and sites of undetermined function. Although some degree of population decline may be implied from the survey evidence, the overall changes in settlement are more suggestive of dispersal of settlement, rather than of significant population decline, and a more extensive form of land use.

On its own, the survey data are insufficient for explaining the demographic changes behind these settlement shifts, not to mention for confidently dating the changing patterns we think we see on the ground. A continuing problem for survey archaeology in Islamic Bilad al-Sham is our inability to distinguish Middle from Late Islamic coarse wares, namely, the omnipresent Handmade Geometrically Painted Wares (generally known by the abbreviation HMGPW) and their slipped, but unpainted, equivalent. HMGPW and plain handmade ware appear as early as the twelfth century CE (Johns 1998) and possibly as early as the late tenth and eleventh centuries (Walmsley and Grey 2001), and variants of both continued to be produced well into the twentieth century (Walker 2009: 55–56; 133, Fig. 56a).[3] The forms and patterns of decoration changed little over much of this period; it has been notoriously difficult to differentiate what is twelfth century from what is fourteenth or eighteenth century. This could potentially mean that sites originally dated to the Mamluk period might actually be Ottoman, exaggerating the scenario of settlement decline suggested by archaeological surveys. There has recently been a concerted (and collaborative) effort among ceramists working in Jordan, Israel, and the Palestinian Territories to stratigraphically separate these wares and develop chronologically meaningful typologies, taking into consideration regional differences (see, for example, Gabrieli in press).

*Excavations*

The results of recent excavations have supported and refined the basic trajectories of settlement change suggested by the surveys. In southern and central Jordan, many of the important archaeological sites of the Mamluk period were abandoned over the course of the fifteenth century. They follow the same general patterns: a gradual contraction in size and intensity of settlement coinciding with a shift from fully sedentary to seasonal settlement, then eventual abandonment. At tell sites, such as those at Hisban and Dhiban, the final phase of settlement was characterized by reuse of ruined structures, the construction of domestic installations (hearths, storage bins) in previously public spaces, and hastily built par-

Figure 10.1 Aerial view of Late Islamic Hisban. Courtesy of David Kennedy, Aerial Photographic Archive for Archaeology in the Middle East (APAAME).

tition walls throughout (Walker and LaBianca 2003: 447–55; Walker and LaBianca 2012: 717). There was almost no year-round reoccupation of such sites until the nineteenth century, coinciding with the application of the 1858 *Tanzimat*-inspired Land Law, which required registration of lands and facilitated the commercialization of agriculture in Jordan (Carroll et al. 2006) (Fig. 10.1).

Although fewer sites of the period have been excavated in the north, those that have been excavated suggest a continuity of settlement into and through the Ottoman period, but on a smaller scale, replicating patterns suggested by the survey data. The 2006 excavations in the historic village of Hubras, described below, to cite one example, document uninterrupted occupation of the village on a not-insignificant scale from the Early Islamic through modern times (Walker et al. 2007).

## Settlement Decline or Settlement Dispersal?

These regionalized shifts in settlement at the end of the Mamluk period cannot be isolated from the concomitant changes in land use. The archaeological evidence from surveys—the weighted distribution of surface sherds, installations related to agriculture and water harvesting, and field systems as they can be read from aerial photos—suggests that the abandonment of many of these sites was accompanied by a shift from extensive to intensive agriculture. Recent pollen and phytolith studies (Walker 2005: 95–105; Laparidou 2013), backed by textual analysis, describe important changes from export market–based to subsistence or local market production, and from rain-fed to irrigated regimes. The Late Mamluk-Ottoman transition in Jordan appears to represent a transformation of the physical and functional landscape. Whether we can call this a period of "decline" per se is a matter of debate, as is the ultimate meaning of abandonment of some (but far from all) settlements in this period.

The importance of changes in land use and land tenure to shifts in settlement has been highlighted in twenty-first-century case studies challenging the notion of settlement decline. In these studies, settlement shifts (described as either "nucleated" or "dispersed") were intimately tied to changes in land tenure and use, changes in the state structures that once controlled access to land, and the character of the local community (where such factors as communal labor and kinship ties came into play).

The tell sites of Mesopotamia, while chronologically remote from the study at hand, offer potential parallels for understanding the social processes behind such settlement cycles. As a settlement system, tells functioned as nucleated communities, which were supported by a fragmented but dense network of small fields and may have developed from the combined pressures of kinship and the need for communal labor and defense (Wilkinson 2010). They would have been, as such, an expression of social systems organized by communal land tenure. The field systems, in this sense, could be compared with the communally held farmland of the traditional *musha'* system, in which small plots were regularly rotated among family units to more efficiently distribute resources to all members. Ethnographic studies in northern Jordan have suggested ways in which organization of work on communally held land can affect field forms and distribution. Fields are clustered near villages, hemming in villages and preventing their physical growth; land is seldom left uncultivated. Tradition (rather than markets) dictates the kinds of crops grown, and production remains largely subsistence based. With the regular reallocation of fields among community members, there is little incentive for investment in the land; the result is limited effort invested in building and land development (construction of outbuildings, terracing, irrigation). The general land-use pattern is compact and agriculture intensive (Palmer 1999).

By contrast, dispersed settlement reflects different land management patterns and can also be related to differences in land tenure and use. Rural England's landscape today largely reflects settlement systems that developed during the medieval era. In western England, the Roman landscape of small, enclosed settlements supported by localized field systems was transformed by the agricultural revolution of the Middle Ages into a dispersed pattern of small hamlets and isolated farmsteads surrounded by small-scale open fields, the result of fragmented patterns of ownership. This process was fully developed, according to recent archaeological and pollen studies, by the fourteenth century CE. The landscape created in this manner was a continuous fieldscape. The change of landscape management that led to dispersal of settlement in England may have resulted from several factors: technological change (the shift to the eight-oxen plow, which required larger and longer fields), the fragmentation of large estates, and changes in land tenure that favored open fields (Rippon et al. 2006).

Privatization of land may also be related to the settlement dispersal identified in the Ermionidha of southern Greece, where distribution of former national lands and monastic estates led to the creation of small family farms over the course of the nineteenth and early twentieth centuries (Sutton 2000: 91, 100). Dispersal of population was one response (possibly of many) to the growing availability of land.

In all of these cases, private landholding and local control over land management (that is, less involvement of the state in local affairs, particularly the agricultural regime), together contributing to some degree of local prosperity, coincided with a phenomenon properly referred to as settlement dispersal. Under these conditions, large towns and villages were abandoned as residents resettled in smaller, more dispersed locales. There is no demonstrable demographic decline, simply a restructuring of settlement favoring smaller, interdependent villages and subvillages. Interdependence and intersettlement, intraregional communication worked to maintain a sense of community that transcended discrete village borders or particular landscape features. In her thought-provoking study of roads and pathways in the northern Troodos of Cyprus, Gibson illustrates ways in which these routes were "intertwined in a series of demographic and economic changes that altered interaction" in the seventeenth and eighteenth centuries CE (2007: 77). These routes gave coherence to a rural landscape transformed by the abandonment of villages and resettlement of entire communities in new locations, as villagers continued to use their old fields, orchards, and churches (76).

The purely archaeological correlates of communal land tenure (associated, in this model, with nucleation) and privatized tenure (identified with dispersed settlement) should be distinctly different. If ethnographic analogies for *musha'* lands reflect similar patterns in the late medieval era—with limited investment in land and regular rotation of plots—then possible archaeological correlates of communal land tenure should be the lack of field scatters (as hand manuring of fields, where such practice was traditional, would be limited) and field walls and outbuildings; low-intensity agriculture; and large tracts of cropped land alternating with tracts of fallow land (Walker 2008: 97; Wilkinson 2010: 60). Private ownership, on the other hand, could take the form of patchwork patterns of smaller fields and continuous cropping, extensive sherd scatters, the presence of agricultural installations, high-intensity agriculture, and well-traveled routes and paths between occupied and abandoned sites (Walker 2008: 97).

## Liquid Landscapes and Historical Demography

It is one thing to observe changes in settlement distribution in the archaeological record; it is an entirely different matter to describe the process or sufficiently identify the factor(s) that triggered human migration. On its own, the archaeological record is not equipped to explain, in a satisfactorily comprehensive manner, the cultural and communal structures underlying movements of peoples in their natural (and socially constructed) landscapes. The concern with migration in and out of villages has generated much scholarship in the disciplines of historical demography and migration studies. The myth of the "immobile village" has been convincingly debunked for Ottoman Palestine (Singer 1992; Singer 1994), Ottoman Cyprus (Given 2000; Gibson 2007), Venetian and Ottoman-era Greece (Sutton 2000; Forbes 2007), and sixteenth- to seventeenth-century Spain (Vassberg 1996). These studies collectively describe normative patterns of rural migration as reflected in the demographically relevant documentary sources of the period (tax registers and censuses, travelers' accounts, land registers, church and monastery records, court files). They describe a range of activities that kept villagers on the move on a daily and seasonal basis and the factors behind communally accepted migrations to other settlements.

In interpreting the social mechanisms behind the abandonment of settlements, we need to distinguish between two distinctly different patterns of mobility: normative migration and disruptive migration. Temporary migration is a natural component of the cycle of peasant life, providing manpower during labor-intensive seasons, such as the grain harvest, the fruit-picking season, and the fall preparation of soils before the winter rains begin (Singer 1992: 49; Mukahala 1992: 247). During these times, peasants, who often live at some distance from their fields, relocate for short periods to other farms and villages or reside seasonally in makeshift housing at the edge of fields. Short-term migration is also one of the few outlets peasants have traditionally had to escape disaster, man-made and natural. The Mamluk-era chroniclers regularly describe the departure of entire village communities during times of armed conflict, drought, and flood. These were, however, almost always short-term moves; migrants usually returned home after the crisis had passed and rebuilt their lives (Walker 2011: 211–12). Many elements of the social life of traditional peasant society required mobility: daily commutes to the fields from villages, annual festivals and markets, pilgrimage, the use of shared facilities (mills, olive presses), the travel of herders and craftsmen, and visitation of former homelands and places of worship and nostalgic places (Given 2000: 227; Gibson 2007: 76). This kind of mobility reinforced the community, and without it, communal ties would dissolve. The rural landscape was full of motion; people were constantly on the move.

Permanent migration can be normative or disruptive, either reinforcing or dissolving the community. Peasants left their homes for good for a variety of reasons, but many of them were political: the violence of a state official who continued to abuse them, insupportable taxes, lack of security and justice (Walker 2011: 212). Recent ethnographic and historical studies of Ottoman Greece have highlighted the roles that labor (for example, the diversification of maritime activities and commercialization of agriculture) and kinship (as entire family groups make the collective decision to relocate) played historically in the abandonment of villages (Sutton 2000; Forbes 2007; see note 2). The full-scale abandonment of one village for another did not necessarily disrupt communal life, particularly if decisions were made collectively and contact was maintained with the former "homeland." Certain kinds of permanent migration were fully normative. Contemporary Arabic texts support this image of a highly mobile rural population in the Mamluk period, where individuals or entire communities relocated without disrupting family ties (Walker 2013).[4] By contrast, the abandonment of groups of settlements, leading to the depopulation of a region, is a disruptive form of permanent migration that should leave a greater trace in the archaeological record. Settlement dispersal and regional migration are, then, different forms of permanent migration that might be conflated in survey data.

Can we effectively distinguish normative from disruptive migrations in the archaeological record? Seasonal migration supporting traditional agricultural work is transient, cyclical, and undisruptive. It leaves no trace in the written record and only the slightest one archaeologically, in the form of field shelters, goat fields, large mills, and olive and grape presses—as built structures or rock-cut installations, watchtowers in orchards and vineyards, and ad hoc inscriptions.[5] Abandonment of one village for another might leave a different pattern on the ground. A variety of settlement forms—keeping in mind that the classical village is only one of them—punctuated the rural landscape of southern Greece in the Ottoman period: small, outlying settlements; scattered housing; work stations; seasonal and exploratory settlements; dispersed homesteads; abandoned villages; and newly created ones (Sutton 2000: 105). In premodern Cyprus, seasonal settlements might be recognized archaeologically by their small, widely spaced structures; clusters of threshing floors; and the absence of communal facilities (Given 2000: 217–18). A site's function could, of course, change with time if occupied on a full-time basis at one point of its history and only seasonally at another. In short, there is an ambiguity in the way seasonal, permanent, fully abandoned, and relocated settlements appear in the archaeological record.

In Ottoman archaeology, heavy use is made today of contemporary Turkish and Arabic documentary and narrative sources—tax registers and land registration files, Shariʿa court registers, travelers' accounts—in an effort to better describe settlement types and locations, document changes in land use, and quantify changes in populations and rural productivity. Some of the same sources are also available for the Mamluk period. The sixteenth-century tax registers are most useful, however, as they list different categories of settlements and of agricultural land and make oblique reference to who owns what kinds of land.[6] The challenge in reconciling such documents to the archaeological record lies in the terminology used by contemporary tax collectors and jurists in describing settlement and land types (see Table 10.1). Our knowledge of the function of off-site features and the ability to identify and describe nonvillage settlement types are not refined enough at this point to associate the land and settlement categories of contemporaries to their archaeological remains. The most difficult terms in this regard are that of the *khirba*, technically a "ruin" (understood as an abandoned settlement), and *mazraʿa*, which is usually defined as a plot of cultivated land associated with an abandoned settlement or a seasonal or isolated settlement (such as a farmstead).

## Rural Migration and Privatization of Land in Late Mamluk Jordan

A narrative that accounts for changes in settlement in late Mamluk Jordan can be compiled through an integrated reading of both textual and archaeological sources. In my own work, I have relied on a range of Mamluk- and early Ottoman-era documentary and narrative sources that are most directly concerned with where people

Table 10.1. Arabic terms found in medieval and Ottoman texts

| Settlement Forms | Categories of Land |
|---|---|
| *madīna* – town | *arḍ/arāḍi* – (farm)land |
| *qarya* – village | *qiṭʿat arḍ* – piece of land |
| *ḍayʿa* – estate, hamlet | *karm* – vineyard, orchard |
| *kafr* – farmstead | *bustān* – garden |
| *al-balad* – countryside, village | *zirāʿa* – farm, farmland, field |
| *khirba* – ruins (of a village), an abandoned village | *filāḥa* – farmland |
| *mazrāʿa* – isolated plot of land (what is left of an abandoned village) | *marʿ* – pasture |
| | *shajarāt* – trees (an orchard) |
| | *mazrāʿa* – field under cultivation |

live, how they use their land, and who owns what types of land. They consist of those loosely economic in function but produced by legal institutions (Shariʿa courts), which include *waqfiyyat*, *fatwa*s, and *sijillat*, the personal papers of judges, and charters; those generated by specifically economic institutions, namely, the tax bureaus (*defter*s); and narrative sources not specifically economic in content but nonetheless informative about rural economic life, such as travelers' accounts, local chronicles, and agricultural manuals. For the Mamluk period, the *waqfiyyat* have proven invaluable for their descriptions of villages, associated settlements, and village land; the kinds of crops grown; how water and land was managed; and what buildings, houses, and lands had become derelict. The Mamluk *waqfiyyat* and early Ottoman tax registers, moreover, list properties that were, at least at one point, in private hands. In the absence of titles to land (the St. Catherine's deeds are a rare exception), they are our best textual evidence for the privatization of land in the fifteenth century.

These sources, and the archaeological record against which they are gauged, suggest a close relationship between the abandonment of settlements from the fifteenth century and the greater availability of land for rural elites through the quasilegal sale of state lands to them by Mamluk authorities. With the collapse of the Mamluk state and the industries and infrastructure that it supported, agriculture reverted to a more diversified and subsistence (or local market-oriented) production, and populations left large settlements for smaller ones, dispersed throughout the countryside. This latter phenomenon appears to have been most marked in those regions of Jordan where rainfall was just enough, or below, the threshold for dry farming of grains. The generally lower rainfall and repeated years of drought in the fifteenth century made this kind of agriculture unfeasible for most communities, which appear to have shifted to small-scale agriculture in irrigated plots, now increasingly held in tenure by local entrepreneurs (Walker 2011: 211–32).

## The Northern Jordan Project

It was, in part, in an effort to test this narrative "on the ground" by investigating fluctuations of settlement in the highlands north of Irbid and comparing this region to central and southern Jordan, that the Northern Jordan Project (NJP) was launched in 2003 (Walker 2005) (Fig. 10.2). Each season a different village and its hinterland have been the focus of archaeological fieldwork, which is combined with archival, ethnographic, architectural, and environmental analysis. The parallel studies are designed to help differentiate human factors from environmental ones that may have contributed to the abatement of settlement in the Late Islamic

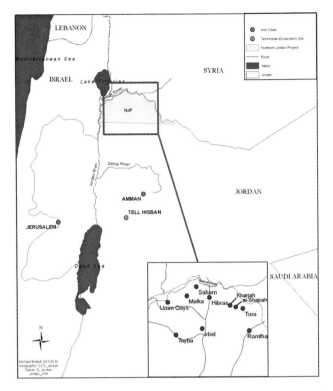

Figure 10.2 Map of Northern Jordan Project study area. Courtesy Michael Brandt, Missouri State University.

period. The frame of reference for the project is that of political ecology, which is concerned with that nexus where state control (land management policies, market pressures, land tenure) and local practice (land use, settlement patterns, and water management) intersect. Four seasons of survey and excavation, which have now completed a transect of all the major microenvironments of the northern highlands, have reinforced the picture of settlement continuity in this region of Jordan, as well as revealed a variety of ways villages can "disappear" from the landscape. Two examples are briefly cited here.

The migration pattern behind the village of Hubras (Fig. 10.3) could be called a case of "change of place within a space." Excavations in 2006 revealed an excellent example of occupational continuity through the Islamic periods. While there is evidence of Byzantine construction elsewhere in modern Hubras, the core of the historic village appears not to have been founded until the construction of the mosque (still standing today) in the Early Islamic period. It is possible that most of the population may have migrated there during the Abbasid period from nearby Abila, the Decapolis and an early Christian town. Environmental studies suggest that the

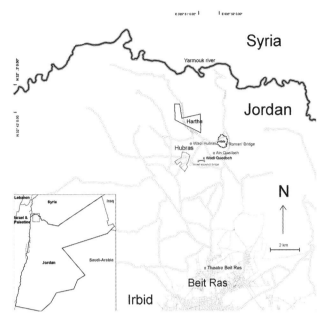

Figure 10.3 Map of northern Jordan, showing the proximity of Abila, Hartha, and Hubras. (Courtesy of Prof. Bernhard Lucke, Erlangen University).

local water supply, ʿAyn Quweilbeh, went dry at that point, and the residents migrated to the nearest available water source, ʿAyn Hubras. The borders among villages in this region have long been blurred: in the Tanzimat era, the lands of Hartha, the village adjacent to the site of Abila, were subsumed by that of Hubras (Walker et al. 2007; Lucke et al. 2012). It is a pattern rather common in Syria: entire communities leave one settlement for another or relocate to a new location while maintaining their old lands.[7] Fieldwork in the Bani Kinanah District, to which Abila and Hubras belong, suggests continuity of settlement on the regional level, with shifts of settlement locally and marked changes in population density overall.

The 2012 survey of the villages of al-Kharja and al-Shajra and their hinterlands revealed different patterns of migration. A section of the western watershed of the upper Wadi Shallala appears to have been abandoned for the opposite side of the wadi by the Abbasid period, in a shift of settlement possibly related to the differences in the drainage systems and soil qualities of the two watersheds and changes in land use.[8] The settlement clusters that developed on the east bank during the Early and Middle Islamic periods, which were characterized by large villages and their satellites, gave way to a more dispersed pattern of settlement and land use after the fourteenth century CE, as has been identified in other regions of Jordan.

## Conclusion

The settlement shifts of the late Mamluk period in Jordan represent a complex phenomenon in which changes in state systems, land tenure and use, and climate all contributed to settlement abandonment. The abandonment of sites in this period, however, reveals distinct regionalisms and made possible the establishment of new, smaller settlements. What has long been described as widespread abandonment of villages and the beginning of the long decline of the rural economy should now be reexamined as a period of settlement dispersal, in which new opportunities in land management and community decision making may have come into play. To what degree these patterns held true for other areas of the Levant, and if the responses to the same impulses by communities outside Jordan were comparable, are important questions worth future investigation.

## Notes

1. "Late Islamic" is a cultural-historical term referring to the material culture of the Levant between roughly 1400 and 1800 CE. It is in wide circulation today among Islamic archaeologists working in Bilad al-Sham (Whitcomb 1992).

2. The term "liquid landscapes" was first coined by Susan Sutton to describe the normative kinds of mobility that characterized the human landscape of early modern Greece as a result of a confluence of political, social, and economic forces (Sutton 2000). It has since become a staple term in both Ottoman archaeology and historiography to describe the parameters of acceptable rural mobility (Forbes 2007).

3. Handmade pottery, in a variety of plain, plain-slipped, and slipped and painted designs, characterizes the ceramic assemblages of northern Jordan and parts of Palestine in the Late Ottoman and British Mandate periods (Crowfoot 1932; Mershen 1985). Red-painted handmade pottery of this sort, such as Palestinian Sinjil ware, continued to be produced as late as the 1980s in the Nablus region (Salem 1999). The range of forms (basins and medium-sized, two-handled jars) and fabric (friable and coarse, frequently incompletely fired, and including much quartzite, grog, and straw) of the late nineteenth-century and early twentieth-century handmade pottery parallels that of wares generally dated to the Mamluk and Ottoman periods. The Late Ottoman–Mandate era wares may have developed out of the Middle Islamic era HMGPW, although an uninterrupted line of continuity cannot yet be demonstrated.

4. Entries in the chronicles of Ibn Hijji "al-Hisbani" (d. 816/1413, his *Tarikh*) and his student Ibn Qadi Shuhba (d. 851/1448, *Tarikh Ibn Qadi Shuhba*), together with the later "diary" of Ibn Tawq (d. 915/1509, his *Ta'liq*), document the migration of families of scholars from Hisban and Ajlun to Damascus over the course of the fourteenth through early sixteenth centuries CE, their establishment of adjacent family cemeteries at Bab al-Saghir, and the regular visitation of and correspondence with relatives in the Transjordanian towns. It is clear from these narratives that the personal networks that flourished in Hisban and Ajlun were re-created in Damascus.

5. Ad hoc inscriptions are those left behind by travelers, rather than formal building inscriptions or tombstones. For Mamluk Jordan, they include Muslim and Christian pilgrims' inscriptions (al-Jbour 2011; al-Salameen and al-Falahat 2007; al-Salameen et al. 2011) and the

so-called caravan texts that can, for this period, record prices, prayers for rain, and various other information useful to fellow travelers of the day (Baramki 1964; al-Jbour 2011).

6. Only one series for southern Bilad al-Sham has been published in English (Hütteroth and Abdulfattah), though one study for Palestine has been published in Arabic and several other registers for Transjordan were edited and appear in print in their original Ottoman Turkish, with Arabic commentary (for a survey of these sources, see Walker 2011: 26). A large corpus of tax-related documents of the period, however, remains unpublished and in the form of hand-written registers; these are currently under study by this author.

7. The latter may represent the land form known by Mamluk historians and Ottoman tax collectors as *mazariʿ*.

8. Personal communication, project geomorphologist Bernhard Lucke, during 2012 field season.

# Bibliography

Baramki, Demetri. 1964. "al-Nuqush al-ʿarabiyya fī al-badiyya al-suriyya." *al-Abḥāth* 17(3): 339–461.

Carroll, Lynda, Adam Fenner, and Øystein S. LaBianca. 2006. "The Ottoman qasr at Hisban: architecture, reform, and new social relations." *Near Eastern Archaeology* 69(3/4): 138–45.

Crowfoot, Grace M. 1932. "Pots, ancient and modern." *Palestine Exploration Fund Quarterly Statement* 1932: 179–87, pls. I–III.

Forbes, Hamish. 2007. "Early Modern Greece: liquid landscapes and fluid populations." In *Between Venice and Istanbul: Colonial Landscape in Early Modern Greece*, edited by Siriol David and Jack Davies, 111–35. Princeton: Princeton University Press.

Gabrieli, Ruth Smadar. In press. "Specialization and development in the handmade industries of Cyprus and the Levant." In *Medieval and Post-Medieval Ceramics in the Eastern Mediterranean - Fact and Fiction,* edited by Joanita Vroom. Amsterdam: Brepols.

Gibson, Erin. 2007. "The archaeology of movement in a Mediterranean landscape." *Journal of Mediterranean Archaeology* 20(1): 61–87.

Given, Michael. 2000. "Agriculture, settlement and landscape in Ottoman Cyprus." *Levant* 23: 209–30.

al-Jbour, Khaled Suleman. 2011. "Bayyān asʿār al-ḥinṭa fī naqsh mamlūkī min al-bādiyya al-urduniyya fī ʿāmay 757 H/1347 M wa 764 H/1363 M." *Journal for History and Archaeology* 5(4): 1–18.

Johns, Jeremy. 1998. "The rise of Middle Islamic hand-made geometrically-painted ware in Bilad al-Sham (11th-13th centuries A.D.)." In *Colloque international d'archéologie islamique*, edited by R.-P. Gayraud, 65–93. Cairo: Institut Français d'Archéologie Orientale.

Laparidou, Sofia. 2013. "Identifying changing agricultural economies as key factors of settlement shifts in medieval Islamic Jordan: a phytolith analysis approach." In *Proceedings of the Eighth International Conference on the Archaeology of the Ancient Near East*, edited by Alison Gascoigne. Wiesbaden, Germany: Harrassowitz.

Lucke, Bernhard, Mohammed Shunnaq, Bethany Walker, Atef Shiyab, and Zeidoun al-Muheisen, Hussein al-Sababha, Rupert Bäumler, and Michael Schmidt. 2012. "Questioning Transjordan's historic desertification: a critical review of the paradigm of 'empty lands.'" *Levant* 44(1): 100–26.

Mershen, Birgit. 1985. "Recent hand-made pottery from North Jordan." *Berytus* 33: 75–87.

Mukahala, Noha Muhammad Hussein. 1992. "al-Zirāʿa fī Bilād al-Shām fī al-ʿAṣr al-Mamlūkī." Unpublished MA thesis, Yarmouk University, Irbid, Jordan.

Palmer, Carol. 1999. "'Whose land is it anyway?' An historical examination of land tenure and agriculture in northern Jordan." In *The Prehistory of Food: Appetites for Change*, edited by Chris Gosden and Jon Hather, 300–302. London: Routledge.

Rippon, S. J., R. M. Fyfe, and A. G. Brown. 2006. "Beyond villages and open field: the origins and development of a historic landscape characterised by dispersed settlement in southeast England." *Medieval Archaeology* 50: 31–70.

al-Salameen and Hani al-Falahat. 2007. "Jabal Haroun during the Islamic period: a study in the light of newly discovered inscriptions." *Arabian Archaeology and Epigraphy* 18: 258–64.

al-Salameen, Zeyad, Hani Falahat, Salameh Naimat, and Fawzi Abudanh. 2011. "New Arabic-Christian inscriptions from Udhruḥ, Southern Jordan." *Arabian Archaeology and Epigraphy* 22(2): 232–42.

Salem, Hamed J. 1999. "Implications of cultural traditions: the case of the Palestinian traditional pottery." In *Archaeology, History and Culture in Palestine and the Near East, Essays in Memory of Albert Glock*, edited by Tomis Kapitan, 66–83. Atlanta: Scholars.

Singer, Amy. 1992. "Peasant migration: law and practice in early Ottoman Palestine." *New Perspectives on Turkey* 8: 49–65.

———. 1994. *Palestinian Peasants and Ottoman Officials: Rural Administration Around Sixteenth-Century Jerusalem*. Cambridge: Cambridge University Press.

Sutton, Susan Buck. 2000. "Liquid landscapes: demographic transitions in the Ermionidha." In *Contingent Countryside: Settlement, Economy, and Land Use in the Southern Argolid Since 1700*, edited by Susan Sutton, 84–106. Stanford, CA: Stanford University Press.

Vassberg, David E. 1996. *The Village and the Outside World in Golden Age Castile: Mobility and Migration in Everyday Rural Life*. Cambridge: Cambridge University Press.

Walker, Bethany J. 2005. "The Northern Jordan Survey 2003—agriculture in Late Islamic Malka and Hubras villages: a preliminary report on the first season. *Bulletin of the American Schools of Oriental Research* 339: 67–111.

———. 2008. "The role of agriculture in Mamluk-Jordanian power relations." In *Le pouvoir à l'âge des sultanats dans le Bilād al-Shām*, edited by Bethany J. Walker and Jean-François Salles. *Bulletin d'Études Orientales*, supplement 62: 79–99.

———. 2009. "Identifying the Late Islamic period ceramically: preliminary observations on Ottoman wares from central and northern Jordan." In *Reflections of Empire: Archaeological and Ethnographic Studies on the Pottery of the Ottoman Levant*, edited by Bethany J. Walker, 37–66. Boston: American Schools of Oriental Research.

———. 2011. *Jordan in the Late Middle Ages: Transformation of the Mamluk Frontier*, Chicago Studies on the Middle East Monograph Series. Chicago: Middle East Documentation Center, University of Chicago.

———. 2013. "Mobility and migration in Mamluk Syria: the dynamism of villagers 'on the move.'" In *Everything Is on the Move: The "Mamluk Empire" as a Node in (Trans-) Regional Networks*, edited by Stephan Conermann. Bonn: University of Bonn.

Walker, Bethany J., Ellen Kenney, Lynda Carroll, Laura Holzweg, Stéphanie Boulogne, and Bernhard Lucke. 2007. "The Northern Jordan Project 2006: village life in Mamluk and Ottoman Hubras and Sahm: a preliminary report." *Annual of the Department of Antiquities of Jordan* 5: 429–70.

Walker, Bethany J., and Øystein S. LaBianca. 2003. "The Islamic *Qusur* of Tall Hisban: rreliminary report on the 1998 and 2001 seasons." *Annual of the Department of Antiquities of Jordan* 47: 443–71.

———. 2012. "Tall Hisban." In *Archaeology in Jordan, 2010 and 2011 Seasons*, edited by Donald R. Keller, Barbara A. Porter, and Christopher A. Tuttle. *American Journal of Archaeology* 116(4) : 716–17.

Walmsley, Alan G., and Anthony D. Grey. 2001. "An interim report on the pottery from Gharan-dal (Arindela), Jordan." *Levant* 33: 139–64.

Whitcomb, Donald. 1992. "Reassessing the archaeology of Jordan of the Abbasid period." *Studies in the History and Archaeology of Jordan* 4: 385–90.

Wilkinson, Tony. 2010. "The Tell: Social Archaeology and Territorial Space." In *Development of Pre-State Communities in the Ancient Near East*, edited by Diana Bolger and Louise C. Maguire, 55–62. Oxford: Oxbow.

CHAPTER 11

# "Presencing the Past"

## A Case Study of Islamic Rural Burial Practices from the Homs Region, Syria

*Jennie N. Bradbury*

Within archaeological and historical discourse, there has been a tendency to portray an idealized and static version of Islamic burial practice. As such, the role of burial is often overlooked in regard to wider rural Islamic society. Using examples from the rural landscape surrounding the modern city of Homs, Syria, this chapter will discuss the diversity of Islamic burial practices that was extant within this area and how they relate to extraurban life across this broad historical period. It will demonstrate how, by taking a broad chronological landscape approach, it is possible to consider how the past may have been reappropriated and integrated into Islamic social rhetoric.

## Islamic Burial Practices Within the Archaeological and Historical Record

> Theoretically at least, a universal and archaeologically
> recognizable Muslim burial exists. (Insoll 1999: 176)

The above quote illustrates commonly held perceptions of Islamic burial practices within the Levant and Arabia. Excavations carried out at cemeteries and burial sites have demonstrated considerable variation over time and space (e.g., Schick 1998: 573; Simpson 1995: 244–45). However, aspects of variability are often downplayed in favor of commonly shared attributes that allow us to identify an "Islamic burial" within the archaeological record (e.g., Frank 2006: 96–97; Insoll 1999: 173,

176; Milwright 2010: 135). The limited number of publications (Schick 1998: 564–65) remains a major problem for making broad-scale comparisons and analyses. Having said this, studies are beginning to illustrate the social processes surrounding burial and to consider why groups may have chosen to either reject or ignore certain parts of Islamic religious doctrine in favor of other traditions and burial practices (e.g., Mershen 2004; B. Walker 2001).

### Graves and Burial Features

Tell el-Hesi remains one of the most well-published Islamic Levantine cemetery studies to date. Excavations at this site have demonstrated both aspects of uniformity, as well as variation within the modes of Islamic burial (Eakins 1993; Toombs 1985). The burials at Tell el-Hesi are characterized by individual internments in simple stone-lined pits (Eakins 1993: 8). In contrast to this, at Tell Hisban, a site that is contemporary with at least some of the burials from Tell el-Hesi, an estimated one hundred individuals were found interred within a common stone-lined grave (B. Walker 2001: 48). Considerable consistency exists in terms of burial orientation and body position at both Tell el-Hesi and Hisban (Eakins 1993: 23; B. Walker 2001: 56); however, these two examples also reflect a more general trend of variation in the nature and form of above- and belowground structures associated with Islamic cemeteries and burials (e.g., Demant Mortensen 2010; Insoll 1999: 192–94; Mershen 2004). There are a number of cases that also caution against dating Islamic burials solely based on the orientation and body position of buried individuals. For example, at Tel Masaikh, several burials that showed "Islamic" attributes in terms of body orientation and position were dated to the Early Roman or pre-Roman period owing to the presence of diagnostic material culture or stratigraphic relationships (Frank 2006: 113–14). These observations demonstrate that the orientation of graves and bodies, as well as the nature of burial, cannot always be used as definitive evidence for the presence of Islamic burials within the archaeological record.

### Grave Markers and Grave Goods

Investigations across this region have unearthed Islamic burials where such items as bricks, stones, and pottery sherds were placed upon graves in order to prevent the body being disinterred by wild animals (e.g., Musil 1928: 671; Granqvist 1965: 56; Simpson 1995: 245). Specific choices may have been made concerning the types of material or ceramic vessels being used to cover the graves. For example, within the Muslim cemetery at Kafr ʿAna, ceramic vessels, possibly originally used as beehives, were used to cover the graves (Taxel 2006: 208). As Bethany

Walker (2010: 150) argues, this presents the opportunity to study the perceived links between death, industry, and household production and recalls Simpson's discussions on the association of Islamic burials with manufacturing areas (1995: 243). In some cases, these vessels appear to have been used to mark the graves (Walker 2010: 150), and despite Muslim law disapproving of the use of inscribed or carved grave markers within Islamic burials (e.g., Simpson 1995: 247), this practice is widespread within both recent and ancient cemeteries within the Levant and beyond (e.g., Da'ādli 2011; Demant Mortensen 2010; Insoll 1999: 193; Mershen 2004: 171). Recent research, such as Demant Mortensen's study of Luristani pictorial tombstones (2010: 13–14, 204–205), has demonstrated that groups employed and upheld local traditions of tribal display and religious expression, although operating within a general Islamic framework. Similar gentle disobedience seems to have existed in relation to the placement and use of grave goods, as exemplified by sites such as Tell el-Hesi (Eakins 1993: 57–68; see Simpson [1995: 245–47, 251] for a general summary of cemeteries and burials incorporating grave goods). It has been suggested that the deposition of valuable ceramics on the surface of modern graves in Oman may reflect a desire to make the grave (and thus individual interred within) stand out from a general background of sociocultural anonymity and uniformity (Mershen 2004: 176). Personal practices are also reflected by the placement of coffee utensils within the grave, which, while not strictly allowed according to Islamic practice, seems to have been a common and widely accepted tradition (e.g., Granqvist 1965: 84). Similar practices may be visible archaeologically; for example, the majority of interred grave goods from such sites as Tabaqat Fahl appear to have been personal items (e.g., Walmsley 1997: 138; although see B. Walker [2001: 58–59] for a discussion of other potential reasons for the deposition of grave goods).

## The Location of Islamic Burials

There has been a limited number of investigations examining the landscape context of Islamic burial practices, particularly in relation to the rural world. Notable exceptions do exist (e.g., B. Walker 2001: 132–33; Schaefer 1989: 52; Simpson 1995: 243), and as the chapters within this volume demonstrate, scholars are beginning to examine aspects of memory, legacy, and landscape much more rigorously in relation to Islamic social practice. The location of Islamic burials and cemeteries has been associated with various other features, such as manufacturing areas in urban locations (e.g., Milwright 2010: 135; Simpson 1995: 243) and the tombs of local saints or holy men in both rural and urban areas (e.g., Insoll 1999: 136–40; Meri 2002: 129, 134–35; Milwright 2010: 135). Other investigations have demonstrated the physical relationship between Islamic cemeteries, tell sites, and ancient ruins (e.g., Simpson 1995: 243), while Bethany Walker notes that unexcavated areas of the tell at Hisban continue to be used for the burial of stillborn infants (2001: 48). The use of separate cemeteries, discrete areas, or different methods of internment for the burial of children and infants is well documented within Islamic practice and more generally the ancient Near East (e.g., Simpson 1995: 244), although this clearly did not take place at all sites, as with, for example, the Ottoman cemetery at Tell Hisban (B. Walker 2001: 48).

The evidence outlined above indicates aspects of consistency and commonality alongside patterns of variability within certain tolerated or accepted limits. Communities were able to modestly deviate from proscribed religious practices, with burial offering the potential to express religious and nonreligious ideas. Leaving grave goods and monuments aside for now, is it possible that a landscape approach to the question of Islamic rural burial practices might further illuminate these variations and the ways in which they have become accepted or integrated into sociocultural practices and traditions?

## Landscape Approaches to the Study of Islamic Rural Burial Practices: The Homs Region, Syria

Investigations over the past decade as part of the Homs Regional Survey Project have revealed a wealth of material dating to the Islamic period (Newson et al. 2009; Philip and Bradbury 2010; Philip et al. 2011), although analysis remains at a preliminary stage and the nature of settlement, occupation, and burial practices within the basaltic landscape northwest of Homs, locally known as the Wa'ar (Fig. 11.1), is only now becoming apparent. From the standpoint of Islamic period activity, the legacy of Roman and Byzantine populations would have shaped the resources with which later communities could work. The basic settlement pattern of nucleated villages, around which buildings, such as tombs, agricultural structures, and public architecture, were present, was established in the Early Roman period and continued into the Byzantine and Islamic periods. For example, just over 50 percent of the sites from the Wa'ar revealing evidence for activity or occupation during the Roman-Byzantine period continued in use or were reoccupied during the Islamic period, and many continued to be used into the early twentieth century (e.g., Newson et al. 2009: 18).

## Islamic Cairns Within the Homs Region and Beyond

Research carried out by the author between 2007 and 2011 across the Wa'ar documented a range of monuments that were classified as cairns. These structures

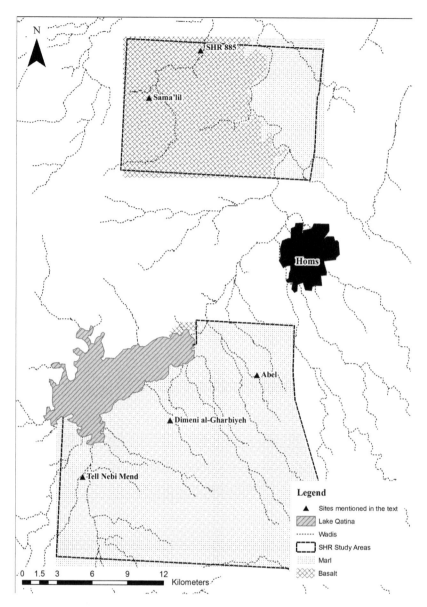

Figure 11.1 The Homs Region, Syria, with sites and areas discussed within the text marked on the map (prepared by author).

varied in morphology, chronology, and possibly even function (Bradbury 2011; Bradbury and Philip 2011). However, most monuments can be assigned to one of three main periods of activity and use: the fourth to third millennia BCE; the Roman-Byzantine period (c. 50 BCE–640 CE); and the third dating, very broadly, to the Islamic period (c. 640–1900 CE). While the periods assigned to the use of these cairns are very broad, they correspond to the main phases of occupation and

activity within the Wa'ar in general (see Bradbury and Philip 2011; Philip and Bradbury 2010; Philip et al. 2011).

During this research, 525 cairns were examined, and surface collection was carried out at 203 of these. Surveys involved recording both the internal (e.g., chambers and cists) and external (e.g., adjoining enclosures) features associated with
cairns. We cannot assume that all of the cairns in this region were used for burial.
No full-scale excavation has been carried out, and owing to looting activities, both
in antiquity and more recently, and taphonomic factors, it is possible that no human
remains survive. Over 80 percent of the cairns surveyed had internal or external
features, including internal chambers and cists, associated external wall lines, and
revetments. Given these elaborations, it is unlikely that the majority of these cairns
are solely the result of clearance activities. We cannot rule out the possibility that
they were originally formed via clearance or "derocking" and subsequently used
for burial; however, a considerable proportion of them may have been built as burial
monuments.

Surface collection was targeted to cover cairn structures and a zone of one meter in diameter surrounding them. A tiny percentage of cairns had artifacts associated with them. In total, twenty-seven cairns were associated with artifacts
that could be dated to the fourth to third millennia BCE, the Roman-Byzantine
period, or the Islamic period. Thirty more could be dated, more broadly, to a Late
Antique to Islamic period (c. 50 BCE–CE 1900). Islamic material (c. 640–1900 CE)
was recovered in association with 30 percent of the cairns (eight of twenty-seven).
Given the very small number of monuments falling into this group, it is very difficult to extract any patterns in terms of the distribution of cairns within the
Islamic period. Having said this, all of the examples yielding evidence for Islamic
period activity were found within five hundred meters of an Islamic settlement. It
is impossible to determine with any certainty whether the Islamic material recovered during the cairn survey pertains to use of these monuments as burial structures. Skeptics could easily suggest that the material culture dating to this period
and found in association with these monuments merely indicates the reuse or use
of these structures as shelters or clearance piles. However, as the examples below
demonstrate, there is increasing evidence to suggest that this is not the case.

### Khirbet es-Sahi, Site 885

The site of Khirbet es-Sahi (also transliterated as Khirbet Sabi, Sabahi) has
produced ceramic evidence for activity dating from the Roman-Byzantine period
into the beginning of the fifteenth century CE (Stephen McPhillips, personal
communication). Surveyed as part of the Homs Regional Survey Project and

Rural Islamic Syria Project the site has revealed a dense arrangement of rectilinear buildings, now largely destroyed by bulldozing and modern agriculture (Fig. 11.2). The village is marked (Kh. Sabi) on the 1932 French-produced map of the region,[1] and to the northeast of the village, a well-maintained Muslim holy man's tomb was recorded. Survey in the area surrounding the rectilinear structures of Site 885 also revealed the presence of several cairns. Other probable cairns were identified on either side of the wadi using satellite imagery analysis (see Bradbury and Philip [2011] for further details of this methodology), although survey of these structures was not possible as they had been destroyed by recent bulldozing and tree planting. The surveyed monuments were located at a distance of around 250 meters from the site and occupied a slightly higher elevation, overlooking the settlement and wadi system. Surface collection from the western cluster of cairns yielded a single Islamic sherd in association with Cairn 486, hardly enough to provide a definitive date for these monuments. No clearly distinguishing morphological features could be identified from the cairns to indicate an Islamic attribution. However, apart from the holy man's tomb, the site of 885 revealed no obvious evidence for an associated cemetery or burial area. The stony nature and shallow soils of the basalt landscape and zone make it highly unlikely that burial sites

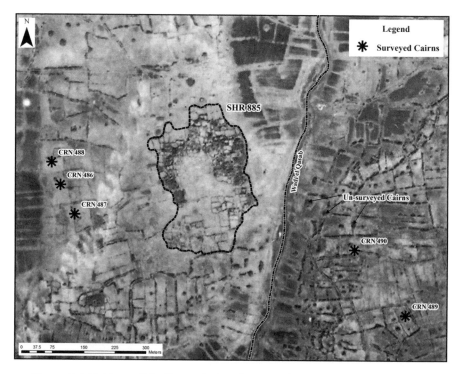

Figure 11.2 Khirbet es-Sahi (Site 885) plotted against the 1950s Russian aerial photograph (author image and declassified aerial photography).

would have been dug into the ground. While we cannot rule out the possibility of burial at some distance from the settlement, the presence of the cairns on either side of the wadi, in close proximity to the village and positioned to overlook both it and the local watercourse, suggests that these were most likely the village burial grounds.

The construction of tumuli and cairns in the post-Roman world is documented elsewhere across this region (e.g., Haiman 1995: 44; Simpson 1995: 243; Stern 1978: 4). Haiman refers to the construction of settlements and temporary encampments dated to the Early Islamic period in the Negev (1995: 44), which are also associated with cairn burials, standing stones, and open-air mosques. Many Western travelers exploring the Levant during the nineteenth century also make reference to simple stone or earthen graves (e.g., Conder, 1892: 264–65; Doughty, 1908: 267). Conder records the use of specific toponyms for local cairns and the myths surrounding them (1889: 205–206), while Burckhardt mentions heaps of stones on both sides of the *hajj* route, marking where pilgrims undertaking this journey had died and been buried (1822: 452). In the deserts of the Levant and Arabia, Arabic inscriptions are found on slabs built into cairns (Winnett and Harding 1978: 3), although in some cases this can be taken as evidence of reuse and reconstruction. Cairns are not solely associated with burial practices, and they have been employed for a range of different functions, including survey and route markers, memorials, and shelters (e.g., Conder, 1889: 202; Glueck, 1935: 95–96, 108; Hole 2009: 264; Palgrave, 1865: 131). Within the Homs region, cairns were observed with shelters or hides built on top of the original structures. Roofs of corrugated iron or troughs for feeding animals were often associated with these features. Canaan records cairns on the road between Jerusalem and Jericho, with stones being thrown on these piles by passing Muslim travelers as they sighted the shrine of Nebi Musa in the distance (1927: 75). Clearly, similarities between pre-Islamic and Islamic cairns should not be overemphasized or interpreted as direct and uninterrupted continuity of practice or meaning. That said, descriptions and depictions of eighteenth- to nineteenth-century CE burials recorded by such early explorers as Conder (1892: 264–65) display remarkable similarities to those of earlier tumuli structures. The presence of stone enclosures, paved areas, and wall lines associated with more recent burial tumuli and shrines in the Homs region and throughout the Levant and Arabia (e.g., Lancaster and Lancaster 2010: 324; Simpson 1995: 241) emphasize the potential long-term similarities that can be seen among these structures.

## Reusing the Material Past: Case Studies from Across the Levant and Arabia

Granqvist, in her study of early twentieth-century village burial practices, suggested that the majority of individuals buried in the village of Artas were not given a new grave. In many cases, internment of individuals would be within the same grave as other family or tribe members. However, she also refers to the reuse of an ancient tomb within the village and notes that despite the fact that this tomb was considered to be an "improper burial" by the shaykh, individuals still chose to be buried there (1965: 56–57).

Of particular interest is the fact that scholars and early travelers recorded the reuse of architectural fragments and archaeological remains within later burials (e.g., Browne 1799: 356; Hogarth 1896: 10; Stark 1942: 234). Hogarth documents the reuse of Roman milestones as grave markers in the cemetery of Kanlu Kavak in Turkey (1896: 10). At Dimeni al-Gharbiya, southwest of Homs, the writer has observed that several graves within the village cemetery incorporate architectural fragments, such as door lintels, presumably reused from decaying and ruined Roman-Byzantine structures within the village (Fig. 11.3). This is something that has also been noted on the Land of Carchemish Survey (Dan Lawrence, personal communication). While we could be dealing with the pragmatic reuse of locally available materials, what is interesting in regard to the example from Dimeni is that the tomb containing the majority of reused architectural fragments was that of a local "holy man." While in some degree of disrepair in 2009, our inquiries indicated that the villagers were very aware of the significance of this grave. This raises the issue of whether the architectural fragments had been specifically selected and used to differentiate this tomb in some way.

Selection and reuse of ancient material culture within medieval burials and sites is a well-discussed phenomenon, particularly within Europe (e.g., Eaton 2000; Moreland 2007: 41; Thäte 2007). The incorporation and reuse of Roman remains during the medieval period in England varied across time and space. However, studies have demonstrated that deliberate reuse and selection of particular types of material culture occurred (e.g., Eaton 2000: 58). Ancient monuments and objects took on new meanings and values as they became integrated into the rhetoric of the medieval world (Eckardt and Williams 2003: 141–43). Within medieval Europe, the flourishing trade in relics, including items of material culture as well as bodily remains, reflects this desire to derive power and value from antiquity (e.g., Walsham 2010). Studies have tended to emphasize the centrality of the Christian "cult of saints," but considerable evidence exists for dynastic groups and individuals throughout the Muslim world trying to assert their power through connections with the past (e.g., Meri 2002: 108–119; P. Walker 2003: 368–71). Meri has

Figure 11.3 Holy man's burial, Dmeini al-Gharbiyeh (image courtesy of Stephen McPhillips).

demonstrated how the sanctity of holy places was reinforced through an association with traditions and legends concerning the ancient world (2002: 35–38). Many medieval shrines and saints tombs have their origins in earlier structures (e.g., Meri 1999: 256). Within this new temporal sphere, ancient objects and monuments could take on different value relations. While perhaps wholly different from those originally intended, these may have created the opportunity for burial monuments and those involved in the use, construction, or reconstruction of these features to demonstrate or renegotiate power structures. While identifying the existence of reuse of ancient remains within the Islamic world is easy, it is more difficult to determine the exact intention of these actions. Archaeologically, we are observing the outcomes of a chain of actions or practices, which makes it difficult to interpret whether we are simply dealing with the opportunistic reuse of readily available building materials or something more meaningful. However, given the multiplicity of Islamic practice and doctrine, especially within the rural world, we have to acknowledge the possibility of ancient ruins, places, and relics being "Islamicized" and, conversely, Islamic practices being "localized" (e.g., Kalanov and Alonso 2008: 175). Such "folk" Islam is well documented across Europe and Central Asia, as well as within the Middle East (e.g., Arakelova 2003; Kalanov and Alonso 2008; Geller 2008). We should not necessarily find it surprising that rural regions in the lands of Bilad al-Sham, not directly within the influence of the main urban schools and centers of Islamic teaching, should adopt and localize Islamic practices and beliefs, and in doing so reinterpret already existing monuments and traditions.

Stark, during her travels in Arabia, documented an area of ruins where a stone-built grave chamber contained an inscribed slab in Hadhrami dialect (1942: 234). The slab, according to Stark (ibid.), commemorated the renovation of this structure and prepared the tomb for a new burial. If the inscription did indeed make specific reference to "renovation" rather than construction, it would indicate that this act was an important step within the burial process, demonstrating an association, or at least an imagined association, with the tomb or its previous owner. If not, and the slab was making reference to the "construction" of a new burial monument within the area, then its proximity to an area of ancient ruins is interesting; why would people choose to place "new" burials in and among ancient ruins or build structures that are visually very similar to ancient monuments? I suggest that this practice was not solely pragmatic, either being linked to the reuse of earlier materials, or to the fact that there are a limited number of ways of burying the dead, particularly within stony landscapes. Rather, in my view, people may have been making informed choices to emulate and reference ancient burial practices, albeit it in a way that was adapted to the sociocultural norms of the Islamic world.

## The "Longevity" of Ruins: Memory and Legacy Within Islamic Burial Practices

Memory is constantly being shaped, negotiated, and renegotiated within the modern world, and the same can be suggested for the past. As Philip has pointed out in regard to the Early Bronze Age, populations did not exist within or upon a blank canvas, and the presence of ancient remains and ruins may have influenced the use and conceptualization of contemporary landscapes (2003). This was almost certainly the case in the Wa'ar where Late Antique–Early Islamic remains would have been very evident features of the landscape. Individuals and groups within the Islamic world would have had the opportunity to exploit and use ancient structures and ruins as they saw fit.

Studies have demonstrated the potential for Islamic cemeteries to be used long after local villages were abandoned (e.g., B. Walker 2010: 132–33). While groups were no longer occupying or cultivating the land surrounding these burial locales, at least on a permanent basis, they continued to use them in order to inter the dead. Granqvist records similar practices with settled Bedouin in the village of Artas, who chose not to inter their dead within the village cemetery but instead returned to and used the tribal burial grounds at Bet Ta'amir (1965: 107). Within the Homs region, sites such as Khirbet Sabi demonstrate that despite no longer being oc-cupied, locales can continue to hold sociocultural significance, in this case due, at least in part, to the presence of a holy man's burial. Investigations of Mamluk period cemeteries in Palestine have demonstrated that no physical associations with village ruins can be determined (B. Walker 2010: 133), possibly suggesting that additional factors were influencing the location of these sites. These observations echo Said's discussions about the interplay between geography, history, and mem-ory, with populations constructing or manipulating the concept of space and place (2003: 54–55). I turn now to these concepts of "imagined geographies" (ibid.) that integrate ancient ruins and landscapes into the Islamic world.

As indicated in the introduction, there are numerous examples of the reuse of abandoned tells and ruins for Islamic cemeteries (e.g., Schaefer 1989: 52; Simpson 1995: 243; B. Walker 2001: 48). Studies emphasize that such sites would have been ideal locations for burial, useless for agriculture, and, in the case of abandoned desert tells, located at a safe distance from the living (e.g., Simpson 1995: 243). In the Homs region, five out of the ten tells used for cemeteries or tombs are still occupied, suggesting that in these cases, there was no attempt to isolate the living from the dead (Table 11.1). The five remaining tells with Islamic cemeteries are all over 0.9 kilometers from modern occupation and occupy highly prominent loca-tions along the River Orontes or the shores of Lake Qattina, with views across the floodplains and surrounding landscape (Table 11.1). The role of tells as "stores" of social memory has been discussed in relation to their continued use over millen-nia (e.g., Steadman 2005). I suggest that the highly visual nature of such sites offers potential for the construction of both real and imagined geographies. Clearly, not all tells within the Homs region have been used for Islamic cemeteries or burials. In fact, discounting those sites that have not been surveyed owing to military use, only 25 percent of tells within the Homs region have been used as cemeteries (ten out of the thirty-nine examples recorded). Equally, some fairly impressive tells from the region show no evidence, as far as we are aware, for having been used as burial sites. Rather than suggesting that the association between tells and ceme-teries is a consistent and uniform pattern within the Homs region, I would argue that the use of specific tells as cemeteries had, and continues to have, meaning and importance for Islamic burial practices. In some cases, groups may have had a

Table 11.1. Tells in the Homs Region, Syria, with Islamic cemeteries or burials, or both

| Major ID | Comments | Maximum Period of Occupation/Activity Determined by Surface Collections | Height of Tell | Cemetery | Shaykh/Holy Man's Tomb | Modern Village/Occupation |
|---|---|---|---|---|---|---|
| SHR 65 | Holy Man's Tomb recorded on tell among ruins and buildings of modern village | seventh century–sixteenth century CE | Low rise | X | X | X |
| SHR 81 | Large Islamic tomb and cemetery located on top of low ovoid tell. The site is located at the junction of the River Orontes and one of the main side wadis flowing into the Homs basalt. | seventh millennium BCE–first century CE | <5 m | X | X | |
| SHR 83 | Cemetery used in recent history. Located on southeastern slopes of the tell. The site is located on the banks of the River Orontes. | seventh millennium BCE–seventh century CE | 10–15 m | X | | |
| SHR 90 | Large cemetery on Tell Shaykh Muhammed. It is located on the banks of the River Orontes. | third millennium BCE–eleventh century CE | 10–15 m | X | | |
| SHR 286 | Cemetery located on Tell Arjun overlooking the River Orontes and with views toward Tell Nebi Mend | seventh millennium BCE–thirteenth century CE | <5 m | X | | |
| SHR 315 | Cemetery located next to mosque and mud-brick buildings of the old village on the top of Tell Nebi Mend | seventh millennium BCE–eleventh century CE | >25 m | X | | X |
| SHR 668 | Old cemetery on tell of Burj el-Qai. Various Arabic inscriptions noted within the cemetery and also a possible holy man's tomb. | third millennium BCE–fifteenth century CE | 5–10 m | X | X | X |
| SHR 748 | Stone-lined graves visible on mound near the deserted village of Khirbet Kafr Abdih. The site has been heavily bulldozed. | seventh century–fourteenth century CE | ? | X | X | |
| SHR 866 | Small cemetery containing possible holy man's/shaykh's tomb, around 100 m east of old village | fourth millennium BCE–twentieth century CE | <5 m | X | X | X |
| SHR 1068 | Recent graves on summit of tell within village. Located alongside River Orontes. | late second–early first millennia BCE | 10–15 m | X | | X |

physical and historical relationship with the tells being used as cemeteries. For example, tells or parts of tells within the Homs region, which have either been recently abandoned or are in the process of being abandoned, often have areas of decayed mud-brick housing and buildings, such as mosques, that are still in use. Personal attachments are often still present; during survey and salvage excavation at Abel, a site located in the southern marls, I spoke to a number of villagers who remembered the buildings that were being excavated. They referred to these structures as belonging to older or deceased family members, and in such cases, it is clear why these places would continue to hold relevance and meaning for local populations. Elsewhere, the possible reasons for an "attachment to place" are not so easily demonstrated. Here, the impressive nature of tells, especially those occupying key positions along the River Orontes, and clearly recognizable features may have been used as material representations of the past, allowing "real or imagined connections" with these locales to be maintained by different populations. The burial of deceased members of society in association with these sites may have even aided in claims to ownership of land in areas that were no longer being occupied (see Philip [2003: 120] for similar arguments in relation to the Early Bronze Age).

While some scholars have explained the reuse of ruins during the Islamic period in association with the wealth of building material available or the presence of reusable features, such as cisterns (e.g., Schaefer 1989: 55), these arguments ignore the role of social memory and the attachment to place. Oliphant made reference to the presence of an eighteenth- to nineteenth-century "Arab stone circle" in the vicinity of the Chalcolithic–Early Bronze Age alignments of stones and dolmens in the al-Mugheir region, Jordan (1885: 182; this material is later covered by Savage [2010]). Other researchers examining this monumental complex also mention the association between the remains and recent features. For example, Conder records the presence of recent tribal markings on standing stones in the region (1889: 184–87). This recalls the slab in Hadrahmi dialect mentioning the potential renovation of a burial recorded by Stark (1942: 234), demonstrating a desire to perhaps reappropriate or reclaim the past.

Returning to the Homs region, several small "ovoid" cairns were recorded on a ridgeline north of the village of Sama'lil (Fig. 11.4). An east–west orientation was noted in some cases; however, there were exceptions. Although the ridgeline is around one kilometer from the settlement, these structures were interpreted by local museum representatives as graves of eighteenth- to nineteenth-century CE inhabitants of Sama'lil. Unfortunately, by the following year, the cairns in this area had been destroyed, which prevented further documentation and analysis. Archaeological and ethnographic research has demonstrated that the distance of separation between the dead and the living (i.e., between the cemetery and the settlement) varies substantially, from the width of a track to the distance of a kilometer or

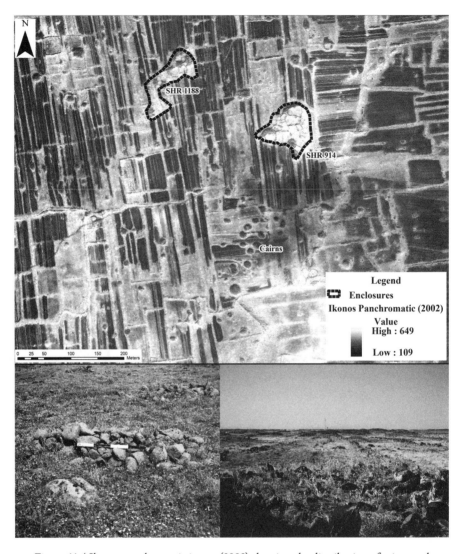

Figure 11.4 Ikonos panchromatic image (2002) showing the distribution of cairns and enclosures across the ridgeline near Sama'lil (base map: courtesy of GeoEye and provided by Durham University).

more (e.g., Simpson 1995: 243). Isolated burials do not necessarily reflect the cemeteries of nomadic groups. Sama'lil lies along one of the main wadi systems of the Wa'ar, and the ridgeline discussed above represents one of the nearest areas of high ground to the village. Thus, the presence of these cairns could be explained as a preference for burial on areas of dry raised ground and rocky outcrops, out of the way of any potential disturbances (e.g., Lancaster and Lancaster 2010: 321; Simpson 1995: 243). The twentieth- to twenty-first-century cemetery of Sama'lil occupies a low-lying area just on the edge of the modern village; it would appear that at least within recent history, the placement of burials on high land was not a key consideration for the inhabitants of this settlement. The ridgeline where the ovoid cairns are located is also home to numerous archaeological features dating, very broadly, to the Late Chalcolithic to Early Bronze Age. These structures are distributed across the ridgeline and include enclosures, possibly representing ancient settlement sites, as well as cairns (Fig. 11.4). The small ovoid cairns are actually constructed in and among these much earlier remains, and a number of large, highly impressive cairns occur alongside the much smaller, more ephemeral "boat-shaped" structures. In the stony landscape of the Wa'ar, archaeological features dating to a variety of different periods are found scattered across the landscape. However, the presence of the cairns and enclosures on the ridgeline would have been a highly visual and impressive reminder of the past. As such, the construction of these possibly Islamic-period cairns on the ridgeline above Sama'lil may not have been solely associated with a desire to locate the burials in an isolated area, away from the chance of disturbance. Instead, the presence of impressive ancient monuments and the potential ability to use such structures to demonstrate ownership within contemporary power relations may have been a factor in influencing the location of later burials.

## Conclusion

As emphasized by a number of other chapters in this volume, mobility, migration, and shifts in settlement and occupation do not necessarily reflect the total abandonment of a geographical locale. Instead, as has been demonstrated throughout this chapter, attachment to "place" can be maintained long after occupation has ceased. One way of demonstrating this may have been through the location of burial sites. The evidence from the Homs region presented here underscores the variability in Islamic rural burial practices and suggests that specific cases may have been shaped and determined by more than just religious practice. Thus, the construction of burial monuments and cairns, alongside and among ruins, may have not only been a visual representation of continuity but also an attempt to reuse and reappropriate the past. Similarly, cemeteries and burials integrating or mimicking ancient remains may have been useful locales for the negotiation of memory and power, with new sociocultural values being attached and drawn from ancient remains. These interpretations offer the potential to take us in new directions. By reexamining the apparent pragmatic reasons for the location of Islamic burials and investigating how other factors may have influenced the placement of these features within the landscape, we might consider internal dynamics of Islamic-period rural communities. Within archaeological circles, there also needs to be a much greater focus placed on aspects of "folk" Islam, especially within the rural world. Rather than starting with an idealized view of Islamic burial (e.g., Insoll 1999; Petersen 2013), we should instead be starting with the archaeology, viewing practices that depart from religious doctrine not necessarily as special cases but as potentially meaningful and deliberate adaptations: the "localization" and potential "ruralization" of Islam. This chapter has touched only briefly upon these subjects, and the findings presented here are preliminary at best. However, it is hoped that it has demonstrated at least one of the ways in which the role of Islamic burial practice can be integrated into a wider discussion of legacy, memory, and sociocultural practice within the rural Islamic world.

## Notes

I would like to thank Stephen McPhillips and Paul Wordsworth for having invited me to participate in this publication and in previous research meetings. Thanks to Dan Lawrence, Graham Philip, Rune Rattenborg, and the anonymous reviewer for their thoughtful comments on drafts of this paper; any errors, of course, remain my own. Finally, my heartfelt thanks and wishes to my colleagues and friends in Bilad al-Sham who made this research possible.

1. Hama (South-West), produced by the Bureau Topographique de l'AFL. The map itself is based on the original Ottoman 1:200,000 mapping. Whether the village of Khirbet es Sahi was still fully occupied or only partially occupied in 1932 is unknown.

## Bibliography

Arakelova, Victoria. 2003. "The Siyāh-Gālesh and deity patrons among new Iranian peoples." *Cahiers de Studia Iranica* 27: 173–78.

Bradbury, Jennie. 2011. *Landscapes of Burial? The Homs Basalt, Syria in the 4th–3rd Millennia BC*. PhD dissertation, Durham University.

Bradbury, Jennie, and Graham Philip. 2011. "The world beyond tells: pre-classical activity in the basalt landscape of the Homs region, Syria." In *Pierres levées, stèles anthropomorphes et dolmens: Standing Stones, Anthropomorphic Stelae and Dolmens,* edited by Tara Steimer-Herbert, 169–80. Lyon: Maison de l'Orient et de la Méditerranée Jean Pouilloux.

Browne, William George. 1799. Travels in Africa, Egypt, and Syria, from the year 1792 to 1798. London: T. Cadell junior and W. Davies, Strand.

Burckhardt, John. 1822. *Travels in Syria and the Holy Land*. London: John Murray.

Canaan, Tawfiq. 1927. *Mohammedan Saints and Sanctuaries in Palestine*. Jerusalem: Syrian Orphanage Press.

Conder, Claude Reignier. 1889. *Syrian Stone Lore; or, the Monumental History of Palestine*. London: Alexander P. Watt.

———. 1892. *Heath and Moab: Explorations in Syria in 1881 and 1882*. London: Alexander P. Watt.

Da'ādli, Tawfiq. 2011. "Mamlūk epitaphs from Māmillā Cemetery." *Levant* 43(1): 78–97.

Demant Mortensen, Inge. 2010. *Luristani Pictorial Tombstones: Studies in Nomadic Cemeteries from Northern Luristan, Iran*. Leuven, Belgium: Peeters.

Doughty, Charles. M. 1908. *Wanderings in Arabia (Being an Abridgement of Travels in Arabia Deserta in Two Volumes, Volume I)*. London: Duckworth.

Eakins, J. Kenneth. 1993. *Tell el-Hesi: The Muslim Cemetery in Fields V and VI/IX (Stratum II). Joint Archaeological Expedition to Tell el-Hesi 5*. Winona Lake, IN: Eisenbrauns.

Eaton, Tim. 2000. *Plundering the Past: Roman Stonework in Medieval Britain*. Stroud, UK: Tempus.

Eckardt, Hella, and Howard Williams. 2003. "Objects without a past? The use of Roman objects in early Anglo-Saxon graves." In *Archaeologies of Remembrance: Death and Memory in Past Societies*, edited by Howard Williams, 141–70. New York: Kluwer/Plenum.

Frank, Constance. 2006. "Funeral practices at Tell Masaikh (Syria): Late Roman and Islamic graves." *Studies in Historical Anthropology* 3: 93–120.

Geller, Florentina B. 2008. *Qura'ān in Vernacular: Folk Islam in the Balkans*. Preprint 357. Berlin: Max-Planck-Institut für Wissenschaftsgeschichte.

Glueck, Nelson. 1935. "Explorations in Eastern Palestine II (1934–1935)." *Annual of the American Schools of Oriental Research* 15.

Granqvist, Hilma. 1965. *Muslim Death and Burial: Arab Customs and Traditions Studied in a Village in Jordan*. Helsinki: Centraltryckeriet.

Haiman, Morchedai. 1995. "Agriculture and nomad-state relations in the Negev Desert in the Byzantine and Early Islamic Periods." *Bulletin of the American Schools of Oriental Research* 297: 29–53.

Hogarth, David George. 1896. *A Wandering Scholar in the Levant*. London: John Murray.

Hole, Frank. 2009. "Pastoral mobility as an adaptation." In *Nomads, Tribes, and the State in the Ancient Near East: Cross-Disciplinary Perspectives*, edited by Jerry Szuchman, 261–83. Chicago: University of Chicago Press.

Insoll, Tim. 1999. *The Archaeology of Islam*. London: Blackwell.

Kalanov, Komil, and Antonio Alonso. 2008. "Sacred places and "folk" Islam in Central Asia." *UNISCI Discussion Papers* 17: 173–85.

Lancaster, William, and Fidelity Lancaster. 2010. "Observations on death, burial, graves and graveyards at various locations in Ra's al-Khaimah Emirate, UAE, and Musandam wilayat, Oman, using local concerns." In *Death and Burial in Arabia and Beyond*, edited by Lloyd Weeks, 319–28. Oxford: BAR International Series 2107.

Meri, Josef, W. 1999. "Re-appropriating sacred space: medieval Jews and Muslims seeking Elijah and al-Khadir." *Medieval Encounters: Jewish, Christian and Muslim Culture in Confluence and Dialogue* 5: 237–64.

———. 2002. *The Cult of Saints Among Muslims and Jews in Medieval Syria*. Oxford: Oxford University Press.

Mershen, Birgit. 2004. "Pots and tombs in Ibra, Oman: investigations into the archaeological surface record of Islamic cemeteries and the related burial customs and funerary rituals." *Proceedings of the Seminar for Arabian Studies* 34: 165–79.

Milwright, Marcus. 2010. *An Introduction to Islamic Archaeology (The New Edinburgh Islamic Surveys)*. Edinburgh: Edinburgh University Press.

Moreland, John. 2007. *Archaeology and Text*. London: Duckworth.

Musil, Alois. 1928. *Manners and Customs of the Rwala Bedouins*. Oriental Expeditions and Studies 6. New York: American Geographical Society.

Newson, Paul, Maamoun Abdulkarim, Stephen McPhillips, Philip Mills, Paul Reynolds, and Graham Philip G. 2009. "Landscape study of Dar es-Salaam and the basalt region north west of Homs, Syria." *Berytus* 51–52: 1–35.

Oliphant, Laurence. 1885. "A dolmen in Judea." *Palestine Exploration Fund Quarterly Statement* 1885, July:181–82.

Palgrave, William, G. 1865. *Narrative of a Year's Journey Through Central and Eastern Arabia (1862–63)*. London: Macmillan.

Petersen, Andrew. 2013. "The archaeology of death and burial in the Islamic world." In *The Oxford Handbook of the Archaeology of Death and Burial*, edited by Sarah Tarlow and Liv Nilsson Stutz, 240–58. Oxford: Oxford University Press.

Philip, Graham. 2003. "The Early Bronze Age of the Southern Levant: a landscape approach." *Journal of Mediterranean Archaeology* 16: 103–31.

Philip, Graham, and Jennie Bradbury. 2010. "Pre-classical activity in the basalt landscape of the Homs region, Syria: the implications for the development of 'sub-optimal' zones in the Levant during the Chalcolithic and Early Bronze Age." *Levant* 42(2): 136–69.

Philip, Graham, Jennie Bradbury, and Farid Jabbour. 2011. "The Archaeology of the Homs Basalt, Syria: the Main Site Types." Studia Orontica 9: 18–55.

Said, Edward. 2003. *Orientalism*. London: Penguin.

Savage, Stephen, H. 2010. "Jordan's Stonehenge: the endangered Chalcolithic/Early Bronze Age site at Al-Murayghât–Hajr al-Mansûb." *Near Eastern Archaeology* 73(1): 32–46.

Schaefer, Jeremy. 1989. "Archaeological remains from the medieval Islamic occupation of the Northwest Negev Desert." *Bulletin of the American Schools of Oriental Research* 274: 33–60.

Schick, Robert. 1998. "The archaeology of Palestine/Jordan in the Early Ottoman Period." *ARAM* 10: 563–75.

Simpson, St. John. 1995. "Death and burial in the Late Islamic Near East: some insights from archaeology and ethnography." In *The Archaeology of Death in the Ancient Near East*, edited by Stuart Campbell and Anthony Green, 240–51. Oxford: Oxbow Monographs 51.

Stark, Freya. 1942. *A Winter in Arabia*. London: John Murray.

Steadman, Susan, R. 2005. "Reliquaries on the landscape: mounds as matrices of human cognition." In *Archaeologies of the Middle East*, edited by Susan Pollock and Reinhardt Bernbeck, 286–307. Oxford: Blackwell.

Stern, Ephraim. 1978. *Excavations at Tel Mevorakh (1973–1976), Part One: From the Iron Age to the Roman Period*. Qedem 9. Jerusalem: Hebrew University of Jerusalem.

Taxel, Itamar. 2006. "Ceramic evidence for beekeeping in Palestine in the Mamluk and Ottoman Periods." *Levant* 38: 203–12.

Thäte, Evam S. 2007. *Monuments and Minds: Monument Re-use in Scandinavia in the Second Half of the First Millennium AD*. Lund, Sweden: Gleerup.

Toombs, Lawrence, E. 1985. *Tell el-Hesi: Modern Military Trenching and Muslim Cemetery in Field 1, Strata I-II. Joint Archaeological Expedition to Tell el-Hesi 2*. Waterloo, Ontario: Wilfred Laurier University.

Walker, Bethany. 2001. "The Late Ottoman cemetery in Field L, Tall Hisban." *Bulletin of the American Schools of Oriental Research* 322: 1–19.

———. 2010. "From ceramics to social theory: reflections on Mamluk archaeology today." *Mamluk Studies Review* 14: 109–57.

Walker, Paul, E. 2003. "Purloined symbols of the past: the theft of souvenirs and sacred relics in the rivalry between the Abbasids and Fatimids." In *Culture and Memory in Medieval Islam: Essays in Honour of Wilferd Madelung*, edited by Farhad Daftary and Josef W. Meri, 364–87. London: I. B. Tauris.

Walmsley, Alan. 1997. "Settled life in Mamluk Jordan: views of the Jordan Valley from Fahl (Pella)." *ARAM* 9: 129–43.

Walsham, Alexandra. 2010. "Introduction: relics and remains." *Past and Present* 206 (Suppl. 5): 9–36.

Winnett, Frederick V., and Gerald L. Harding. 1978. *Inscriptions from Fifty Safaitic Cairns*. Toronto: University of Toronto Press.

# CHAPTER 12

# Sustaining Travel

## The Economy of Medieval Stopping Places Across the Karakum Desert, Turkmenistan

*Paul D. Wordsworth*

Desert landscapes offer an unusual perspective on the rural Islamic economy—unusual in that the majority of studies with an ostensibly rural outlook focus on sedentary agricultural areas, where farming and related trades are primary economic activities (good examples include Adams [1965] and Miller [1991]). Deserts and steppes have been examined with regard to transhumant or seminomadic populations, linked to an economy of pastoralism (Donner 1989; Jabbur 1995; Marx 1992), but these activities are rarely labeled as *rural*. Given the fundamental definition of rural landscapes in contrast with urban space, it would seem logical to overcome this division and talk of a continuous region, not restricted to fertile zones. However, landscapes beyond the boundaries of permanent cultivation are different insofar as many economic activities are linked to the need for movement. It is for this reason that perspectives on economies of movement have the potential to contribute greatly to the understanding of desert landscapes.

This study centers on what I have loosely termed "stopping places" in the Karakum desert, which stretches for over 350,000 square kilometers in the modern state of Turkmenistan (Fig. 12.1). The somewhat awkward terminology, "stopping places," arises from an attempt to move away from otherwise loaded nomenclature. Caravanserais, for example, feature frequently in research on the architecture of Central Asia and Iran, yet refer to only one particular phenomenon. Semantic nuances between the different terms for these desert outposts will become apparent in the following discussion, but they all share a common definition as nodal points in the landscape that show evidence of human movement over a sustained period.

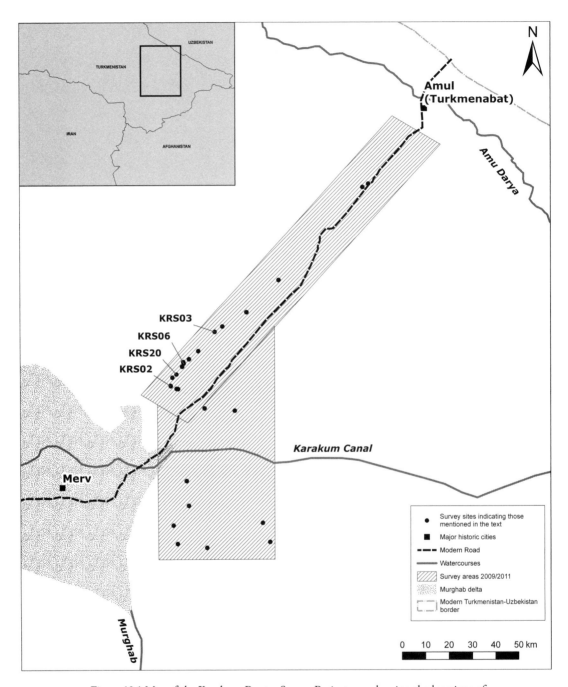

Figure 12.1 Map of the Karakum Routes Survey Project area showing the locations of the twenty-six sites recorded in detail (inset—general location map) (prepared by author).

The data have been gathered as part of wider research into medieval routes across the Karakum, collected through archaeological landscape survey (the Karakum Routes Survey Project, henceforth KRS) since 2009. One of the primary motivations in analyzing this landscape was to understand the complexity of regional and interregional travel beyond the traditional concept of the "Silk Routes" and the "Great Khurasan Road"—the major historical trade arteries that have come to characterize this region.

Three broad themes highlight the economic processes underpinning the establishment, the function, and ultimately the abandonment of the desert stopping places: construction, hydroeconomies, and food and pastoralism. Presented below is a brief discussion of the evidence for these activities, followed by some reflections on the related aspects of the interdependence or independence of these outposts. Finally, this paper offers some preliminary conclusions on the characterization of these economies of movement, and some ideas as to how this concept can be a useful paradigm for exploring this and other desert landscapes.

## The Landscape of the Karakum

The Karakum possesses all of the characteristic features associated with what one might typically term "a desert." From a climatic perspective, the vast central, eastern, and northern sections fall below the two-hundred-millimeter isohyet in average annual precipitation. Low rainfall, coupled with an extreme continental climate, means that the landscape can be considered a "cold desert" (for example, as defined on the Köppen-Geiger classification; see Peel et al. [2007] for a summary of this system). Comparable environments are found throughout the lowlands of Central Asia and the desert areas of Iran. Vegetation is relatively sparse and restricted to drought-tolerant species (such as *Haloxylon sp.*, sand sedge [*Carex physodes*], and *Artemisia sp.*: Rustamov 1994: 78–79), while the soil largely comprises sand, some of which accumulates into shifting dune formations. Permanent natural standing water is absent, as are rivers, except for those in the southernmost region (the Murghab and Tejen), and the Amu Darya, dividing the Karakum and Kyzylkum deserts. In 1988, the Karakum canal was completed (indicated on Fig. 12.1), diverting water from the Amu Darya across the desert to the lands of southern Turkmenistan (see Institut Geografii Rossiĭskaia Akademiia Nauk and Institut Pustyn' Akademiia Nauk Turkmenskoĭ SSR [1977] and Orlovsky [1999] for a discussion of its construction and environmental impact). Underground aquifers are generally hypersaline, although some brackish and fresh "lenses" of water are tapped by wells.

The city of Merv, situated in the fertile Murghab delta, has long been considered an oasis and a waystation for those wanting to cross the Karakum. Of the routes passing through Merv, the best known is that running east and west of the city, connecting Iran and the Near East with Central Asia and beyond. This major arterial flow of traffic crossed the desert between the Murghab delta and the Amu Darya (medieval Jaihun, classical Oxus). The major historical river crossing at Amul is still in use, under the more modern names of Chardzhou or Türkmenabat, although several others were in use at different times. The route between the Amul and Merv therefore became known as the northeastern segment of the "Great Khurasan Road" (Le Strange 1905: 9).

## Fieldwork Methodology

The first stage of the landscape survey was to undertake a desk-based assessment, collating a wide range of historical and modern cartographic materials, satellite and aerial imagery, geographical data, and information from historical studies and previous scientific expeditions.[1] This information was digitized and combined in a geographical information system (GIS) platform, which allowed the cross-comparison and synthesis of the raw data in a single framework.

KRS fieldwork was initially conducted over two short seasons (2009 and 2011), targeting the anomalies identified from the satellite imagery as well as known or previously mapped sites. A final season completed the survey work in 2013 but the results are not incorporated here. The primary objectives for the fieldwork were threefold. First, by visiting features mapped remotely, it was possible to inform the process of recognition and digitization, allowing for a more detailed interpretation and the confirmation of key "signatures." Second, it was possible to undertake comprehensive photographic recording and topographic mapping of the sites, which revealed new information about their form and function, as well as providing dating information where architectural details survive. Third, the collection of material culture, particularly ceramic sherds, from the surface of the sites enabled a broad chronological date range to be established for each site and gave insights into their functionality.

A total of twenty-six archaeological sites were confirmed through fieldwork (Fig. 12.1), while a number of other apparent features have been mapped but are yet to be ground-truthed. Of these twenty-six sites, fifteen contained architectural remains, including large caravanserais and smaller towers (Fig. 12.2). The eleven nonarchitectural sites were identified through surface material alone.

Figure 12.2 Kite photograph of one of the best-preserved architectural sites in the survey area (KRS20): the caravanserai known locally as Akcha Kala (white castle) (photograph by Alexis Pantos).

## Economies of Construction

Economic investment in construction is easily overlooked or underplayed when considering vernacular architecture or small-scale infrastructure in rural archaeological contexts. Building materials are often locally gathered or produced, or sourced through a regular trade agreement that ensures a certain level of supply. The predominance of mud brick as a building material in the traditional architecture of Central Asia and Iran reinforces this idea, as the basic primary materials are almost ubiquitously available locally. In the context of the Karakum, however, water is extremely scarce. Clay-rich soils are also limited in their distribution, and where they do occur, they are often compacted and hyperdesiccated, and thus difficult to work. Finally, other materials, such as temper for the bricks (often straw or chaff) or gypsum to create plaster, would have to be imported, as they are not widely available. These constraints mean that the mud-brick architecture of the Karakum represents a specific economic process, which reflects the nature of these desert outposts.

All of the fifteen architectural sites identified were constructed from earthen materials, following regional architectural traditions (Fig. 12.3). Three basic forms of earthen architecture are common: sun-dried mud bricks (also known as "cured" or "raw" bricks), fired bricks, and rammed earth or *pakhsa*. The raw materials for all three are earth, water, and temper, although the amounts used in each case vary greatly (Fodde 2009:153–54). Most of the structures identified used a combination of the three earthen architectural types. Fired bricks usually form the

Figure 12.3 Photographs from two of the architectural sites located, showing two different construction techniques. Top: Arch at KRS03 constructed in unfired mud brick. Bottom: External wall of KRS02, showing the *pakhsa* blocks used in its construction (photograph by Alexis Pantos).

foundation courses as a method of preventing rising water percolation and as decorative elements in other parts of the building. Heavy *pakhsa* blocks form the lower courses of the large outer and load-bearing walls, while more versatile mud bricks form the upper courses and were used in such architectural details as arches.

Production sites for mud bricks and *pakhsa* are difficult to identify archaeologically, particularly without excavation, as the only visible remains would be an extraction point for soil and in some instances a mixing place. Comparative ethnographic evidence suggests that in the majority of instances bricks such as these are made as needed on the site where they are to be used, assuming the raw materials are at hand (Wulff 1966: 109), although high-quality soils with a reliable composition are valued (Fodde 2009: 154; Gaigysyz Jorayev, personal communication). While sand is abundant throughout the Karakum, discrete flat areas of compacted clay deposits, known as *takyr*, occur across certain parts of the desert (see below for a discussion of these in relation to water). It is therefore feasible to suggest that the earthen component of raw mud bricks would be obtainable in a desert context, providing the site was located close to a *takyr* or where the soil geology contains a higher percentage of silt clay.

Water is harder to obtain, which would arguably restrict construction work to the wettest months each year. However, as Wulff observed in Iran, cured bricks are traditionally manufactured in the hottest months, when they will dry in the sun in one or two days (1966: 110). Wells fed by underwater aquifers and surface water collection yield very limited resources throughout the year, and it is highly unlikely that they would produce enough for sustained brick production. *Pakhsa* is almost always created in situ (the term refers both to rammed earth between wooden boards and to cob-built walls), which suggests that it would be necessary to obtain at least enough water to enable this process at the sites where this technique was used.

Finally, temper may be added to sun-dried bricks and *pakhsa* as a bonding agent. Chaff or straw is traditionally added to the brick mixture to prevent cracks occurring as the earthen matrix dries out, but in instances with suitable soil mixes, this addition may not be necessary (Fodde 2009: 153, 155). While significant plant material can be found in the desert, very little of it would be suitable as temper, as the most frequently occurring plants are woody shrubs. Work has yet to be carried out to determine specifically the composition of the mud bricks and *pakhsa* blocks in the buildings, but it is likely that where temper was used, it was brought from rural agricultural lands in the oases.

By contrast with sun-dried building material, fired bricks require much more selectively sourced earth, given that they must include a high clay component and be free of impurities (often achieved by slaking the clay in water; see Wulff 1966: 115). The resulting matrix of the fired bricks is free from large inclusions, and they do not normally appear to include substantial amounts of vegetation-based temper. The initial drying process is similar to that of cured bricks, but following this, they are fired in a kiln. Several aspects of this process suggest that fired-brick production is unlikely to have taken place at desert outposts because of the need for clean, high-quality clay and the high amounts of water used, as well as the required construction of kilns and the fuel to charge them with.

Evidence from the archaeological survey suggests that, contrary to the observations above, fired bricks were manufactured at several of the sites, indicated by the remains of kilns. Unlike those recorded by Wulff in Iran (1966: 177), designed for high capacity and repeated firings, the kiln remains at the outposts are much smaller scale. The buried remains range in size from around three to five meters in diameter, but none have been excavated thus far and so their actual extent and layout is unknown. Their use is attested by the presence of large numbers of partially fired and overfired brick fragments, as well as vitrified earth associated with brick making. In most instances, for example, at KRS20 where three installations were identified with certainty, the kilns are located relatively close to the main structure (Fig. 12.4). Where this is the case, it is reasonable to assume that they provided bricks for the initial construction of the main building, and then were no longer used.

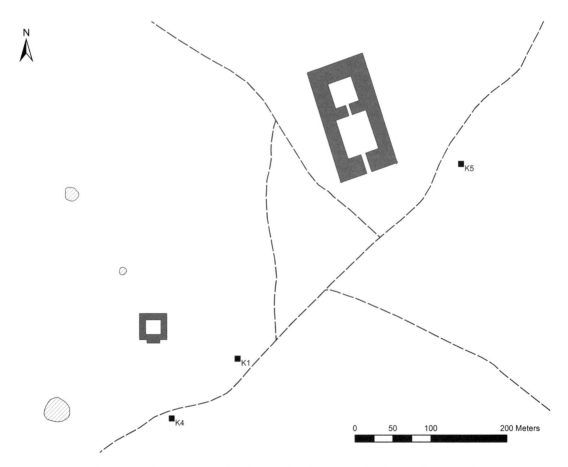

Figure 12.4 Plan of KRS20 showing the locations of the brick kilns (prepared by author).

Given the specificity of the raw materials, it is almost certain that clay would have been imported for these purposes, and water would have been needed in significant quantities from nearby sources. Although desert shrubs might seem uneconomical as firing fuel, archaeological evidence suggests that saxaul (*Haloxylon persicum*) in particular was commonly used as firing fuel for kilns throughout the region (Herrmann and Kurbansakhatov 1995: 52; Bonora and Vidale 2008: 160).

In some of the better-preserved structures, it is clear that wood was also used as a construction material. At KRS20, "Akcha Kala," beam slots high in the walls suggest that planks of wood would have supported a second floor. Trees large enough for wooden beams are absent from the desert and are unlikely to have been found in large numbers in the nearby settled oases, although archaeobotanical evidence of a wide range of woods has been found at Merv (Herrmann et al. 1996: 20). The use of these timbers therefore demonstrates the medium or long-distance import of material for use in constructing the monuments.

Evidence of early Islamic occupation was also found in the south of the survey area, at sites where there were no historical architectural remains present (Fig. 12.1). These assemblages of material culture were located in sheltered depressions, adjacent to modern shepherding stations, usually in conjunction with a well. The economy of these sites is discussed further below, but the presence of this material highlights the existence of outposts that may have been the locations of temporary installations or structures made from materials that would be difficult to visualize archaeologically in such a rapidly changing sandy landscape, such as tents. How far then is the "built environment" representative of the full economic range of desert stopping places? Historical sources from the eighteenth and nineteenth centuries describe major routes avoiding structural remains entirely, instead erecting tents at rest stops, in spite of the significant danger of raids on caravans (Burnes 1834: 48–49). In most instances, the presence of a well suggests that some initial investment must have been made to ensure a drinkable water supply at a given point. The provision of water in the desert highlights an economic system in its own right, applicable across the study area.

## Hydroeconomies

There is no doubt that in order to be able to cross this part of the Karakum in the premechanized era, it was necessary to rely on local water sources in the desert. Even if it were possible to transport enough for human consumption, it is impossible to carry enough for animal needs as well. In one probably exaggerated account, Nader Shah commanded huge numbers of wells to be dug at stages across this part of the desert in order to allow his army to cross from Bukhara to Merv in the winter of 1740–1741 (al-Kashmiri 1788: 52–53).

Wells allow the harnessing of groundwater aquifers, which exist across the desert at varying depths below the surface, fed by rainwater percolation in the wet months. In some areas, a brackish or freshwater lens floats above the underlying, highly saline groundwater. Examining modern wells across the study area, they range in depth from 5 to 10 meters below the surface in the northern region to over 180 meters in the southernmost area examined, in order to tap drinkable water. The water they draw also varies greatly in its salinity, sometimes being only brackish at best. Salinity changes over time, often leading to the abandonment of wells for new ones, frequently dug very close by.

Archaeological evidence for wells is very scarce. They are often small in diameter, with little or no superstructure, and once they are abandoned, the shaft will collapse or fill in very rapidly. Isolated derelict wells in this region thus are impossible to identify through remote prospection or even ground survey. In many instances, however, the site of a well remains unchanged over several centuries, when the geological and geomorphological conditions of a given locale continue to allow freshwater to be drawn from that point. This is illustrated at the sites in the southern half of the survey area, which all coincide with watering points, inhabited by modern shepherd communities. It is not possible to discern whether any of the well shafts are premodern in origin, as they have without exception been reinforced with modern materials (largely concrete) and sometimes reuse historical materials found nearby. It is only the juxtaposition of dense ceramic scatters around these wells that indicates that they were occupied in the premodern era.

One commonly observed architectural solution to extend the seasonal availability of water in this region is the underground or semisubterranean cistern, or *sardoba* (unnumbered plural *sardobalar*). Known also in Iran as *ab anbar* (Beazley 1982: x), these constructions allow the conservation of water resources, which would otherwise evaporate in a desert environment. Very few historical *sardobalar* remain intact in Turkmenistan, but three archaeological examples can be seen at Merv from different periods (two of which have been reconstructed and are still functional; Herrmann 1999: 106). Only one example has been tentatively identified in the study area, by the Soviet survey of the same area undertaken in the 1950s (Masson 1966: 118–19). According to their information, a *sardoba* existed at a point near the site of Takhmalaj (site code KRS06) until the early twentieth century, at which point it was destroyed by local farmers. The resulting deep circular pit and the adjacent spoil mound were documented during our survey (KRS08), which also noted two brick kilns very close by, presumably used in the reservoir's construction.

Although the survey has not yet unearthed evidence for other historical *sardobalar* in the desert, it seems very likely that this method was used for water storage. The construction and maintenance of these structures would form an important part of the economic role of the outposts, while the establishment of water reservoirs would have provided reliable stopping points, even into the arid season. It is unsurprising, therefore, that many of the extant examples in Iran display quite elaborate architectural forms (Siroux 1949: 125–31), given that their endowment is of significant value to the traveler.

One perplexing issue concerning the use of reservoirs is the source of the water itself, given that regular replenishment from a stream or *qanat* is not possible. Fleskens and colleagues (2007) have documented ethnographic evidence for water harvesting, which relies not on subterranean aquifers but on the seasonal inundation of large, flat, impermeable expanses of clay (*takyr*), present in some areas of the Karakum. In a modern context, water collected via channels on the surface of *takyr* is directed either into large open pits (*khakh*) or into concrete *sardoba*.[2] Archaeological evidence for a similar practice was discovered by Soviet archaeologists in the northern Karakum, at the site of Ak-Yaila (Vishnevskaya 1958). Their survey reconnaissance and exploratory sondages established that the caravanserai structure included a *sardoba* that was filled with *takyr*-accumulated water via a ceramic pipe, carrying the water some 850 meters (232–34).

In 2011, we examined again the location of the alleged *sardoba* at KRS06, which is indeed at one end of a large *takyr* formation. It seems likely that the reason for this placement, two kilometers distant from a large, seemingly contemporary caravanserai complex, is to make use of the natural environment and collect water in this manner. Owing to the geomorphology of the desert, *takyr* are only present in the northern half of the survey area. The existence of what are effectively seasonal lakes correlates with the presence of built structures, and it is possible to suggest that this type of hydroeconomy was better suited to the needs of the caravanserais. One argument that might corroborate this is pointed out in the modern ethnographic study: that the water gathered from *takyr* is significantly less brackish than the water from wells (Fleskens et al. 2007: 18), owing to the fact that it does not absorb the same amount of soluble salts from the subsurface geology. This would potentially provide a higher quality of water for travelers, albeit in a limited supply, as the *sardoba* would only be replenished by the winter rains. Seasonality forms cyclical economic frameworks for trade and travel, which are seldom discussed in the archaeological literature. The interplay of the two types of sites observed in this survey, harnessing both well water and precipitation, suggests that routes taken through the desert are highly seasonal and that the practice of travel may change throughout the year accordingly.

*Food and Pastoralism*

The extreme range of annual environmental conditions in the Karakum also dictates the availability of food and fodder, both for travelers and for raising livestock. Although the climate is severe and the soils are largely poor, the desert has a rich floral and faunal ecosystem (Walter and Box 1983), which is actively exploited by modern pastoralists (Fig. 12.5). Among the native plants, there is very little that would be suitable for human consumption, although the collection of some edible wild species is attested historically (O'Donovan 1882: 235–36). Meanwhile, there is also no archaeological or historical indication that even small-scale agriculture was practiced in this part of the Karakum in the premodern period. Archaeobotanical investigation has yet to be undertaken at remote outposts such as these in the Karakum desert, but the results of such a study would be invaluable in understanding the sites more fully. Considering the data presently available, it seems as though most food for human consumption would have been

Figure 12.5 KRS23, one of the sites in the south of the survey area, in the same location as a modern pastoralist outpost (photograph by Alexis Pantos).

imported from the Murghab delta and the small agricultural band along the Amu Darya, as well as further afield for foodstuffs unobtainable in these zones.

Fodder for transport animals would be needed in significant quantities at desert outposts, but this would vary depending on the time of year and the type of transport used. While horses would enable passage across the desert at some speed, they also are less tolerant of the range of available shrubs in the desert. It is for this reason that nineteenth-century sources concerning the movement of Turkmen tribes and foreign armies in the deserts of Iran and Central Asia mention the forage that they carry with them (Yate 1887: 251; Ferrier 1856: 84). Camels, meanwhile, are able to browse on the native desert flora, including green shoots of saxual (*Haloxylon persicum*) (Khanchaev 2005). Taking into account the physical suitability of camels for crossing large sandy tracts, it is unsurprising that in later historical accounts, the composition of caravans was weighted strongly in favor of them, although they were normally accompanied by some horses (Burnes 1834: 13; O'Donovan 1882: 442). Nevertheless, it is likely that stocks of more nutritious wild fodder would have been harvested at stopping places when seasonally available, for year-round use.

Aside from the economic impetus to provide food for passing transport, there remains the question of how the practice of pastoralism relates to movement in the desert. The raising of sheep and goats on seasonal pastures in the Karakum most likely has a very deep history indeed, although unlike the archaeology of the settled deltas in the early periods of occupation, very little can be said about the desert in prehistoric times (Kohl, for example, describes the Karakum as an impassable barrier rather than pastoral lands [2002: 164]). Although before the Saljuq Empire there are several mentions of supposedly nomadic peoples in this broad region—for example, the enigmatic Ghuzz—it is unclear which specific territories they inhabited (Peacock 2010: 21), or whether they would have shepherded flocks as far southwest as the Karakum desert. It is in relation to the Saljuq and Turkmen migrations that the first descriptions of pastoralist activity in the desert can be found, when they pleaded for the right to settle the deserts of Khurasan with their flocks and were granted the lands by Mahmud of Ghazna (Gardīzī 2011: 95–96).

Long-standing occupation of the desert regions is supported by preliminary dates obtained from the ceramic material gathered at the sites, which in the southern area range from the Sasanian or early Islamic period to the fifteenth century.[3] As these sites also coincide with modern shepherd outposts, it is logical that this region (if not the whole of the Karakum) would also have supported pastoralist activities in the past. As highlighted above, the wells allow shepherds and their flocks to be based in the desert throughout the year, although modern practices attest varying levels of seasonal movement, particularly in more northerly and westerly areas (Behnke et al. 2008). Herds of sheep and goats find a wide variety of native shrubs to browse, and if their grazing patterns are managed effectively, it is possible to maintain them annually around the same watering points. On the basis of livestock raising, these outposts would have been able to establish a strong economic relationship with the settled agricultural zones both at Merv and on the Amu Darya, particularly given that in both these regions the zone of irrigated land is limited and therefore highly valued. Camel herding, for milk and hair as well as for transport in the premechanized era, would also have been a viable economic activity in the desert.

## Discussion and Conclusion

Ultimately, trade and travel are phenomena concerned not with the movement of objects but with the movement of people. The importance of the social perspective is shown clearly by the example of desert guides, attested in nineteenth-century literature as a fundamental requirement for crossing the deserts of Central Asia (for example, Yate 1887: 26) on account of the often ephemeral nature of tracks and seemingly few landmarks. It is necessary to rely on a guide who knows or has (or at least professes to have) journeyed a given route before, and this individual knowledge differentiates the new or occasional traveler from the habitual merchant or caravan leader, and from those who reside in different regions of the desert on a permanent or semipermanent basis. One of the main shortcomings of an attempt to analyze travel from archaeological survey evidence is its failure in representing the social aspect of who is traveling which routes and with what purpose. While the discussion here concentrates solely on economic factors in the existence of the desert outposts, the motivation of specific individuals or groups should not be underplayed. Although later historical accounts illuminate the character of desert travel in some detail (Floor 1999), there is a lack of comparable detailed information on social aspects of journeys from the early Islamic period.

Nevertheless, the archaeological observations presented above begin to highlight aspects of the economic infrastructure that surround movement in the Karakum desert. From the perspective of construction, it can be demonstrated that while substantial investment is indisputably necessary in order to create large outposts in terms of capital, planning, and labor, the raw resources for the majority of constructions are to be found locally, and the manufacture of materials, such as fired brick, is widespread and highly localized. Evidence for more elaborate arrangements beyond the use of basic materials includes the construction of upper stories supported by wooden beams, which would have needed to be imported from some distance away. Architectural remains, meanwhile, are restricted to the northern group of archaeological sites, in spite of the presence of archaeological material in other regions.

In terms of water resources, again a significant dichotomy is apparent between northern and southern practices, and it is pertinent to consider whether *takyr* harvesting would have proved advantageous for those wanting to control water supply in the northern area. Harvesting water runoff requires a certain degree of coordination, and in many instances, the *takyr* themselves require maintenance to remove encroaching vegetation or drifting sand (Fleskens et al. 2007: 20). Undertaking this seasonal activity and conserving good-quality drinkable water in brick *sardoba* would enable outposts to provide for travelers through an otherwise barren landscape at different times throughout the year. The wells seen today in the southern region would have had much the same function, but their superior numbers attest to the fact that their northern counterparts may represent the harnessing of a much scarcer and possibly guarded resource. Without entering the debate on the degree of nomadism practiced in historical periods by desert peoples in the Karakum, it is sufficient to highlight that climatic and modern ethnographic data support the hypothesis of a large stable economy for livestock herding, based on seasonally available desert vegetation.

Ceramic sherds were common at all of the sites identified, sometimes accompanied by a limited number of coins and metallic objects, as well as small amounts of glass and other materials. The initial inspection of the assemblages suggests that they can reasonably be considered representative of daily use rather than residual incidental material discarded by transient caravans. Nevertheless, the distribution of this material demonstrates that one of the fundamental economic relationships between the outposts and the travelers was that of provision of materials, as well as more basic foodstuffs. It also suggests that both in the north and in the southern survey regions, outposts were established with a certain degree of permanence, conducive to the use and discard of significant quantities of ceramic material. The trilateral interdependence between urban centers, travelers, and the stopping places is thus a defining characteristic of movement in the desert, and the data presented here suggest that it was not restricted to single highways but can be seen across a complex network of tracks and pathways.

## Notes

1. Full details of the general survey methodology for the KRS will be outlined in a forthcoming publication of the results.

2. The word *sardoba* is not just applicable to historical reservoirs. It is also used to refer to modern storage tanks, which are common across the desert but usually constructed from concrete and often filled either from a tanker or with piped water.

3. The study of the survey ceramics is ongoing (see also the discussion below), and I must thank Dave Gilbert, University College London, for providing these dates and for undertaking an overview assessment of the material.

## Bibliography

Adams, Richard McC. 1965. *Land Behind Baghdad*. Chicago: University of Chicago Press.

Beazley, Elisabeth. 1982. *Living with the Desert: Working Buildings of the Iranian Plateau*. Warminster, UK: Aris & Phillips.

Behnke, Roy, Grant Davidson, Abdul Jabbar, and Michael Coughenour. 2008. "Human and natural factors that influence livestock distributions and rangeland desertification in Turkmenistan." In *The Socio-Economic Causes and Consequences of Desertification in Central Asia*, edited by Roy Behnke, 141–68. NATO Science for Peace and Security Series. Dordrecht, Netherlands: Springer.

Bonora, Gian Luca, and Massimo Vidale. 2008. "An aspect of the Early Iron Age (Yaz I) Period in Margiana: ceramic production at Site No. 999." In *The Archaeological Map of the Murghab Delta*, vol. II: *The Bronze Age and Early Iron Age in the Margiana Lowlands: Facts and Methodological Proposals for a Redefinition of the Research Strategies*, edited by Sandro Salvatori and Maurizio Tosi, 153–94. Oxford: Archaeopress.

Burnes, Alexander. 1834. *Travels into Bokhara: Being the Account of a Journey from India to Cabool, Tartary and Persia. Also, Narrative of a Voyage on the Indus from the Sea to Lahore with Presents from the King of Great Britain*, vol. 2. London: John Murray.

Donner, Fred. M. 1989. "The role of the nomads in the Near East in Late Antiquity (400–800 C.E.)." In *Tradition and Innovation in Late Antiquity*, edited by Frank M. Clover and R. Stephen Humphreys. Wisconsin Studies in Classics. Madison: University of Wisconsin Press.

Ferrier, Joseph P. 1856. *Caravan Journeys and Wanderings in Persia, Afghanistan, Turkistan, and Beloochistan; with Historical Notices of the Countries Lying Between Russia and India*. London: John Murray.

Fleskens, Luuk., A. Ataev, B. Mamedov, and W. P. Spaan. 2007. "Desert water harvesting from takyr surfaces: assessing the potential of traditional and experimental technologies in the Karakum." *Land Degradation and Development* 18(1): 17–39.

Floor, Willem. 1999. "The Bandar 'Abbas-Isfahan route in the Late Safavid Era (1617–1717)." *Iran* 37: 67–94.

Fodde, Enrico. 2009. "Traditional earthen building techniques in Central Asia." *International Journal of Architectural Heritage* 3(2): 145–68.

Gardīzī, 'Abd al-Ḥaiyy ibn al-Ḍaḥḥak. 2011. *The Ornament of Histories: A History of the Eastern Islamic Lands AD 650–1041, the Persian Text of 'Abd al-Hayy Ibn Zahhak*, translated by Clifford Edmund Bosworth. London: I. B. Tauris.

Herrmann, Georgina. 1999. *Monuments of Merv: Traditional Buildings of the Karakum*. London: Society of Antiquaries of London.

Herrmann, Georgina, and Kakamurad Kurbansakhatov. 1995. "The International Merv Project: preliminary report on the third season (1994)." *Iran* 33: 31–60.

Herrmann, Georgina, Kakamurad Kurbansakhatov, and St. John Simpson. 1996. "The International Merv Project: preliminary report on the fourth season (1995)." *Iran* 34: 1–22.

Institut Geografii Rossiĭskaia Akademiia Nauk and Institut Pustyn' Akademiia Nauk Turkmenskoĭ SSR, ed. 1977. *Remaking of Nature Under Socialism: Desert Development in the V. I. Lenin Karakum Canal Zone.* Problems of the Contemporary World 54. Moscow: Social Sciences Today Editorial Board, USSR Academy of Sciences.

Jabbur, Jibrail S. 1995. *The Bedouins and the Desert: Aspects of Nomadic Life in the Arab East*, edited by Suhayl J. Jabbur, translated by Lawrence I. Conrad. Albany: State University of New York Press.

al-Kashmiri. 1788. *The Memoirs of Khojeh Abdulkurreem, a Cashmerian of Distinction, Who Accompanied Nadir Shah, on His Return from Hindostan to Persia; from Whence He Travelled to Baghdad, Damascus, and Aleppo, and After Visiting Medina and Mecca, Embarked on a Ship at the Port of Jeddeh, and Sailed to Hooghly in Bengal. Including the History of Hindostan from AD 1739 to 1749: With an Account of the European Settlements in Bengal, and on the Coast of Coromandel*, translated by Francis Gladwin. Calcutta: William Mackay.

Khanchaev, Khojageldi. 2005. "Pasture ration of Arvana camels in desert pastures." In *Desertification Combat and Food Safety: The Added Value of Camel Producers*, edited by Bernard Faye and Palmated Esenov, 209–10. NATO Science Series v. 362. Amsterdam: IOS.

Kohl, Philip L. 2002. "Archaeological transformations: crossing the pastoral/agricultural bridge." *Iranica Antiqua* 37: 151–90.

Le Strange, Guy. 1905. *The Lands of the Eastern Caliphate: Mesopotamia, Persia, and Central Asia from the Moslem Conquest to the Time of Timur.* 3rd ed. London: Frank Cass.

Marx, Emanuel. 1992. "Are there pastoral nomads in the Middle East?" In *Pastoralism in the Levant: Archaeological Materials in Anthropological Perspectives*, edited by Ofer Bar-Yosef and Anatoly Khazanov. Monographs in World Archaeology no. 10. Madison, WI: Prehistory Press.

Masson, Mikhail. E., ed. 1966. *Средневековые Торговые Пути Из Мерва в Хорезм и в Мавераннахр (в Пределах Туркменской ССР) Srednevekoviee Togoviee Puti Iz Merva v Khorezm i v Maverannakhr (v Predelakh Turkmenskoĭ SSR). Труды Южно-Туркменистанской Археологической Комплексной Експедиции* (Trudy Yuzhno-Turkmenistanskoĭ Arkheologicheskoĭ Kompleksnoĭ Ekspeditsii) XIII. Ashgabad, Turkmenistan: Akademisk Nauk Turkmenskoĭ SSR.

Miller, James M. 1991. *Archaeological Survey of the Kerak Plateau.* ASOR Archaeological Reports. Atlanta: Scholars Press.

O'Donovan, Edmund. 1882. *The Merv Oasis: Travels and Adventures East of the Caspian, During the Years 1879–80–81, Including Five Months Residence Among the Tekkés of Merv*, vol. 2. London: Smith, Elder.

Orlovsky, Nicholas S. 1999. "Creeping environmental changes in the Karakum Canal's zone of impact." In *Creeping Environmental Problems and Sustainable Development in the Aral Sea Basin*, edited by Michael Glentz, 225–44. New York: Cambridge University Press.

Peacock, Andrew C. S. 2010. *Early Seljūq History: A New Interpretation.* Routledge Studies in the History of Iran and Turkey 7. London: Routledge.

Peel, Murray C., Brian L. Finlayson, and Thomas A. McMahon. 2007. "Updated world map of the Köppen-Geiger climate classification." *Hydrology and Earth System Sciences* 11: 1633–44.

Rustamov, Igor G. 1994. "Vegetation of the deserts of Turkmenistan." In *Biogeography and Ecology of Turkmenistan*, edited by Victor Fet and K. I. Atmuradov, 77–104. Dordrecht, Netherlands: Kluwer.

Siroux, Maxime. 1949. *Caravansérails d'Iran et Petites Constructions Routières.* Cairo: Imprimerie de l'Institut Français d'Archéologie Orientale.

Vishnevskaya, Olga. A. 1958. "Раскопки караван-сараев Ак-яйла и Талайхан-ата (Raskopki karavan-saraev Ak-aiĭla i Talaĭkhan-ata)." In *Археологические и этнографические работы Хорезмской экспедиции*, 1949–1953 (Arkheologicheskie i *étnograficheskie raboty Khorezmskoĭ ekspeditsii, 1949–1953*), edited by Sergeĭ P. Tolstov and Tat'iana A. Zhdanko, 431–66. Moscow: Akademia Nauk SSSR.

Walter, H., and Elgene O. Box. 1983. "The Karakum Desert, an example of a well-studied eubiome." In *Temperate Deserts and Semi-Deserts*, edited by Neil E. West, 105–59. Ecosystems of the World 5. Amsterdam: Elsevier.

Wulff, Hans E. 1966. *The Traditional Crafts of Persia: Their Development, Technology, and Influence on Eastern and Western Civilizations*. Cambridge, MA: MIT Press.

Yate, Arthur C. 1887. *England and Russia Face to Face in Asia: Travels with the Afghan Boundary Commission*. London: W. Blackwood.

# Conclusion

## Some Reflections on Rural Islamic Landscapes

*Alan Walmsley*

The relatively recent focus on archaeological landscapes in the rural milieu, the expressed subject of this volume, may be regarded as an innovation of some importance in contemporary archaeology, and in many ways, that is true if the steady appearance of publications over the last two decades is anything to go by (Ucko and Layton 1999; Wilkinson 2003; Davies and Davis 2007; Athanassopoulos and Wandsnider 2004). Yet the study of landscape—in this case, applying the word in a more general sense—as an inseparable part of archaeology has early roots, finding widespread application once the heat of antiquarianism had passed. As the focus of archaeological endeavor began to shift from long-known, individual sites of great magnitude to the discovery of unknown archaeological horizons, the implementation of regional survey programs intuitively brought in an assessment of the countryside. In much of the Islamic world, archaeological work of the nineteenth and early twentieth centuries CE was often linked to the colonial ambitions of the great powers, and the extraordinary detail sought and recorded by the survey teams shows just how intense and deliberate they were in maximizing the retrieval of strategic information during their missions. It may be mistaken to portray all nineteenth- and early twentieth- century survey work as blatantly imperial in objective, but its usefulness in empire building was unquestionable, nonetheless. The detail preserved in these publications, and occasionally archives, is often staggering in scope and providential given the changes wrought on the region over the last half century. Geographical features, routes, distances, resources (especially water), population centers, and modern inhabitants (their "character," often seen as distinctly other) all attracted attention, as well as the obvious archaeological mounds, architectural ruins, and antiquities. We can only marvel at the achievements of the adventurers that strode so purposefully over the territories of the Middle East, Central Asia, and North Africa in a very different age from ours, where success and even survival was often dependent on the abilities of the individual and the hospitality of the local population. Yet publications (there is no need here to go into details) reveal how acutely aware were our pioneers in recording the fullness of their experiences, even if we lament how much more they must have seen but did not think to present, or could not.

There were many blind spots inherent in early regional work as the result of limited objectives, restricted interests, and team competencies. The emphasis was primarily on site location and identification (especially the detection of uncharted biblical, Hellenistic, Persian, and Roman places) and the countryside that separated them, and how those spaces were and could be crossed. Never far from the overt scholarly objectives were covert geopolitical interests, however constrained in their presentation. Not unexpectedly, after a heady rush of early "discoveries," the archaeological emphasis switched to the excavation and generally unspoken cultural "repossession" of historical sites seen to be of great cultural and religious significance to Western belief systems: Old Testament cities, hallowed ground in the life of Jesus, and monuments to the Classical Tradition and its aftermath. It has taken a long time to recognize and commence a process by which this inherently biased approach in early work can be transcended (Athanassopoulos 2004) and to grasp the extent to which such flawed attitudes have negatively affected advances in the archaeology of the Islamicate world.

This volume on the tangible expression of cultural traditions from landscapes in the Islamic Middle East and Central Asia demonstrates the many significant advances in thought and approach achieved since the 1980s. The papers provide a long-overdue statement on the value and variety of rural archaeology in documenting and understanding the Islamic world and sets out the challenge of defining discipline aspirations and the means to achieving these goals. In his introduction, Tony Wilkinson documents a century of survey work on the Islamic countryside but notes that the entirety of rural landscapes has been often overlooked. A system of land use that was intensive in nature and stretched unbroken over the landscape has been obscured by an emphasis on documenting sites with tangible remains, and only scanning rapidly the space between—little more than more localized versions of the work done a hundred years ago. If one maps the degree of ground reconnaissance programs in Jordan, for instance, and plots the sites discovered on a map of the country, remarkably the zones surveyed and sites found taper off substantially around the limits of cultivation, as if what lay beyond (eastward) was insignificant, unconnected, and vacant territory. Yet in Jordan, evidence for pre-Islamic and Islamic-period occupation in the steppe landscape of the *badia* and the desert further east is substantial and prominent, such as with rock-carved pictograms, pre-

Islamic inscriptions in North Arabian dialects, and desert kites. Map those in, and a thickly populated landscape once dismissed as barren (of people and culture) becomes immediately visible. Only in Early Islamic times has it been less challenging to populate a map with "red dot" (in this case, squares) sites in the *badia* and desert territories (see Bartl, Chapter 3), representing not much more than an immodest monumentalizing of a long-established settlement tradition by Arab groups, an architectural branding of the landscape that began in earnest during late antiquity.

Practitioners of Islamic archaeology have their work cut out for them, as these papers reveal. Wilkinson conveniently sets out the common themes that link many of the chapters, specifically, connectivity, the impact of long-distance travel on settlement profiles; land and settlement, in which lifestyle changes deliberate of forced impacted settlement profiles; water management, the harnessing of scarce groundwater and the harnessing of water as an energy source for financial benefit through sophisticated irrigation systems; rural sustenance, especially the role of seasonality and procurement methods; technology, notably the village-based production; and burial, notably the prominence and persistence of cemeteries as community markers in the rural landscape. Wilkinson summarizes these themes more fully, but here we can see how the bar has been raised so very high from the 1990s and we are challenged by a situation in which old-style approaches just will not do anymore (as more information is missed than recovered, and conclusions skewed). New methods will require not only an expansion and upgrade of field techniques but also access to a plurality of sources: historical, oral accounts, ethnography, traditions, cartography, archival documents, environmental studies, geomorphology, architectural stratigraphy, statistical analysis, and the full spectrum of archaeological sciences regularly applied in fieldwork. The binding of disparate data from an assortment of researchers trained in different academic traditions is no easy task, yet the likely results from applying a wide-ranging and cohesive research strategy promises outcomes that will be both more complete and more compelling. As scholarship still struggles to explain many aspects of Islamic history, archaeology is in an enviably strong position to question old beliefs, proffer new alternatives, and substantiate them with an evidential base that is sound while being provable and refinable through further testing.

The chapters presented in this volume identify a number of issues in need of particular attention in the years ahead. Compelling among these topics is the undeniable necessity to identify and implement the appropriate methods and research design needed to solve advanced research questions, especially in areas that remain significantly understudied. By giving definition to those areas of research crucial in the study of the rural Islamic world, significantly new research questions will be recognized. One major field needing particular attention is the role and impact of irrigation technologies in the countryside, both on the regional and interregional scale. Existing research in Syria and Spain, for example, has highlighted the major impact of irrigation programs on rural settlement and the economic activities it encouraged: agricultural, pastoral, and manufacturing. The work of Bartl (1994) and Berthier (2001), among others, demonstrated the intertwined relationship between canal cutting and burgeoning rural settlement profiles in early Islamic Syria, at which time investment in the countryside peaked due to abundant financial resources and growing demand due to the rise of sprawling urban centers (Madina, Makka, Damascus, Rusafa, al-Raqqa, and later Baghdad and Samarra being the obvious cases; see also the comments of Wilkinson in the introduction) and the monetary and provisioning requirements of the Umayyad and Abbasid armies. A similar trend is also observable in Umayyad Spain, with evidence of considerable rural growth fueled by irrigation projects, including those based on *qanat* technology.

A significant development in the last decade or two has been an accelerating recognition and documentation of rural settlements primarily devoted to resource exploitation and manufacturing activities, often associated with a local increase in agricultural activity. A clear example of this mutually sustaining development in the rural exploitation of a wide spectrum of resources has been documented in the southern Wadi Araba and the Negev desert (Avner and Magness 1998), where villages were established in Early Islamic times to mine mineral ores, especially copper, and to support high-earning production activities, such as copper smelting, pottery firing, and shell working. The investment required in setting up these villages, as well as their uniform characteristics and standard room dimensions, indicates that they were built at the direction of a single body made up of local notables, most likely Bedouin *shaykhs* who were at liberty to harness the skills of the nomadic population. The primary function of the Wadi Araba and Negev enterprises was to meet a burgeoning urban demand, notably the markets of Ayla (al-Aqaba) but also the more distant towns of Bayt Jibrin, Ghazza, and Asqalan, thereby productively bringing the resident Bedouin populations of the urban hinterlands within the political and cultural orbit of the Islamic elite.

During different periods, the development of concentrated pockets of the political and religious elite similarly created a super-hot focal point of commodity demand, with an impact that radiated out from the commercial hub so created. One instance is the well-documented Umayyad *qusur*, which at least in their earlier manifestations present as individually inspired projects but, in the last decades, tend toward architectural gigantism and greater uniformity—a preview of Abbasid-period preferences. At Hallabat in Jordan, the discovery of rare Persian turquoise-glazed jars in an Umayyad context illustrates the economic drawing power of an elite group in the countryside (Bisheh 1985). Archaeologically, the presence of Ayyubid and Mamluk elites in the major fortified sites of south Jordan has been documented through comparative ceramic studies, in which a distinct difference could be detected with high-quality, color-glazed vessels found in the castle towns with the village-produced handmade geometric painted wares discovered scattered throughout the thickly populated rural areas (Brown 1991, 2000).

More detailed research into the important role of demand for food and commodities in the Islamic economy, building on a still-growing body of information on production and supply, is of considerable importance if the complexities of socioeconomic systems are to be understood. Of note, for example, is the central question of the development and contraction of regions and their towns due to, for instance, the vagaries of political fortunes or environmental challenges, such as climate change and overexploitation of the land. Such matters remain of prime importance in the modern world.

In that Islamic archaeology was partnered to Anglo-European adventurism in the Islamicate world, regional coverage has been very patchy. Syria-Palestine in Early Islamic times has been relatively well covered due to a roll-on effect of intensive work into the Classical tradition and its late antique (Christian) inheritance in that region. Further east, the coverage is patchier, which is a mismatch with the importance of Iraq and the Persianate world in the Islamic periods that followed the exceptional, but distinctive, Umayyad era. While interest in North Africa profited from a century of French colonial interventions, the Iberian Peninsula is entering an exciting period of rediscovery. Likewise, the rural economy in Ottoman Eastern Europe has been a great unknown despite its relevance to contemporary events, as has interest in the subject come about owing to, in major part, shifting attitudes in the pertinent European countries. Similarly, Wordsworth, in Chapter 12, reveals how new approaches can demolish outdated and inhibiting approaches. His research shows categorically how so-called empty spaces are nothing of the sort, but are richly populated and bound into regional networks to such an extent that they are crucial to their operation. The chapters in this volume reveal just how far we are from being able to adequately document and explain the economic foundations of the rural Islamic world and its central role in the social formation of Islam: this observation stands as an important contribution to the debate. With the chapters in this volume, then, much is laid bare and many issues made clear, and the path forward better defined because of them.

## Bibliography

Athanassopoulos, Effie-Fotini. 2004. "Historical archaeology of medieval Mediterranean landscapes." In *Mediterranean Archaeological Landscapes: Current Issues*, edited by E.-F. Athanassopoulos and L. Wandsnider, 81–98. Philadelphia: University of Pennsylvania Museum of Archaeology and Anthropology.

Athanassopoulos, Effie-Fotini, and LuAnn Wandsnider, eds. 2004. *Mediterranean Archaeological Landscapes: Current Issues*. 1st ed. Philadelphia: University of Pennsylvania Museum of Archaeology and Anthropology.

Avner, Uzi, and Jodi Magness. 1998. "Early Islamic settlement in the Southern Negev." *Bulletin of the American Schools of Oriental Research* 310: 39–57.

Bartl, Karin. 1994. *Frühislamische Besiedlung im Balīḫ-Tal/Nordsyrien, Berliner Beiträge zum Vorderen Orient, Band 15*. Berlin: Dietrich Reimer.

Berthier, Sophie. 2001. *Peuplement rural et aménagements hydroagricoles dans la moyenne vallée de l'Euphrate, fin VIIe–XIXe siècle: Région de Deir ez Zor-Abu Kemal, Syrie. Mission Mésopotamie syrienne, archéologie islamique, 1986–1989*. Damascus: Institut français d'Études arabes de Damas.

Bisheh, Ghazi. 1985. "Qasr al-Hallabat: an Umayyad desert retreat or farmland." In *Studies in the History and Archaeology of Jordan*. Amman, Jordan: Department of Antiquities.

Brown, Robin M. 1991. "Ceramics from the Kerak Plateau." In *Archaeological Survey of the Kerak Plateau*, edited by J. M. Miller, 168–279. Atlanta, GA: Scholars Press.

———. 2000. "The distribution of thirteenth- to fifteenth-century glazed wares in Transjordan: a case study from the Kerak Plateau." In *The Archaeology of Jordan and Beyond: Essays in Honor of James A. Sauer*, edited by L. E. Stager, J. A. Greene, and M. D. Coogan, 84–99. Winona Lake, IN: Eisenbrauns.

Davies, Siriol, and Jack L. Davis, eds. 2007. *Between Venice and Istanbul: Colonial Landscapes in Early Modern Greece, Hesperia Supplements*. Princeton: American School of Classical Studies at Athens.

Ucko, Peter J., and Robert Layton, eds. 1999. *The Archaeology and Anthropology of Landscape: Shaping Your Landscape, One World Archaeology*. London: Routledge.

Wilkinson, Tony J. 2003. *Archaeological Landscapes of the Near East*. Tucson: University of Arizona Press.

# Glossary

*amir* (Ar.)—prince, emir
*ard* (Ar.)—(farm)land
*badia* (Ar.)—low rainfall steppe lands of the eastern Levant
*birka* (Ar.)—reservoir
*dirham* (Ar.) silver coin
*diwan* (Ar./Per.)—government administrative office
*fals* (Ar.)—small copper coin
*fatwa* (Ar.)—written legal advice
*gargur* (Ar.)—bell-shaped mesh fish traps
*hadrah* (Ar.)—tidal fish traps
*hajj* (Ar.)—annual Islamic pilgrimage to Mecca
*haysub* (Ar.)—irrigation engineer
*karm* (Ar.)—vineyard, orchard
*khakh* (Turkic)—pit dug in hard clay desert surfaces to collect natural rainwater
*khan* (Ar./Tr./Pers.)—caravanserai
*khirba* (Ar.)—ruins (of a village), an abandoned village
*kizan* (Ar.)—large water jar
*kurgan* (Rus.)—tumulus or mound, normally associated with burial
*madina* (Ar.)—town or city
*mihrab* (Ar.)—marker or architectural feature indicating the direction of the qibla
*mshash* (Ar.)—holes dug in dry river beds (wadi beds) to gather water
*musha'* (Ar.)—system of agricultural land rotation, or common ownership practiced in the
    Levant
*noria* (Ar.)—water-lifting wheel
*pakhsa* (Rus.)—blocks of rammed earth used in building construction
*qadi* (Ar.)—judge
*qanat* (Ar./Per.)—underground canal tapping groundwater aquifers along changes in topo-
    graphic relief, normally with a system of ventilation holes
*qarya*—(Ar.) village
*qasr* (Ar., pl. qusur)—castle, fortress or fortified palatial residence
*qibla*—(Ar.) direction from a given point towards the ka'ba (Mecca), the direction of prayer
    (also more generally the direction of prayer)
*qulayl* (Ar.)—container for vegetables
*rawda* (Ar.)—natural topographic depressions and points of natural rainwater collection (ter-
    minology particularly associated with landscapes on the Arabian/Persian Gulf littoral)
*sabkha* (Ar.)—coastal salt flats, periodically inundated by saline or brackish water
*sardoba* (Per./Turkic)—underground domed reservoir (terminology used mainly in Central Asia,
    Iranian equivalent: ab anbar)

*shamal*—(Ar.) north wind (Arabian/Persian Guf)

*sijill* (Ar.)—Ottoman court register

*tahun* (Ar.)—water mill

*takiyya* (Ar.)—Sufi convent

*takyr* (Turkic)—area of compacted impermeable clay, subject to seasonal inundations during heavy rainfall

*tannur* (Ar.)—semi-subterranean clay oven,

*Tanzimat* (Tr.)—Ottoman imperial administrative reforms of the mid-nineteenth century

*tapu tahrir defter* (Ar. /Tr.)—Ottoman taxation assessment document

*tasa* (Ar.)—small cup

*tepe* (Turkic)—hill or mound. Often associated with the remains of an archaeological site (as *tall*, Ar.)

*waqfiyya* (Ar.)—endowment records

*zur* (Ar.)—irrigated valley floors

# Contributors

**Pernille Bangsgaard** (ArchaeoScience, Natural History Museum of Denmark) completed her PhD at Copenhagen University: an ethnographic and zooarchaeological study of faunal material from the Scandinavian Joint Expedition to Sudanese Nubia. She has worked on projects in Greece, Sudan, Jordan, Syria, and Bahrain, and has recently held the position of Director of Environmental Studies of the Qatar Islamic Archaeology and Heritage Project. She now heads the ArchaeoScience unit, at the Centre for GeoGenetics, the Natural History Museum of Denmark.

**Karin Bartl** (German Archaeological Institute, DAI) is director of the German Archaeological Institute in Damascus. She is a Near Eastern archaeologist and specialist in Early Islamic settlement archaeology, renowned in particular for her survey work in the Balikh Valley in northern Syria. She has directed survey and excavation projects in Jordan, Syria, and Lebanon, and has authored numerous publications over the course of her career.

**Jennie N. Bradbury** (University of Oxford) completed her PhD at Durham (U.K.) in 2011, with an innovative and well-received thesis looking at landscapes of settlement and burial in western Syria. She has worked on projects in Syria, Jordan, Kuwait, Oman, and Lebanon. Her particular research interests focus on the use of GIS in landscape archaeology and traditions of death and burial in the Levant. She is currently a Research Associate on the Endangered Archaeology in the Middle East and North Africa (EAMENA) Project at the University of Oxford.

**Robin M. Brown** (Independent scholar, Watertown, MA) is a researcher working on aspects of medieval Islamic and Ottoman era archaeology and history in Jordan and its region. She was a Fulbright scholar at the American Center of Oriental Research in Amman and published key papers and book chapters on Islamic pottery before turning her attention to an important synthesis of zooarchaeological research into questions of agricultural subsistence. Her recent work has focused on palatial architecture in medieval Jordan. She is also working with the Harvard Semitic Museum (Cambridge, MA) to publish portions of the Islamic collection.

**Alison L. Gascoigne** (University of Southampton) is a lecturer in medieval archaeology. Her research focuses on the archaeology of the early medieval Middle East and Central Asia. In recent years, she has directed several archaeological projects, including the investigation of Tinnis, a provincial urban center in northern Egypt, and has conducted landscape survey around the site of Jam in central Afghanistan. She has published an analysis of a corpus of ceramic material from the latter site in the journal *Iran*.

**Ian W. N. Jones** (University of California, San Diego) is currently a doctoral candidate in anthropology, specializing in the Islamic archaeology and material culture of Jordan. His primary research into early second millennium CE copper extraction and smelting practices in the Faynan region of southern Jordan draws upon field research conducted alongside international specialists collaborating in the Edom Lowlands Regional Archaeology Project.

**Stephen McPhillips** (University of Copenhagen) is a researcher and teacher of Islamic archaeology and art who has worked extensively on archaeological projects in Syria, Jordan, and Lebanon. He completed his PhD on Islamic material culture at the University of Sydney, Australia, in 2006 in collaboration with the Syrian-French Citadel of Damascus Project after having worked at the French institute in Damascus. He is now working on rural Islamic archaeology and ethnography initiatives in Lebanon and Greece, as well as collaborating in projects in Jordan and the Arabian peninsula.

**Phillip G. Macumber** (Independent scholar and Qatar Islamic Archaeology and Heritage Project) is a hydrogeologist and geomorphologist who also has a degree in Middle Eastern studies. He has worked on Arabian archaeological sites since 1980, in Jordan, Oman, and Qatar, and previously on sites in Australia. He was head of the Hydrogeology Section in the Department of Water Resources in Oman, where he examined the relationship between groundwater systems and the major Mediterranean and Indian Ocean precipitation sources. His PhD, on groundwater-surface water interactions, examined the hydrological instability in the Australian landscape and the hydrology and chemistry of lake systems, enabling a reevaluation of the nature of the widespread salinity problems affecting southern Australia. These skills have since been brought to bear on the archaeology of Qatar.

**Daniel Mahoney** (Institute for Social Anthropology, Austrian Academy of Sciences) has recently completed his PhD in Near Eastern Languages and Civilizations at the University of Chicago, under McGuire Gibson. He is currently working as a postdoctoral researcher for the Visions of Community: Comparative Approaches to Ethnicity, Religion and Empire in Christianity, Islam and Buddhism (400–1600 CE) project at the Austrian Academy of Sciences in Vienna.

**Astrid Meier** (Orient-Institut Beirut) is a historian and specialist of Ottoman administrative and juridical archives, who has published widely in English, German, and French on many aspects of Ottoman Syria. She has recently turned her attention to the relationship between the city and the rural world, and the transformations of this relationship that resulted from global, imperial, regional, and local developments between 1750 and 1850.

**David C. Thomas** (La Trobe University) recently completed his doctoral thesis at La Trobe University, Melbourne, which examined in detail the landscapes of the twelfth- to thirteenth-century Ghurid empire, centered in what is now Afghanistan. He has also conducted fieldwork across North Africa, the Middle East, and Central Asia, most recently working in Afghanistan on the study of the settlement around the famous Minaret of Jam.

**Bethany J. Walker** (Annemarie Schimmel Kolleg, University of Bonn), a historically trained archaeologist, directs two long-term field projects in Jordan and actively consults on Crusader and Islamic ceramics at eastern Mediterranean sites. She is founding editor of the newly launched *Journal of Islamic Archaeology* and serves on numerous American and French editorial boards, as well as the Board of the American Center of Oriental Research in Amman. Walker's current research centers on rural society and migration in the Mamluk period, environmental and agricultural history, indigenous peasant knowledge in the Middle and Late Islamic periods, and frontier studies, topics on which she published extensively in monograph and article form.

**Alan Walmsley** (University of Copenhagen) is an archaeologist and a historian, specializing in the archaeology, architecture, art, and numismatics of the Islamic World and in the contribution of these disciplines to cultural and heritage studies. In his work, he seeks new ways of comprehending the origin and development of Islamic society down to modern times by applying contemporary approaches to the analysis of visual culture: architecture, decorative ornamentation, and material objects. During thirty-eight years in the Middle East, he has directed five major archaeological programs in Jordan and the Arabian Gulf, more recently with an expanded heritage component in recognition of the growing appreciation of preserving and presenting the past. He is a fellow of the Society of Antiquaries of London and a member of the Royal Danish Academy of Sciences and Letters.

**Tony J. Wilkinson** (Durham University) conducted research into archaeological landscapes across the Middle East, investigating a wide range of time scales and environments. Most recently, he headed the Fragile Crescent Project, analyzing settlement change in Syria, Turkey, and Iraq. His book, *Archaeological Landscapes of the Near East*, served as a benchmark for studies in Near Eastern archaeology and has twice been awarded prizes in the United States.

**Paul D. Wordsworth** (University of Oxford) researches the archaeology of medieval landscapes in Central Asia and the Caucasus. He is particularly interested in rural infrastructure and the relationship between urban and rural settlement organization, and he is exploring these themes in the northeastern regions of the early Islamic world, including in Azerbaijan, Afghanistan and Turkmenistan. He completed his PhD at the University of Copenhagen on the archaeology of travel and movement in the Karakum desert, Turkmenistan, which drew upon his background in geographic information systems analysis and archaeological landscape survey.

**Lisa Yeomans** (University of Copenhagen) completed her PhD at University College London on zooarchaeological and historical evidence of the tanning, leather-dressing, and horn-working industries in post-medieval London. Lisa is one of the foremost specialists in marine archaeozoology working in the Middle East today. She has excavated at a wide range of archaeological sites, having also been a member of the long-running Giza (Egypt) and Çatalhöyük (Turkey) excavation projects. Lisa is currently a post-doctoral researcher working on fish remains from excavations in Qatar and on the mammal and bird faunal assemblages from Epipalaeolithic and Neolithic sites excavated in Eastern Jordan as part of the Shubayqa Project.

# Index

Abbasid, 2, 34, 39, 42–44, 46, 47, 81, 89 n.15, 136, 143, 157, 194, 195, 240

Abel, 213

Abila, 194–195

Abu al-Fida' (Sultan of Hama), 84, 85, 89 n. 7

Achaemenian, 170

Aden, 130, 131, 133

Ahangaran valley, 174, 175

Ain Muhammad, 42

'Ajlun, 86, 111, 114, 196 n. 5

Aktangi, 174

Aleppo, 152, 161 n. 23

Amuq, 3, 145, 160 n. 3

Antioch, 145, 147, 162 n. 38

Aqaba, 5, 84, 111, 240

Araba, 111, 125 n. 4, 185, 240

al-Arish, 42

'Arja, 118, 121

Artas, 208, 211

Assyrian, 12

A'waj (river), 19, 21, 23–24

Ayyubid, 74, 75, 78–83, 88, 88 n. 2, 89 n. 14, 130, 240

Azraq, 52, 63, 64, 65 n. 16; n. 17

Baghdad, 11, 12, 240

Bahrain, 96, 106

Balikh (River/valley), 2, 3, 7, 11, 12, 14 n. 4, 160 n. 3

Bamiyan, 174, 178

Band-i Amir, 154

Basra, 11

Beirut, 157, 158

Beqa', 146, 157, 158

Bet Ta'amir, 211

Bilad al-Sham (Levant), 50–51, 111, 124, 184, 186, 196 n. 1, 197, n. 6, 210

*birka. See* cistern

Birkat al-Hajj, 62

Birkat al-Nabatiya, 62

Bor Bator, 46

Bronze Age, 13 n. 1, 122, 125 n. 4, 210, 213, 215

burial (human), x, 1, 3, 10, 200–216, 239

Busayra, 185

Byzantine, 3, 12, 13 n. 1, 62, 64 n. 4, 65 n. 13, 81, 112, 157, 194, 203–205, 208

Caesarea, 157, 160

Cairo, 85, 86

camel, 9, 34, 46, 48, 52, 62, 77, 85, 86, 88, 97, 171, 231–232

canal, 3, 7, 11, 12, 14 n. 4, 19, 23–27, 31 n. 15, 60–61, 146, 155, 158, 161 n.17, 162 n. 38, 221, 240

caravanserai 5, 62, 155, 156, 219, 222–223, 229

*castrum/castellum*, 61

cattle, 74, 76–80, 89 n. 14; n. 16; n. 17, 97, 104, 106

Celebi, Murad, 156

cemetery, 201, 203, 206, 208, 211–214. *See also* burial

ceramics (pottery): coarsewares and handmade pottery, xi, 196 n. 3; and graves, 201–202; regional studies and survey 3, 71, 88 n. 3, 96, 233, 234 n. 3; and local traditions, 5; and chronology, 35, 43–44, 54–55, 62, 113, 116, 205, 222, 228, 231; and elites, 240–241; and nomadism, 174, 178–179; and water resources, 229; production (Yemen), 129–140; technology, 121

charcoal, 116, 118–124, 125 n. 8

Chisht-i Sharif, 176–177

cistern, 9, 51, 54, 56, 58–63, 64 n. 3, 65 n. 8; n. 13; n. 16, 74, 79, 81–83, 131, 213, 228

copper production, 111–124, 240

court (judicial), 6, 19–30, 156, 192, 193

Crusader, 74–76, 78–83, 86, 88, 88 n. 2, 89 n. 15

dam, 51, 59, 61, 63, 131, 146, 157, 161 n. 13; n. 15; n. 16; n. 22, 162 n. 33

Damascus, 7, 19, 21–22, 26, 28, 30 n. 1; n. 6; n. 7, 62, 155–158, 160 n. 4; n. 9, 196 n. 4, 240

Darayya, 19, 24–26

Darb Zubayda, 2, 5, 6

Darwish Pasha, 156

desert, 2, 50, 73, 95, 219–233, 238–240; burial, 10, 207, 211; desert castles, 51–52 ; wild fauna, 85, 105–106; Karakum desert. *See* Karakum; nomadic pastoralism, 96, 171, 173, 230–232; travel, 5, 11, 219–233; water provision/ management, x, 1, 5, 7, 12, 62, 227–229, 233 n.1

Dhamar, 130, 132, 133, 137

Dhamar Plain, 130–139

Dhiban, 73–75, 77, 79, 81–83, 85, 89 n. 12, 186

Dimeni al-Gharbiya, 208

*diwan*, 22, 173

Doha, 40, 106

*dusut*, 114

Ephesus, 157

Euphrates, 11, 160 n. 3

Faynan, 10, 111–124, 125 n. 1; n. 8

Fayshakh, 46

Firuzkuh. *See* Jam

fish, 9, 76, 77, 84, 89 n. 17, 98–103

fishing traps, 9, 98–100

Frankish, 75, 80, 88 n. 2, 89 n. 7; n. 9; n. 15

Furayha, 42, 46

Fuwayrit, 39, 41, 42

*gargur*. *See* fishing traps

Ghab plain, 147

al-Ghariya, 42

Ghazni, 172

Ghiyath al-Din (Sultan), 172, 180 n. 1

Ghur, 169, 172, 174, 175, 179

Ghurid, 169–179

Ghuwairiya, 40

glass, 166, 132, 233

goats. *See* sheep

Gumbad-i Shuhada', 176

al-Hadiya, 42

*hadra*. *See* fishing traps

Hadramawt, 133, 136

*hajj*, 5, 11, 62, 64, 65 n. 12, 207

Hama, 84, 146, 147, 155–157, 159, 216 n. 1

al-Hamdani, 132

Harat, 172, 180 n. 1

Hasi, 131

Hassiya, 154

Hawran, 145, 152, 158, 160 n. 3

Hawsh Sayyid 'Ali, 146

Hays, 134, 136

Hellenistic, 63, 157, 238

Helwan, 42

Himyarite, 5, 135

Hisban, 73–75, 77, 79–86, 89 n. 10; n. 14; n. 15, 20 n. 90, 186–187, 196 n. 4, 201, 203

Homs: burial landscape, 10, 200, 203–205, 207–208, 211–213, 215; Homs dam, 161, n. 16; Homs lake (Lake Qattina), 147, 211; water use, 147; rural economy, 146, 157; regional survey, 3, 143, 160 n. 5, 161 n. 20, 203; water mills, 150, 155–159

Hormuz, 4–5, 9, 11

horse, 9, 76–77, 85, 86, 88, 97, 104, 131, 171–173, 231

Hubras, 187, 194–195

al-Husayniyya, 19, 25

al-Idrisi, 132

Ilkhanid, 170

'Imm, 147

Indian Ocean, 12, 130, 135, 136

iron, 111, 114, 116, 121, 125 n. 7, 152, 153, 173, 174, 207

Iron Age, 88 n. 4, 113, 121, 123

irrigation, x, 7, 9, 12–13, 23, 42–43, 143, 145, 150, 155, 158, 159, 160 n. 3, 161 n. 13; n.21, 188, 193, 232, 239–240

Isfahan, 154

Istanbul, 7, 22, 157

*jaghli* (water mill), 145, 154, 157, 158

Jalalabad, 172

Jam (Afghanistan), 5, 169–172, 176–179, 180 n. 1

Jam (Iran), 8

Jarash, 157, 160 n. 3

al-Jebelain, 133

Jisr al-Shughur, 147

al-Judayda, 19, 25

Jamailiya, 44, 46

al-Jumayl, 42,

Jusih, 158, 162 n. 38

al-Juzjani, 169, 172, 174, 178, 179

Kabul, 172

Kafir Qal'a, 174

Kafr 'Ana, 201

Kaminj, 172

al-Kanakir, 19–21, 24–26, 28, 30

Karak, 65 n. 18, 73–75, 77–79, 81–86, 185

Karakum, 5, 7, 9, 219–233

Karana, 45, 47

Kashan, 179

Kawd am-Saila, 133
*khan*, 156
Khanfar, 133
al-Kharja, 195
Khirbat al-Nahas, 113, 121
Khirbat Faynan, 112, 122–124, 125 n. 1
Khirbat Nuqayb al-Asaymir, 10, 112–124
Khirbet es-Sahi, 205–206, 216 n. 1
Khurasan, 172, 179, 221, 222, 231
al-Khuwair, 42
Khwarazm-Shah, 174
kiln, 134, 136, 137, 225–228

Labweh, 158
Lala Mustafa Pasha, 156, 162 n. 30
*Laodicaea ad Libanum* (Tal Nabi Mand), 150
Lashkar-i Bazar, 172
late antiquity, 239
Late Roman, 3, 13 n. 1, 52–53, 55, 63, 65 n.12

al-Maghribi, ibn Sa'id, 84
Mahkamat al-Bab. *See* court
Makin, 43
al-Makki, Muhammad, 146–147, 156
Mamluk: administration and elites, 75, 85, 156,
    179, 240; archaeology of Jordan, 122, 151;
    cemeteries, 211; fauna and faunal remains,
    78–83, 85–86, 89 n. 14, 90 n. 20,; inscriptions,
    196 n. 5; Jordan (Transjordan), 30 n. 5, 88 n. 1,
    184–188, 190–193, 196, 197 n. 7; pottery, 196 n. 3;
    settlement and land use, 73–75, 184–188,
    190–193, 196, 197 n. 7; water mills, 154–156, 159
Manjak, (Amir) Sayf al-Din, 155
Maqrizi, 85
Masjid-i Sangi, 176
Maurian, 11
Mecca, 5, 45
Medina, 5
migration, 154, 169, 171, 184, 190–195, 196 n. 4,
    215, 231
*mihrab*, 34, 41, 44, 46, 48
miller/milling, 1, 7, 161 n. 22, 191
millstone, 147, 150, 152–154, 156, 161 n. 22;
    n. 29
mining, 105, 111, 119, 120, 123, 132, 137, 240
Mongol, 169, 172, 174, 179
mosque, 25, 30 n. 6, 34, 41, 44, 46–48, 132, 176,
    180 n.1, 194, 207, 212–213
*mshash*, 52, 243
Mu'azzamiyyat Darayya, 19, 25
Mughal, 172
al-Mugheir, 213
Muhammad b. 'Ali b. 'Amran, 132
Muhayriqat, 42

Mu'izz al-Din, 172
ibn Munqidh, Usama, 84–85, 89 n. 13, 161 n. 28
Murayr (Qala'at), 42, 95
al-Murra, 97
Murwab, 43, 45
Musayka, 39, 42–43
Muscat (Sultanate of), 95
al-Muwaqqar, 52, 63–64, 65 n. 16

Nabataean, 63
al-Na'im, 96–97
al-Nasir Ahmad, 86
al-Nasir Muhammad, 85
Negev/Naqab, 46, 48 n. 2, 207, 240
Neo-Assyrian, 11, 13 n. 1
Neolithic, 35, 43, 53
networks, 82, 171, 178, 188, 196 n. 4, 233, 241;
    communication, 10; defensive, 75, 80;
    hydraulic, 26, 143, 145–146, 150, 158–159, 160
    n. 3; maritime, 11; roads, 82, 233; trade, 4, 84,
    86, 130,177, 179
nomads/nomadic, 1, 34, 40, 46, 48, 52, 73,
    96–97, 106, 154, 169–175, 178–179, 214, 219,
    231, 233, 240
*noria*, 146–148, 156, 243
al-Nufur, 19–20, 25

Öljeitü, Sultan, 170, 172
Orontes, 143–147, 150–159, 160 n. 5, 161 n. 23,
    162 n. 38, 211–213
Ottoman, xii, 6–7, 21, 22, 30 n. 5, 88 n. 2, 130,
    132, 146, 196 n. 2; n. 3, 241; administration,
    19–20, 22, 25, 27–30, 147, 244; fauna and
    faunal remains, 74, 78–81, 83, 85, 88, 89 n. 7;
    forts and watchtowers, 62, 137, 154; Greece,
    191; maps, 216 n. 1; settlement archaeology,
    73, 75, 184–186, 188, 190, 203; sources,
    192–193, 197 n. 6; water mills, 147, 154–159,
    160 n. 12, 162 n. 35
ovicaprids. *See* sheep

Palaeolithic, 53
Palmyra (Tadmur), 145, 154
Parthians, 170
Persian (period), 238, 240–241
pigs, 76–80, 89 n. 14–17
pigeons, 85, 105–106
Pishawar, 172
pottery. *See* ceramics

Qa'a, 158
Qala'at Fassu'a, 62
Qarakhanid, 174
al-Qaraw, 133

Qashgai, 154
Qasimi, 130
qasr, 53, 55, 61, 64, 65 n. 10, 243
Qasr Ain al-Sil, 64
Qasr al-Hayr al-Gharbi, Qasr al-Hayr al-Sharqi,
    50, 65 n. 14
Qasr Azraq, 52, 63–64, 65 n. 16–17
Qasr Kharana, 50–51, 63
Qasr Mushash 5, 9, 50–64, 64 n. 1; n. 5
Qattina. *See* Homs Lake
*qibla*, 34, 41, 44, 46, 243
Qusayr, 146, 161 n. 17
Qusayr 'Amra, 50–51, 63–64
Qutayfa, 62

al-Rabadha, 2, 11
Raqqa, 11, 240
Rastan, 147, 161 n. 18
Rasulid, 142
*rawda*, 39, 45, 47, 243
Rawdat al-Faras, 39
Red Sea, 111, 130, 134–135
Resafa-Sergiupolis (Rusafat al-Hisham), 50
reservoir, 51, 56, 58–60, 63–64, 65 n. 16,
    228–229, 233 n. 2, 234
Rikayat, 43
Roman, ; archaeology, 55, 65 n. 12; 161 n. 15,
    238; burials and cairns, 201, 207; *castrum* and
    related, 61, 64, 65 n. 10; n. 15; empire, 1;
    mining, 112–113, 123; relationship with subse-
    quent periods, 12, 188, 203, 208
Roman–Byzantine, 203–205, 208
Rujm al-Khayyat (al-Rujm), 19–21, 24–25, 28, 30
Rüstem Pasha, 156
Ruwayda, 42, 39

Sa'sa', 19, 24–26
*sabkha*, 37, 39–40, 42, 47, 243
Sahab, 63
Sahnaya, 19, 25
Saljuq, 143, 172–173, 231
Sama'lil, 213–215
Samanid, 174
Samarra, 11
San al-Fuzayra, 41, 46–47
Sanaa, 130–131
Sanjar (Sultan), 172–173
*sardoba*, 228–229, 233 n. 2, 243
Sasanian, 12, 231
satellite imagery, 3, 206, 222
Shagra, 35, 40, 46
Shah Shuja', 172
Shah-i Mashhad, 176
Shahrak, 172

Shahristan, 174
Shaizar, 147, 155
al-Shajra, 195
Sharma, 133, 136
Shasabanid. *See* Ghurid
Shawbak, 73–75, 77–79, 81–83, 85–86, 89 n. 11
sheep (and goats), 9; Afghanistan, 171, 173, 178,
    191; Bedouin, 52,; faunal remains (Jordan), 74,
    76–83, 87, 89 n. 14; n. 17; n. 18; Karakum
    (Turkmenistan), 231–232; Qatar, 97–98, 103,
    104, 106; water and, 62
Siraf, 4, 7–9, 11, 14, 160 n. 3
Sistan, 179
slag, 113, 115–124, 125 n. 8
smelting, 111, 116, 119–123
Sohar, 7, 11, 14 n. 4
sugar, 114, 121, 185
sulfur, 132, 137
survey (archaeological), xi, 1–3, 6, 9, 12, 237–238;
    Qatar, 40, 96; Jordan, 113, 121, 123, 184–187,
    191, 195–195, 238; Yemen, 129–132, 134–137,
    139; Syria, 144–145, 160 n. 5, 203, 205–208, 211,
    213; Afghanistan, 177; Karakum (Turkmenistan),
    220–223, 226–230, 232–233, 234 n. 3

Tabaqat Fahl (Pella), 89 n. 15, 202
Tadmur. *See* Palmyra
Tafila, 185
Taiwara, 175
*takiyya*, 156, 244
Tall Hamrat al-Qurayma, 53
Tel Masaikh, 201
Tell el-Hesi, 201–202
Thaqab, Qala'at al-, 46
Tihama, 133–134, 136
tobacco pipes (Ottoman), 134–135
Tripoli, (Lebanon), 155
Turayna, 41, 45–47

Ubaid, 13, 35, 43
Umayyad, 30 n. 6, 51–52, 55, 64, 65 n. 10, 81,
    89 n. 15, 157, 161 n. 15, 172, 240–241
Umm al-Kilab, 43–45
Umm al-Ma', 43
Umm al-Shuwayl, 42
Umm Bab, 41, 46
Umm Jassim, 42
Umm Said, 40
Ustrushana, 173
'Utub, 94, 100

Wa'ar (Jabal), 203, 205
wadi: cisterns, 64 n. 3; dams, 59–60; and
    farming, 88 n. 6; and groundwater, 63;

hunting in, 86; in Jordan (Transjordan), 52–53, 59–61, 63, 65 n. 9, 73, 118, 123, 185, 195; in Qatar, 41; settlement in, 185, 195; in Syria, 161 n. 22, 206–207, 212, 214; water resources, 9, 41, 52–53, 59–61, 63, 65 n. 9, 243

Wadi al-'Araba, 111, 125 n. 4, 185, 240

Wadi al-Dubayan, 43

Wadi al-Ghuwayb, 113, 123

Wadi al-Salmina, 123

Wadi Farasa, 73–75, 77, 79–81, 83, 88 n. 6, 89 n. 17, 90 n. 18

Wadi Faynan. *See* Faynan

Wadi Hasa, 185

Wadi Mushash, 53–54, 57, 59–60

Wadi Sirhan, 63, 65 n.12

*waqf* (*awqaf*), 145, 156–159, 160 n. 4, 162 n. 30

*waqfiyya*, 193, 244

Wasit, 11

water mill, 7–8, 14 n. 4, 143–159, 160 n. 3; n. 5, 161 n. 21, 161 n. 26, 161 n. 29, 162 n. 35, 244

well (water), 23; Arabia, 7; Qatar, 7, 9, 12, 34–36, 39–48, 95, 97; Jordan, 52, 63, 65 n. 15; n.16, ; Yemen, 131,; Karakum (Turkmenistan), 221, 225, 227–229, 233; saxaul (*Haloxylon persicum*), 119, 122–123, 227

Wu'ayra, 73–75, 77, 79–83, 86, 88 n. 6, 89 n. 17, 116

Yoghbi, 43

Zabid, 136

Zamin-Dawar, 169

Zhafar, 5

al-Zubara, 9, 11, 39, 41–43, 94–96, 100, 102–107

*zur*, 143, 152, 155, 244

# Acknowledgments

This volume was made possible through the input and support of many colleagues and friends. We would particularly like to thank the following individuals and organizations for their contributions and assistance.

The authors of the individual chapters in the volume not only contributed their own research but also provided critical input and stimulated debate across the themes discussed.

The following people were instrumental in organizing the workshop at which the ideas for the volume were first conceived: Alan Walmsley (University of Copenhagen), for his support all the way through this initiative; Bodil Egede Fich and Pernille Bangsgaard (Statens Naturhistoriske Museum, Copenhagen); Hanne Nymann and the Materiality in Islam Research Initiative (University of Copenhagen); Salwa Amzourou and Nikoline Tyler (University of Copenhagen); and Rune Rattenborg (Durham University); and the Geological Museum, Copenhagen, for hosting this event.

The workshop was made possible with the financial support of the C. L. David Foundation, Copenhagen.

Special thanks go to Deborah Blake at the University of Pennsylvania Press for guiding us through each step of the publication process. Thanks also to our anonymous reviewer for insightful comments.

Our own personal thanks go to Robin M. Brown for her kind support at every stage in preparing the book.

\*   \*   \*

The editors wish to pay special tribute to Professor Tony J. Wilkinson, who passed away while this book was in press. It is a privilege to have had the opportunity to work with a scholar whose impact on the discipline of Near Eastern archaeology cannot be overstated and who was prominent in encouraging the integration of Islamic periods in the study of historical landscapes. We greatly value his contribution to this publication and his positive input at the research meeting that inspired it.